THE CONTINUING SPIRIT

BY NORMAN BEASLEY

THE CROSS AND THE CROWN
The History of Christian Science

THE CONTINUING SPIRIT

THE
CONTINUING
SPIRIT

by NORMAN BEASLEY

Duell, Sloan and Pearce
New York

MANUFACTURED IN THE UNITED STATES OF AMERICA

VAN REES PRESS • NEW YORK

Foreword

As readers of *The Cross and the Crown* know, that history of Christian Science confined itself, largely, to the beginnings and the widening acceptance of the teachings of Mary Baker Eddy while she was here, in person.

Within a few weeks after publication of the book in October, 1952, I began receiving letters asking that another history be written that would cover the years since the passing, in 1910, of the Discoverer and Founder of Christian Science.

The requests became so many that, in the spring of 1953, I discussed such a book with the publishers. They felt, as did I, that there was need for it; and they agreed that, if written, the book should be done on the basis of my own independent research, as was *The Cross and the Crown*. And so it was.

The research was carried on in sources wholly outside the Archives of The Mother Church, and no official assistance was requested, or given, in the writing of these books. My single purpose was to present, in the two books, an independent, documented history of what Mary Baker Eddy left to her followers.

NORMAN BEASLEY

Contents

Introduction   ix

1. Words of Eternal Purpose   3
2. A Builder of Churches   18
3. To Ask God to Heal the Sick Is against the Law   46
4. A King Interferes   78
5. "Whose Neighbour Am I?"   96
6. Dedicated to Accomplishment   112
7. Protection Was Provided   134
8. All Survived That Could Survive   156
9. A Name Is Restored   182
10. That Which Is to Be   204
11. All Churches Closed   227
12. Expansion and Extension   247
13. Without Malice, without Guile   267
14. The Home on the Hill   287
15. Unless Youth Is Drawn   317

Appendices

(1) People v. Cole   329
(2) People v. Vogelgesang   343

(3) Deed of Trust   348

(4) Decision of the Supreme Judicial Court of
     Massachusetts in the matter of the Trustees   353

(5) Letter of John V. Dittemore   376

(6) Statement from The Christian Science Board
     of Directors at the annual meeting (1938) of
     The Mother Church   378

(7) Youth Forums   382

(8) Christian Science Board of Lectureship   384

Index   389

Introduction

Mary Baker Eddy was ruled by one conviction, and was governed by one desire. Her single conviction was that God is All-in-all. Her one desire was to be of His ministry. Her teaching was, that unless identified with God, life is a word without meaning.

Knowing that Jesus never spoke of life as less than eternal and knowing, too, that the Apostle Paul spoke of life as "hid with Christ, in God," Mrs. Eddy accepted, without reservation, the fact that God *is*. She believed that when Jesus said, "Take no thought for your life," He meant precisely what He said. Having no doubts to shadow her faith, she trusted God in all things.

There are brief moments when you and I trust Him in all things. In these brief moments we perceive that life is everlasting; we understand that eternity dwells in us, and we in it; and we know there are no limitations of any kind—not even those we were so sure existed.

THE CONTINUING SPIRIT

CHAPTER ONE

Words of Eternal Purpose

THERE was a great deal of speculation following the passing of Mary Baker Eddy on December 3, 1910, about the future of the Christian Science movement.

Some said, as did the *Manitowoc* (Wisconsin) *Daily Herald,* "The church will topple and fall without the cohesive influence of her captaincy"; some said, as did the *Cedar Rapids* (Iowa) *Evening Times,* "The effect of Mrs. Eddy's death upon the church will not be momentous."

The *Boston Transcript* examined the growth of Christian Science, pointed out that it was growth that had "come in a period we are used to calling especially commercialized, narrow and sordid," and observed, "That may account for its growth, but it can hardly account for its origin, which was certainly due to the genius of one woman."

The *New York Post* had a different view of Mrs. Eddy, and foresaw a poor future for her church:

"It might seem out of place to dwell at present upon the harm which has been done by Mrs. Eddy's doctrines. This we will only say has been, in our opinion, very great, and has involved both needless physical suffering and mental and moral injury. But institutions grow and thrive by their good qualities, not their bad.

"Christianity itself was called an *excitabilis superstitio* at first; and it would be almost as great a mistake to call Christian Science nothing but a superstition. Its ultimate fate, however, now that its founder is gone, is problematic.

"A part of its membership will doubtless be reabsorbed into the Christian churches, which are themselves now doing something to win over those who believe in mental healing. Other Christian Scientists will fall away, for one reason or another, and the impetus of the cult, which there is some reason to believe has already been checked, will probably drop off with the years.

"Yet, whatever may become of this singular association, its founding by a woman like Mrs. Eddy, and its long and seemingly inexplicable dominance by her, will remain a problem to try the wits of students of religious vagaries."

But, whatever the predictions, the Christian Science movement has continued, and has grown greatly—because, in providing for its future, Mary Baker Eddy left nothing to chance.

She protected her books by copyrighting them, and marked them with a Cross and a Crown; [1] she provided against interference in the government of her church by publishing a *Church Manual* and by stipulating in this *Manual*:

> The Church Manual of The First Church of Christ, Scientist, in Boston, Mass., written by Mary Baker Eddy and copyrighted, is adapted to The Mother Church only. It stands alone, uniquely adapted to form the budding thought and hedge it about with divine Love. This Manual shall not be revised without the written consent of its author.
>
> [Article XXXV, Section 1.]

---

[1] Later, the marking was recognized as a trademark.

And stipulated again:

> No new Tenet or By-law shall be adopted, nor any Tenet or By-law amended or annulled, without the written consent of Mary Baker Eddy, the author of our textbook, Science and Health.
>
> [Article XXXV, SECTION 3.]

She did more. Looking upon The Mother Church as "God's gift, foundation and superstructure [to which] no one could hold a wholly material title," [2] she conveyed the edifice and the land upon which it stands to the keeping of The Christian Science Board of Directors, and, in so doing, stipulated that neither the edifice nor the land could ever be bought, sold, or mortgaged.

In addition, in the *Church Manual,* she provided:

> The edifice erected for The First Church of Christ, Scientist, in Boston, Mass., shall neither be demolished, nor removed from the site where it was built, without the written consent of the Pastor Emeritus, Mary Baker Eddy.
>
> [Article XXXIV, SECTION 3.]

Nor was that all. In the deed of trust by which she conveyed the property, she provided: "If said building is burned, the Directors shall proceed forthwith to rebuild the church." She did these things, believing "The First Church of Christ, Scientist, our prayer in stone, will be the prophecy fulfilled, the monument upreared, of Christian Science." [3]

Also, she created The Christian Science Board of Directors, established it in perpetuity, lifted it above de-

---

[2] *Miscellaneous Writings,* p. 140.
[3] *Miscellaneous Writings,* p. 141.

pendence upon passing favor by giving to it the authority of choosing its own membership—then charged it, and all succeeding Christian Science Boards of Directors, with the protection of her church, the preservation of her teachings, and the administration of church government.

So is it that in her teachings, in her *Church Manual* with its explicit directions, and in her instructions to The Christian Science Board of Directors, Mary Baker Eddy still stands between her church and every effort to tamper with its authenticity.

Although medical opinion said she was dying, Mrs. Eddy was healed in 1866 while reading the Bible. For the next years, she did little else but study the Scriptures to learn how the healing was done, and how it could be done again. She found what she believed was the way and named her discovery Christian Science.

She was determined to do all she could, in every way she could, to protect her discovery so that the principle of Christian healing would not be lost as it had been lost in the third century after the crucifixion.

That is why she took such great care in protecting what she believed to be the truth. Accepting righteousness as the sum of God's law and purity of heart as the perceiver of His truth, she saw Christian Science as a religion tributary only to God. Seeing it this way, she looked upon the *Church Manual* as an instructor to be heeded, an authority to be obeyed, and she sought to write into its rules the same impartiality that occurs in the rules that were heard in a sermon on the shores of a sea in Galilee.

She knew that impartiality would prosper her church, as she knew that adherence to the *Manual* would prevent its dissolution; and she said this, in a letter to The Christian

Science Board of Directors under date of February 27, 1903:

> Never abandon the By-laws nor the denomina-
> tional government of The Mother Church. If I am
> not personally with you, the Word of God, and my
> instructions in the By-laws have led you hitherto
> and will remain to guide you safely on.

Nothing in the government of this church speaks of ceremony; nothing waits on bell or scepter. The sole requirement of those who are students of Christian Science is that
they follow their "Leader only so far as she follows Christ." [4]
In this instruction, Mrs. Eddy did not mean herself as a
person; nor did she mean Christ as a person.

Interpreting Christian Science as a spiritual movement,
she established it as a humanly leaderless movement—even
as the early Christian church established its leadership not
in the crucifixion of the human Jesus, but on the teachings
of the incorporeal Christ . . . *even as,* in the words of Paul,
Christ is the head of the Church.

Understanding the Christ as the presence of God, Mrs.
Eddy acknowledged God as the only source of good; accepted spiritual consciousness as the eternal element; and
saw all life as immortal, and not as a clock running down.
She believed the truth of God is the science of God. She believed Jesus's healings scientific in the strictest sense of the
word. She believed the science of God to be knowable, and
His law to be demonstrable.

It was this concept of God that separated her from intellectualism, which said that nothing definite is known about
Him; from ecclesiasticism, which pictures Him as a personal
deity; and from materialism, which rejects Him because it
cannot find Him under a microscope or in a test tube.

---

[4] *Message to The Mother Church,* 1901, p. 34.

A world given to intellectualism, or ecclesiasticism, or materialism could scarcely be expected to accept her assurance that *whatever ye shall ask in prayer, believing, ye shall receive* was a completely scientific statement, and completely provable.

As a Leader, Mary Baker Eddy saw all life in the light of truth, and early in her work she learned that revealing God is not done without disapproval. She was denounced from the pulpit and in the press; she was ridiculed by Mark Twain, and in his lectures on "Natural Religion" in Edinburgh, Scotland, in 1901-2, William James regarded her teachings as unworthy of "the compliment of explicit attention." *The Journal of the American Medical Association* demanded laws prohibiting the practice of Christian Science; in cities and towns her followers were arrested and jailed, their homes defaced, their families ostracized, employment denied them, their businesses boycotted.

It was a type of malice old in history. Its counterpart was present in the palace of the high priest on the night of Gethsemane, was present on that day when a monk named Luther dared to challenge Pope Leo X by placing the Scriptures above papal authority.

Nor was it strange. As the words of Jesus and Luther threatened the entrenchments of ecclesiastical domination, so did her words. And as all inspired minds live above the turbulence of their times, so did she. She recognized bigotry for what it is—not a defense of God, and not a defense of religion, but a defense of the trappings of organization.

However, this is not to say that Mrs. Eddy disputed the need of organization. In 1909, she singled out Judge Clifford P. Smith for specific instructions about organization and its application to her church.

In the *Permanency of The Mother Church and Its*

Manual [5] Judge Smith told of being invited to see Mrs. Eddy. At her request, he had prepared a legal paper covering a change in the disposition of her personal estate and, in the company of three others, he went to see her. It was his first visit to her home.

After some discussion, the legal paper was signed and, as the visitors were preparing to leave, Mrs. Eddy asked Judge Smith to stay.

"Mrs. Eddy then spoke to me for fifteen minutes or so," recalled the jurist. "She began by saying that organization is necessary for a religion or church which intends to attain much size. She said she had always, from the time of the first organization of the Christian Scientist Association, felt this to be true. She said she now saw that it was essential, and without it the Christian Science movement would be left unprotected.

"She continued by saying that the organization should fit the occasion; that is, the Christian Science movement needed an organization corresponding to its character and purpose. She spoke of the Christian Scientists who go about saying we need no organization as 'not knowing what they are talking about.' She also said, in substance, 'Organization is a simple matter, for all of its importance. It is simply a matter of doing things by working together.'

"In closing, she spoke of its being desirable that I be well informed on this subject, and to use what she had given me in writing. In later years, when the entire organization of The Mother Church was threatened, I appreciated the value of what Mrs. Eddy had said to me and perhaps why she had chosen me to receive her instruction and had advised me to be well informed on the subject. . . ."

[5] Copyright, 1954, The Christian Science Publishing Society, Boston, Massachusetts.

And, as Judge Smith pointed out later in his article, Mrs. Eddy's "writings contain much information on the subject" of organization.

It is instruction on how to stand together, and strive together, in discovering how rich we all are when we hear, as did Isaiah, "Fear not: for I have redeemed thee, I have called thee by thy name; thou art mine."

Perceiving that Jesus disclosed all of Himself when He said, "A new commandment I give unto you, That ye love one another; as I have loved you," Mrs. Eddy believed this "new commandment" a precept for all who recognize in Him, as did Peter, *the Christ, the Son of the Living God.* Accepting divine love, the new commandment, as the great virtue, she taught it as a fundamental of Christian Science.

One day she was asked if, when she spoke of this love, she meant "love of person."

Her answer was prompt, "No, I mean love of God," and she explained that divine love needs no object to call it forth, is available always, attainable always, and, being divine, is love that may be trusted in all eternity. Not being a sentiment, it is love that is power set free, and authority that is its own proof. In it is only that which is right. Being divine, it is the gate to the kingdom.

It was inevitable that Mrs. Eddy, in accepting divine love as a fundamental of Christian Science, should seek impartiality as a fundamental on which to establish her church, and as a principle in its *Manual.* She was aware that the center purpose of all materialism is to obscure the presence of God so that humanity may not understand, and may not perceive, even as in the day of Isaiah's prophecy "which saith, By hearing ye shall hear, and shall not understand; and seeing ye shall see, and not perceive."

In writing the *Church Manual,* Mary Baker Eddy also

had a center purpose: to make sure there would be no mis-use of Christian Science.

That is why, in the *Manual,* it is stipulated: "This Manual shall not be revised without the written consent of its au-thor"; and stipulated again: "No new Tenet or By-law shall be adopted, nor any Tenet or By-law amended or annulled, without the written consent of Mary Baker Eddy, the author of our textbook, Science and Health."

Adopted in 1895, and given its final revision in 1910, the *Manual* had appeared in eighty-nine editions by the time of Mrs. Eddy's passing in 1910.[6] Without change of any kind from its eighty-ninth edition, which was published in 1910, it remains the law of The Mother Church, The First Church of Christ, Scientist, in Boston, Massachusetts.

Mrs. Eddy attached the greatest importance to the *Church Manual,* and thought of its Rules and By-laws as originating "not in solemn conclave as in ancient Sanhedrim [and] not arbitrary opinions nor dictatorial demands, such as one per-son might impose on another." Instead, she wrote of them as Rules and By-laws that "were impelled by a power not one's own . . . hence their simple, scientific basis, and detail so requisite to demonstrate genuine Christian Science, and which will do for the race what absolute doctrines destined for future generations might not accomplish." [7]

In *Miscellany* (p. 230) she said, "Notwithstanding the sacrilegious moth of time, eternity awaits our Church

[6] *Seventy-third Edition the Authority.* Sect. 2. The Board of Directors, the Committee on Bible Lessons, and The Board of Trustees shall each keep a copy of the Seventy-third Edition and of subsequent editions of the Church Manual; and if a discrepancy appears in any revised edition, these editions shall be cited as authority. (*Church Manual,* Article XXXV, SECTION 2.) The seventy-third edition was published in 1908.

[7] *Miscellaneous Writings,* p. 148, and used as a foreword in the *Church Manual.*

Manual, which will maintain its rank as in the past, amid ministries aggressive and active, and will stand when those have passed to rest." Also in *Miscellany* (pp. 25-7), she strongly advised her followers: "Adhere to the teachings of the Bible, Science and Health, and our Manual, and you will obey the law and the gospel."

Mrs. Eddy regarded obedience to the *Manual* as essential if her church was to endure; and no one obeyed it more willingly than did she, as Adam H. Dickey recalled in the *Christian Science Journal* (April, 1922) when he wrote, "She has been known to correct some simple thing she herself was doing on finding that it was not in accord with the Manual."

This obedience was in full keeping with her convictions. She did not start her church with the thought of abandoning it. She knew that obedience to the laws of God discloses the perfect gifts that are waiting, and that are ours.

In her letter of February 27, 1903, when she counseled The Christian Science Board of Directors, "Never abandon the By-laws nor the denominational government of The Mother Church," she requested the placing of her letter "upon our church records," and advised them further:

> The present and future prosperity of the cause of Christian Science is largely due to the By-laws and government of 'The First Church of Christ, Scientist,' in Boston. None but myself can know, as I know, the importance of the combined sentiment of this Church remaining steadfast in supporting its present By-laws. Each of these many By-laws has mastered or forestalled some contingency, some imminent peril, and will continue to do so. . . .

It is because "each of these many By-laws has mastered or forestalled some contingency, some imminent peril, and will continue to do so" that it is not possible to overstress the importance of the *Church Manual* in the continuing strength of the Christian Science movement. The Mother Church cannot survive without adherence to the *Church Manual,* and the Christian Science movement cannot exist without The Mother Church.

All this, Mary Baker Eddy foresaw.

This is why in the *Manual*—in it and under it—she gave to The Christian Science Board of Directors the great responsibility of serving her, and continuing to serve her teachings when, as she said, "I am not personally with you." She established them as her representatives, and as her administrators in all the affairs of The Mother Church; and she made them accountable, not to the church membership, but to each other, and accountable together in perpetuity to her through the *Church Manual.*

She knew this authority of representation and power of administration would be needed if her church, and her teachings, were to remain unchanged. In her own efforts to persuade a disbelieving world that "God will heal the sick through man, wherever man is governed by God," [8] she had encountered hostility. She knew that as the world was hostile to her, so would it be hostile to her representatives.

A world accustomed to thinking of disease as normal and educated to being afraid could scarcely be expected quickly to agree that there is no need to be afraid, that all disease is illegitimate, and that it is an impeachment of God to believe He is in league with sickness or with evil of any kind. Hers were teachings that rejected, and rejected completely,

[8] *Science and Health,* p. 495.

any argument that God sends sickness and death, or visits suffering upon humanity.

There were those who doubted, as there were those who doubted the disciple James:

> Let no man say when he is tempted, I am tempted of God: for God cannot be tempted with evil, neither tempteth he any man.... Every good gift and every perfect gift is from above, and cometh down from the Father of lights, with whom is no variableness, neither shadow of turning. Of his own will begat he us with the word of truth, that we should be a kind of first fruits of his creatures.

Mary Baker Eddy never questioned the goodness or the power of God. She believed that in healing the sick, raising the dead, feeding the multitude, and stilling the tempest, Jesus was expressing the goodness of God and expressing, as He said, "not my own will, but the will of the Father which hath sent me." Believing His words, Mrs. Eddy did not believe "the will of the Father" was expressed that only a few might see, that only a neighborhood might be remembered.

She believed in expressing this will, Jesus was establishing "what he said by demonstration, thus making his acts of higher importance than his words [and proving] the principle, which heals the sick and casts out error, to be divine." [9]

She maintained, "It is the duty and privilege of every child, man and woman to follow in some degree the example of the Master by the demonstration of Truth and holiness"; and to this conviction, she added: "Christians claim to be

---

[9] *Science and Health,* p. 473.

his followers, but do they follow in the way he commanded? Hear these imperative commands: 'Be ye therefore perfect, even as your Father which is in heaven is perfect!' 'Go ye into all the world, and preach the gospel to every creature!' *'Heal the sick!' "* [10]

To her, these were words of eternal purpose for all who accept His love, who follow wherever He may go, and who hear His voice wherever they may be.

These, or very similar, words must have been in her mind on that day when she detained Judge Smith and told him "the Christian Science movement needed an organization corresponding to its character and purpose." Having accepted the Christ teachings as the essence of Christian Science, she could have had but a single thought on how best to protect the Christian Science movement. It must have been her thought that the best protection is Christian Science.

To have the Scriptures understood spiritually was her high undertaking, and her work was to establish universal acceptance of the knowledge that "The true theory of the universe, including man, is not in material history but in spiritual development. . . . It is this spiritual perception of Scripture, which lifts humanity out of disease and death and inspires faith." [11]

But the world does not yet believe *God created man in his own image, in the image of God created he him; male and female created he them;* nor yet accept Mary Baker Eddy's spiritual interpretation of the foregoing verse from Genesis: "To emphasize this momentous thought, it is repeated that God made man in His own image, to reflect the divine Spirit." [12]

[10] *Science and Health,* p. 37.
[11] *Science and Health,* p. 547.
[12] *Science and Health,* p. 516.

It was in her acknowledgment of God as perfect and eternal, and as man created in the image of God, that Mrs. Eddy found her life and her work. This was a conception that made of prayer a customary thing, and an acknowledgment that to live in God is to understand not one truth, but all truth.

Mary Baker Eddy was not a halfway believer in God. Accepting without condition the precept that "the kingdom of God is within you," she found communion within herself, and, by applying this pure instruction, dwelt with Him, spoke with Him, and listened to Him, in prayer.

For almost ten years after discovering what she believed was the way Jesus healed her hope was that the Christian church would test her revelation. She was sure Jesus healed in accordance with God's law. And because it was God's, she was sure that this law operates not temporarily, but eternally; and there were words she asked all people to believe, as Jesus asked His disciples to believe the last time He appeared to them, which was "as they sat at meat":

> "Go ye into all the world, and preach the gospel to every creature. . . . And these signs shall follow them that believe; in my name shall they cast out devils; they shall speak with new tongues; They shall take up serpents; and if they drink any deadly thing, it shall not hurt them; they shall lay hands on the sick, and they shall recover."

She believed these words to be as binding as when He spoke them—on all who think of themselves as His people.

Because she spoke beyond their liking, her very name offended the materialists. Yet, though she was despised of them, they were not deaf to her. Her words were a challenge that did not subside because she would not retract. She only added.

To keep insisting that the best security humanity can have is to get on with the unfinished task of understanding God does not make for popular listening in a world mesmerized by test tubes and blueprints. To say, and keep saying, that morals are the real basis of the world's wealth and to repeat, and repeat again, that the true profit of humanity comes from the investment it makes in principle are verities not in focus in a world taught by its Caesars to believe that theft of a neighbor's land is wealth and that conquest is principle.

As her search for spiritual understanding of the Bible was a high undertaking, so the preservation of her findings is a high responsibility. If they are to continue to benefit humanity, these findings must remain unadulterated.

This she knew; and knew that, once there is substitution of ritual for solitude with God, the time will come when there is only ritual; and knew that, in her own church, there would come those who, in the wisdom of the world, would open the books of her teachings and seek to change this, and to change that, until the changes would be a thousandfold, and left would be only what they had done, unless, in perpetuity, there were those who stood guard over her teachings and who, in standing guard, were buttressed by elemental law.

The elemental law is the *Church Manual*. Standing guard is, as said, the high responsibility Mrs. Eddy gave to The Christian Science Board of Directors.

CHAPTER TWO

A Builder of Churches

T HE wisdom back of Mrs. Eddy's decision to establish The Christian Science Board of Directors in the way she did, and to give the Directors the high responsibilities she gave them, was soon apparent.

Not until she was no longer here in person was it realized, generally, that there could be no further revisions in the *Church Manual*, in *Science and Health with Key to the Scriptures*, and in her other writings. Because it was the government of her church, the *Manual*, particularly, was the subject of much discussion, and much criticism.

"It is not possible," said some, "for the church to survive under a set of rules which makes it impossible for us to keep in tune with the times," and it was argued, "Mrs. Eddy could not have intended that we should be compelled to remain within fixed By-laws when she, herself, made changes to meet new situations."

Yet, before them were her words:

> No new Tenet or By-law shall be adopted, nor any Tenet or By-law amended or annulled, without the written consent of Mary Baker Eddy, the author of our textbook, Science and Health.

Undeterred, the doubters began searching for ways to get around her words. In numbers they were not many, but they were persistent.[1] One of the things they seized upon was the action of The Board of Directors in deleting the name of Mary Baker Eddy, Pastor Emeritus, from the Listing of Church Officers as published in the *Manual* in 1911.

They were not familiar with the circumstances surrounding the bestowal of the title, Pastor Emeritus, upon Mrs. Eddy. This honor was one that was given her in April, 1895, when, by appointment of The Christian Science Board of Directors, she was, "for the time and for all generations to come," made Pastor Emeritus of The Mother Church.

It was done because "she is our Pastor Emeritus, not merely because she once officiated as pastor and minister of the early church organization, but because as Discoverer and Founder of Christian Science, her discovery will ever minister to the needs of suffering and sinning humanity, healing the sick and comforting the sorrowing through the impersonal truth she revealed."

Having bestowed the honor, it was within the power of the Directors to take it from view if the circumstances were such that they believed the continued appearance of her name among the Church Officers was causing public misunderstanding; and it was. At the time, gossip was spreading over the world that the Directors were keeping Mrs. Eddy's name among the Church Officers in anticipation of her resurrection and return, in person, to her church.[2]

The doubters manufactured another argument. On June 13, 1904, Mrs. Eddy presented a small rosewood casket to

---

[1] At the time, there seemed to be nothing that portended serious disagreement, but serious disagreement came within the decade.

[2] In 1912, a memorial was completed in a cemetery in Cambridge, Massachusetts, where Mrs. Eddy's body was buried. Built by individual contributions, the memorial has no significance. It is only a reminder to humanity that Mary Baker Eddy was once here, in person. Other than that, it is solely a gesture—made to the world, to meet the terms of the world.

The Mother Church; and, in offering it, she said, in part, to the church membership:

> Permit me to present to you a little gift that has no intrinsic value save that which it represents—namely, a material symbol of my spiritual call to this my beloved church of over thirty thousand members; and this is that call: In the words of our great Master, "Go ye into all the world," "heal the sick," cast out evil, disease, and death; "freely ye have received, freely give." [3]

The following day at the annual meeting of The Mother Church in Boston the casket was opened. In it was a gavel,[4] and a note from Mrs. Eddy:

> My Beloved Brethren:—You will please accept from me the accompanying gift as a simple token of love.

Inasmuch as the gavel was for the President of The Mother Church, the doubters read into its presentation much more than an ancient symbolism of authority. By the act of presenting a gavel to the President of The Mother Church, they said, in order to meet changing conditions, Mrs. Eddy gave authority to a President, chosen each year, rather than to a Board of Directors, established in perpetuity.

Their claim was that, when assembled in annual meeting, the membership of The Mother Church was "a deliberative body"; and they referred to an action by the members in the

---

[3] *Miscellany,* p. 172.

[4] The wood of the head of the gavel was taken from the first chapel at Yale University. Built in 1761, the chapel was torn down in 1893 to make room for Vanderbilt Hall. The wood in the handle was grown on the farm which was Mrs. Eddy's birthplace in Bow, New Hampshire.

annual meeting in 1902 to support their argument. In that year, the membership approved a resolution which stated:

"Recognising the need for providing an auditorium for The Mother Church that will seat four or five thousand persons, and acting in behalf of ourselves and for the Christian Scientists of the world, we agree to contribute any portion of $2,000,000 that may be needed for this purpose." [5]

The argument was that this action was binding on The Mother Church because when the members were assembled in annual meeting, "they became a court of last resort in all affairs pertaining to The Mother Church"—an argument that disclosed a misconception of the nature of the government of The Mother Church.

The resolution to build an auditorium was a voluntary action taken by those members who were in attendance at the annual meeting. In no way did it bind the Church. In no way could it bind the Church. Voting power in The Mother Church was held by The Christian Science Board of Directors, as was stipulated in the *Manual*, as is still stipulated, and as was confirmed in 1921 by decision of the Supreme Court of the Commonwealth of Massachusetts.

When Mrs. Eddy organized The First Church of Christ, Scientist (The Mother Church), on September 23, 1892, she gave to the Directors and to those who were called First Members the responsibility of administering the affairs of her church. She named the Directors, and she named twelve persons, including the Directors, as First Members. These twelve were authorized, by her, to increase their numbers, as First Members, to thirty-two.

In turn, the thirty-two First Members were authorized to increase their numbers within certain limits, with seven

[5] Known as the Extension to The Mother Church, the auditorium was completed, and dedicated on June 10, 1906.

First Members being "a quorum for the purpose of transacting business for the Church." Authority to transact church business was divided, with the Directors and the First Members each having specific duties. In 1901, Mrs. Eddy wrote a new By-law giving to the Directors full responsibility for transacting the business of The Mother Church. Appearing in the *Church Manual* in 1901, this By-law stated:

> The business of The Mother Church hitherto transacted by the First Members shall be done by The Christian Science Board of Directors.

In 1903, the First Members became known as Executive Members. Except for the exclusive duties of serving as Readers and as President of The Mother Church, they had no church functions. In 1908, their titles were abolished, and their exclusive functions ceased.

Also, prior to 1902, and the agreement to "contribute any portion of $2,000,000 that may be needed" to provide an auditorium for The Mother Church, there were other and specific acts by Mrs. Eddy denying that "when assembled in annual meeting, the membership of The Mother Church is a deliberate body."

At no time did Mrs. Eddy communicate with the membership of The Mother Church in affairs that concerned the business of the church. All such communications were sent to the First Members and to the Directors; and, beginning in 1901, all such communications were sent to the Directors.

The *Church Manual* states:

> The business of The Mother Church shall be transacted by its Christian Science Board of Directors. [Article I, Section 6.]

Equally clearly, the *Church Manual* also states:

> The regular meetings of The Mother Church shall be held annually, on Monday following the first Sunday in June. No other than its officers are required to be present. These assemblies shall be for listening to the reports of Treasurer, Clerk, and Committees, and general reports from the field.
>
> [Article XIII, SECTION 1.]

In other words, attendance at the annual meeting is a requirement for officers—and only for officers—of The Mother Church. These meetings are not held for the purpose of transacting business. They are held for the purpose of listening to specific and to general reports.

In the June, 1904, issue of the *Christian Science Journal,* Mrs. Eddy explained the government of The Mother Church:

> The Magna Charta of Christian Science means much, *multum in parvo,*—all-in-one and one-in-all. It stands for the inalienable, universal rights of men. Essentially democratic, its government is administered by the common consent of the governed, wherein and whereby man governed by his creator is self-governed. The church is the mouthpiece of Christian Science,—its law and gospel are according to Christ Jesus; its rules are health, holiness, and immortality,—equal rights and privileges, equality of the sexes, rotation in office.[6]

When, in 1901, Mrs. Eddy gave to the Directors the responsibility of managing all the affairs of The Mother Church it was for the one purpose, as has been told, of for-

[6] *Miscellany,* pp. 254-55.

ever placing the government of her church in the care of a group answerable only to her and, in her absence, answerable only to the *Church Manual*.

She did it this way because, already in 1901, membership in The Mother Church had spread far beyond Boston. Mrs. Eddy foresaw a day when membership would be world-wide and only a few, comparatively speaking, would be in attendance at the annual meetings. As a result, if members attending the annual meeting were to govern the church, church affairs would be in the hands, and at the disposal of, a minority of the membership.

By making The Christian Science Board of Directors responsible for the well-being of The Mother Church she denied to any minority, at any time, the chance to control its affairs, fortified her church against the possibility of its government's ever becoming government by proxy, eternally protected it from tampering. In shaping its government, she made each member eligible to serve the church. Consequently, all Directors, and all who serve its ministry, are from its membership.

The branch churches are local organizations. As such, their members meet at regular intervals, and act as congregations in church affairs, choosing their own officers and managing their own affairs. In branch churches, as in The Mother Church, all have equal rights, including eligibility to serve the church in any capacity.

The care Mrs. Eddy took in establishing The Mother Church was in keeping with her purpose to make its government, and its teachings, as exact as the Word she sought to obey. The same exactness was written into *Science and Health*. Yet the argument was heard that, with Mrs. Eddy gone, *Science and Health*, the *Manual*, and Mrs. Eddy's other writings were out of date. The criticisms had their precedents.

When published in 1895, the *Manual* was given a mixed reception. There was fretting and complaining; it was said that there was no need for rules and by-laws in a church in which, by church law, the only preachers are the Bible and *Science and Health*.

The critics were not familiar with the responsibilities of leadership. Not only did Mrs. Eddy have a multitude of problems in connection with establishing The Mother Church, but there had to be guidance for the branch churches and societies that were springing up all over the country. Only she could give this guidance, and she was called upon constantly.[7]

With churches and societies multiplying, and having these and many other activities to watch and to initiate, it was neither practicable nor possible for Mrs. Eddy to continue her personal correspondence with all who sought her guidance.

Two needs were apparent. There must be uniformity in organization, in services, and in other essentials of church government, if the movement was to grow; and there must be protection for the organization of The Mother Church and for the teachings there imparted.

To find the way to solve these problems, Mrs. Eddy sought

[7] To all appearances, *Science and Health* was a failure when published in 1875. The first edition comprised 1,500 copies. Not all were sold. The second edition was in two volumes; 1,000 copies were printed. One volume contained so many typographical errors that it was destroyed. In 1881, although urged to abandon the book, she refused and brought out a third edition.

By 1890, the total sales of her book had reached 15,000 copies. By 1894, eighty-five editions had been published; in 1906, the edition number of *Science and Health* (cloth binding) was 417 and, in leather binding, the edition number was 418.

In 1906, Mrs. Eddy discontinued numbering the editions.

guidance from the one source she considered valid. In prayer, she found her answer. The time came when the *Manual* was ready. Its impartiality was recognized; and the time also came when, as Mrs. Eddy said it would, the *Manual* was "acknowledged as law by law."

Although it may not have seemed so to the doubters, it is plain that Mrs. Eddy's desire was that no By-law should become invalid when her approval, or consent, was no longer obtainable. There was her letter of February 27, 1903, to The Christian Science Board of Directors in which she counseled steadfast support of the *Manual.*

In the *Manual* (Article XXV, Section 2) The Christian Science Publishing Society is required to pay over to the Treasurer of The Mother Church, at stated intervals, the net profits of the business of the Society; and the Treasurer "shall hold this money subject to the order of The Christian Science Board of Directors, which is authorized to order its disposition only in accordance with the By-laws contained in this Manual."

Writing in the *Christian Science Sentinel* (July 3, 1926) George Wendell Adams expressed the view that "had Mrs. Eddy not intended her church to continue to function under the *Manual,* it would have been without reason for her to have provided in her will for property valued at approximately $2,590,000 to be given to this church in trust, to be used for the extension of the religion of Christian Science as taught by her, and also to have provided . . . that the net profits of the Publishing Society be paid to this church to be dispensed subject to its Rules and By-laws."

Also neglected by the doubters was another teaching of the Leader they professed to respect.

Having become accustomed to thinking of her as being here in person, the doubters had fallen into the habit of thinking of her as a person. In so doing, they neglected to heed a published letter written by her in declining a request by a clergyman to see her, and to talk with her.

In part, her letter read: "Those who look for me in person, or elsewhere than in my writings, lose me instead of find me." [8]

In 1886, in a sermon preached in Boston, she called upon all who heard her words to realize "that the worshippers of a person have a lower order of Christianity than he who understands that the Divine Being is more than a person, and can demonstrate in part this great impersonal Life, Truth, and Love, casting out error and healing the sick. This all-important understanding is gained in Christian Science, revealing the one God and His all-power and ever-presence, and the brotherhood of man in unity of Mind and oneness of Principle." [9]

She asked no more of her enemies than that they judge her by what she taught; and she called upon them, as she did upon her own people, to break away from reliance upon personality, reliance upon personal sense.

Among the last of her written messages is one entitled *Personality* and, to indicate its importance, she wrote a subtitle: *Personal Contagion*. In this message (*Miscellany,* copyright, 1909, pp. 116-18), she identified the dwelling place of Christian Science:

> "In the beginning was the Word, and the Word
> was with God, and the Word was God." (St. John)
> This great truth of God's impersonality and indi-

[8] *Miscellany,* p. 120.
[9] *The People's Idea of God,* p. 13.

viduality and of man in His image and likeness, individual, but not personal, is the foundation of Christian Science.

She knew that insofar as we yield to the temptation of deifying persons, we turn against God and grant a victory to idols. She knew that no person, however powerful, can protect the people of a nation or the people of the world. She knew only God can do that.

Believing that all good is in God, Mrs. Eddy was certain that the destiny of man cannot be found in an inventory called history. She was sure it can be found only in the high laws and in truths that have eternity for their unfoldment.

These were teachings that were not understood by materialists; nor did the materialists understand that, without God, humanity is defenseless before every threat that is made against it. In her teachings, disaster of every kind is without support in higher law, while study of this law leads from truth to never-ending truth and brings men into their inheritance of all that is good, all that is God.

Many years ago she began saying these things, and nearly twenty years after her passing, Charles P. Steinmetz, the genius in electricity, was interviewed by Roger Babson in *Forbes Magazine* (January 15, 1928) and predicted:

"I think the greatest discovery will be made along spiritual lines. Here is a force which history clearly teaches has been the greatest power in the development of men and history. Yet we have merely been playing with it, and have never seriously studied it as we have studied the physical forces.

"Some day people will learn that material things do not bring happiness and are of little use in making men and women creative and powerful. Then the scientists of the world will turn their laboratories over to the study of God and prayer and the spiritual forces which as yet have scarcely been scratched.

"When this day comes, the world will see more advancement in one generation than it has in the last four."

On page 382 of *Science and Health,* Mrs. Eddy said it her way: "If half the attention given to hygiene were given ... to the spiritualization of thought, this alone would usher in the millennium."

At the moment of her own healing in 1866, Mrs. Eddy saw a great truth. She saw the ever-presence of God, with its healing truth; and she found in this ever-presence not personality, but universal love. Being universal, she saw it as love that belongs to all, and love that is given to all—on the same terms.

She saw it as love that cannot be borrowed, cannot be bought, and cannot be stolen—but can be found. She perceived that all that is needed to find is to give—and also perceived that unless there is love of our fellow men there is no love of God.

On that day of perception in 1866, Mary Baker Eddy put her own personality "under my feet," and sealed her teachings in "the covenant of everlasting love." [10]

Advising her students that "pondering on the finite personality of Jesus, the son of man, is not the channel through which we reach the Christ, or Son of God, the true idea of divine Principle." [11] Mrs. Eddy also cautioned her students against expecting to receive the benefits of Christian Science by speculating about her personality.

In the almost forty-five years of her pilgrimage, she never ceased to caution against it; early, she began preparing her followers for the time of her personal absence.

[10] *Miscellany,* p. 131.
[11] *Miscellaneous Writings,* p. 309.

In 1885, she used the *Christian Science Journal* to announce that she did not take patients. Having taught others how to heal, she was anxious that nothing should interfere with their progress and anxious, too, that they, and all who came for help, should learn to look away from her and better understand that healing has its origin in God, not in person.

In 1889, at the height of its prosperity, she closed the Massachusetts Metaphysical College where she had held classes in Christian Science since 1881, and went to Barre, Vermont, for a short rest. Then, instead of returning to Boston, she moved to Concord, New Hampshire, that she might be released for her great purpose of bringing the world to understand that, unless men are free to obey the laws of God, it is useless to talk of any other freedom, and that men who are free spiritually cannot live in a manner unworthy of them.

From Concord, early in 1890, she sent word to all her students that she was not to be "consulted, verbally or through letters," on personal or organizational matters. On June 6, 1891, she wrote to the members of the Christian Scientists' Association of the Massachusetts Metaphysical College:

> My Beloved Students:—You may be looking to see me in my accustomed place with you, but this you must no longer expect. When I retired from the field of labor, it was a departure, socially, publicly, and finally, from the routine of such material modes as society and our societies demand. Rumors are rumors,—nothing more. I am still with you on the field of battle, taking forward marches, broader and higher views, and with the hope that you will follow.

The eternal and infinite, already brought to your earnest consideration, so grow upon my vision that I cannot feel justified in turning aside for one hour from contemplation of them and of the faith unfeigned. When the verities of being seem to you as to me,—as they must some time,—you will understand the necessity for my seclusion, and its fulfillment of divine order. "Wherefore come out from among them, and be ye separate, saith the Lord."

All our thoughts should be given to the absolute demonstration of Christian Science. You can well afford to give me up, since you have in my last revised edition of Science and Health your teacher and guide.[12]

Mrs. Eddy's use of the apostle Paul's plea to the congregation in Corinth when calling upon the members of the Christian Scientists' Association of the Massachusetts Metaphysical College to "come out from among them, and be ye separate," was not by chance.

She, too, was a builder of churches. She, too, knew disappointment.

Having organized a church in Corinth, Paul used his experience with an almost wholly Greek membership to spread Christianity over Asia Minor and into Europe. Now, with backsliders appearing, he pleaded with the Corinthians:

Be ye not unequally yoked together with unbelievers; for what fellowship hath righteousness with unrighteousness? and what communion hath light with darkness? And what concord hath Christ with Belial? or what part hath he that believeth with an infidel? And what agreement hath the

[12] *Miscellaneous Writings,* pp. 135-36.

temple of God with idols? for ye are the temple of
the living God; as God hath said, I will dwell in
them, and walk in *them;* and I will be their God,
and they shall be my people.

Wherefore come out from among them, and be
ye separate . . .

Paul was repudiated by some in Jerusalem. They said
he was not a true Christian because he was not of the twelve,
nor of those who knew Jesus in Jerusalem, in Capernaum,
in the hills of Judea; and while Paul was in Ephesus they
sent agents to Galatia to stir up rebellion. Writing from
Rome, Paul admonished the Galatians:

Do I now persuade men, or God? or do I seek to
please men? for if I yet pleased men, I would not
be a servant of Christ. But I certify you, brethren,
that the gospel which was preached of me is not
after men. For I neither received it of men, neither
was I taught *it* but by the revelation of Jesus Christ.

In 1888, when she was away from Boston and in Chicago,
Mrs. Eddy was repudiated by thirty-four members of the
Christian Scientists' Association of the Massachusetts Metaphysical College, who seized the records of the Association,
corrupted her teachings, and organized their own "Christian Science" churches.

Paul reminded the Galatians that they were "all the children of God by faith in Christ Jesus," and, by placing them
completely within the teachings of Jesus, rejected any dependence they might have had on Judaic discipline. Mrs.
Eddy's teachings were equally radical. She broke sharply
with a theology that, for centuries, had patronized two
deities, God and the devil, had divided man into two parts,

soul and body, and life into two phases, here and hereafter.

She identified God as Truth and as Spirit, the devil as evil and as a lie; she defined the body as matter, matter as mortal mind, and mortal mind as nothing; she spoke of man as spiritual and as perfect, created, as the Bible says, in the image of God, and in the likeness of God; she believed life to be without end. She, too, placed her people completely within the teachings of Jesus by instructing them to follow her "only so far as she follows Christ"—and instructed them to search the Scriptures and judge for themselves if, in her teachings, she did follow Christ.

Paul was arrested in Jerusalem, faced trial in Rome, was found guilty of being a Christian, and, probably, was executed in A.D. 64; because she was a Christian Scientist, Mrs. Eddy was the subject of nearly half a century of ridicule and scorn, and in her last years enemies sought to destroy her by pleading with the court to declare her insane.

Paul could have multiplied his churches had he been willing to include charms and incantations in his teachings; Mrs. Eddy could have done likewise had she been willing to include mesmerism and spiritualism. Paul's churches were forced to be in constant touch with each other in an atmosphere of self-protection; Christian Science churches were closely knit for the same reason. The enemies of Paul were ecclesiasticism, gnosticism, and the Roman government; the enemies of Mrs. Eddy were ecclesiasticism, dissemblers, and local governments.

Paul's final instructions were written in Rome, not long before his death. Epaphroditus had come to him with a gift of money from the Philippians that he might defend himself in the court of Nero. In gratitude, Paul wrote his moving and tender farewell to his church in Philippi:

Only let your conversation be as it becometh the gospel of Christ: that whether I come and see you, or else be absent, I may hear of your affairs, that ye stand fast in one spirit, with one mind, striving together for the faith of the gospel; Wherefore, my beloved, as ye have always obeyed, not as in my presence only, but now much more in my absence, work out your own salvation with fear and trembling. For it is God which worketh in you both to will and to do *his* good pleasure. And the peace of God, which passeth all understanding, shall keep your hearts through Christ Jesus.

At the close of Sunday morning services in The Mother Church, The First Church of Christ, Scientist, in Boston, Massachusetts, on December 4, 1910, the First Reader paused before he pronounced the benediction—then went on, his eyes holding to the pages of a book open before him as, carefully, he read aloud:

My Beloved Students:—You may be looking to see me in my accustomed place with you, but this you must no longer expect. When I retired from the field of labor, it was a departure, socially, publicly, and finally, from the routine of such material modes as society and our societies demand. Rumors are rumors,—nothing more. I am still with you on the field of battle, taking forward marches, broader and higher views, and with the hope that you will follow. . . .

A hushed quietness settled over the congregation, and kept it standing, as realization came to its members that they had heard Mrs. Eddy's farewell, that she had gone on, taking that which belongs to her, their love, and leaving that which belonged to them, her love.

In the comment and speculation that marked her passing, there were a few paragraphs in *The Woman's National Daily,* of St. Louis, Missouri, which seemed to interpret better than did most newspaper and magazine editorials the place this woman held in the minds of her own people:

"It is peculiarly human to venerate and sanctify our ancestors and stone those who seek to better life while we are living it. But a comparatively few years ago a man died whose life had been spent in causing the world to swim in blood and misery. The world trembled and gasped in relief as he died, and then proceeded to glorify him as it had groveled at his feet while he lived. He had emptied a million homes of their breadwinners, caused more widespread misery and distress than any man who ever lived, and built a world empire which crumbled before he was gone; yet when Napoleon Bonaparte died all the world bowed its head in tribute to the beating he had given it.

"Two nights ago a frail little old gentlewoman died who, too, had built an empire, but not of blood and misery. A million hearts silently mourned her for a moment, but in accordance with her own teachings it was only a tribute of love and loyalty for the brighter, better viewpoint of their own life and death she had taught them.

"There was no pomp; but a few brief words following the usual services, and the announcement that a loved and revered Leader had exchanged a mortal form for an immortal one. She had shed no blood, destroyed no homes, shackled no nation, but what she had done was to take away a little human misery and substitute a happier, better attitude toward life.

"She taught nothing new, for what she taught was but a

different view of the first thing—the beginning and the end. We may differ from that view, but none can even now doubt but that she was one of the most remarkable souls that has appeared in human guise.

"We cannot know how much of such rare human lives is abnormal genius and how much a message and a lesson put in understandable, humanly tangible form by divine Love. Certainly, whether we agree with the teachings, or reject them, the lesson is the same and the world grows better with each such lesson. We stoned her for a time, as usual, and perhaps she will soon be forgotten, or perhaps future generations will cloak her with divinity.

"At any rate, the world owes that frail woman a greater debt than it owed the world conqueror, and if her works be of life they will live; and if not they will die, but the fact that even a single life has been made better will not be lost in the world's melting pot from which through countless centuries a great purpose, beyond our human understanding, is being worked out. Some time in the future, perhaps, the race will stone the bloody monster who seeks to make it swim in blood to gratify his own lust, and honor the pure of heart, who seeks to brighten it; but we are not yet quite that civilized.

"I have never read Mrs. Eddy's book or teachings, but I have seen some results of them which compelled both honor and respect, and I believe that all are agreed that a reasonable way of judging a tree is by its fruit. Nothing could have been finer than the way of her going and its reception by the multitude whose Leader and loved teacher she has been."

As with Paul, Mrs. Eddy was a teacher well within the definition: "He teaches who gives, he learns who receives."

That she chose, as did Paul, the most difficult work of all is not surprising. Identifying herself with her work, and identifying her work with God, she could do nothing else than choose as she did, and do as she did.

In all the years of her ministry, she never spoke of God as less than All.

In this stand she was in conflict with scholasticism, which seeks to confine Him within the limits of its doctrinal explanations. Mrs. Eddy did not believe that any doctrine which seeks to limit God is to be trusted; however much a qualification of limitation might be acceptable to scholasticism, it was not acceptable to her. She believed, as she said in *Science and Health* (p. 275), that "God, Spirit, is All-in-all, and there is no other might nor Mind."

This belief that God is All-in-all and, therefore, limitless, is the essence of her teaching.

It was this conviction that brought her into conflict with doctrines that interpreted Christianity in terms of formalism. She regarded formalism as a creature of materialism and made her position clear in *Science and Health* (p. 256) by stating: "A finite and material sense of God leads to formalism and narrowness; it chills the spirit of Christianity."

There is no evasion in Mrs. Eddy's teachings, and no compromise. In her teachings every attempt to lessen God as Spirit is an attempt to establish Him as matter so that mortal mind may have dominion over mankind—and every effort to formalize Him is an effort to destroy His allness by making him an accessory to ceremony.

Believing communion to be within, she had no need for ceremony; accepting the great fact that God's presence is always at hand, she felt no security in tradition. In the injunction, "They that worship him must worship *him* in spirit and in truth," she found the way into communion and, knowing there was One who rejected the temptations of tradition, she stood her ground with Him: *And he said unto them, Full well ye reject the commandment of God, that ye may keep your own tradition.*

In Mrs. Eddy's teachings the way into understanding is the same for all. Instruction is the same; all walk in the same steps; progress is the same; and, as grace and truth were the companions of Jesus, so may they be the companions of all men. All that is needed to be in their company is to acknowledge their presence.

Mrs. Eddy was sure that in the Kingdom of God all men are equal, all men have access to the same Source, and each must be his own minister in the understanding that, as truly as Jesus recognized His relationship to God, just as truly will all men, when they recognize their relationship to God, know that they, too, are sons of the eternal Father, each and every one.

The world may disagree, but hers are teachings whose only ritual is love of God, whose only sacrament is love of our fellow men.

The protection of that love is the single assignment she gave to The Christian Science Board of Directors.

Serving as Directors in 1911 were Ira O. Knapp, Stephen A. Chase, Adam H. Dickey, Archibald McLellan, and John V. Dittemore. So great was the cooperation given them by the great majority of Mrs. Eddy's followers that, in the first full year after her passing, the growth in membership in The Mother Church exceeded, as the Treasurer reported, "all previous records in the history of our denomination."

In the year ending March 31, 1912, 65 churches and societies—a new one every few days—were organized in the United States, in Canada, in Europe, in South America, in

Australia, and in New Zealand. During the same fiscal year, the number of persons devoting themselves wholly to the practice of Christian Science healing increased to 5,193 from a total of 4,870 at the close of the preceding year. This increase of 323 practitioners was the largest in any one year since the beginning of the movement.

This growth did not take place unnoticed.

Before 1911, laws prohibiting the practice of Christian Science had been introduced into nearly every state legislature. In 1911, the freedom of Christian Scientists to practice their religion was threatened in the Congress of the United States. In this year, United States Senator Robert L. Owen of Oklahoma introduced a bill into the Senate calling for the establishment of a department of health under which would be placed the physical well-being of all persons living in the United States and its territories.

In arguing for passage of the legislation, Owen said:

"The health service established by this act shall have no power to regulate the practice of medicine or the practice of healing, or to interfere with the right of a citizen to employ the practitioner of his own choice, and all appointments made within the health service, including the head of the service, shall be made without discrimination in favor of or against any school of medicine, or of healing."

The senator's assurances were not convincing to Christian Scientists, nor, for that matter, to medical groups, although the proposed legislation had the strong backing of the American Medical Association.

In the bill, in Section 3, was this provision:

"It is the province and duty of the department of health to foster and promote all matters pertaining to the conservation and improvement of the public health and to collect and disseminate information relating thereto."

Medical groups, as distinguished from the American Medical Association, were concerned with what the proposed legislation portended. In making it "the province and the duty of the department of health to foster and promote all matters pertaining to the conservation and improvement of the public health," members of different medical groups detected the encroachment of state medicine. They were aware of division of opinion within their own ranks as to which school of medicine was best, and probably felt as did the justices of the Supreme Court of North Carolina who, after considering a medical dispute before them, stated:

"Some M.D.'s doubtless believe that all treatment of disease, except for their own system, is quackery. Is this point to be decided by the M.D.'s themselves . . . or is the public the tribunal to decide by employing whom each man prefers? . . . The law says that the M.D.'s may examine and certify whether an applicant is competent to be one of their number . . . but they cannot decide for mankind that their own system of healing is now and ever shall be the correct one, and that all others are to be repressed by the strong arm of the law." (State v. Biggs, 133 N. C. Reports 729, 64 L.R.A. 139.)

Conscious of the smallness of their own knowledge in the broad subject of health, medical groups saw, as did William Lloyd Garrison, the great danger of establishing, by law, the supremacy of the superficial. Speaking before a committee of the Massachusetts legislature in 1896, Garrison said:

"One has only to read the candid opinions of eminent physicians of long practice to realize how tentative and purely experimental is the science of medicine. The death of a patient under 'irregular treatment,' although it may be demonstrated that the greatest care and intelligence were used, is heralded abroad as something scandalous and dreadful, but if any regular physician were to make public the deaths coming to his knowledge from misapprehension of the disease, or because of mistaken remedies used, the public might well be alarmed.

"A statement of the truth is not to disparage the noble body of men and women who give their lives and thoughts to this divine service of humanity, but it is to remind them of their fallibility, and to bespeak their tolerance for others having the same high end. . . ."

Opposing the Owen bill was an organization calling itself the National League for Medical Freedom. Identifying the League as a mixture of patent-medicine vendors, homeopaths, osteopaths, and Christian Scientists, *The Journal of the American Medical Association* charged the members with opposing laws of sanitation as well as pure-food laws and with seeking to destroy public confidence in the medical profession.

In the *Congressional Record* (June 23, 1911) was an editorial from the official organ of the American Medical Association in which it also was stated:

"The members of the so-called League for Medical Freedom have been grossly imposed upon and have been grossly misrepresented as to what they truly stand for. . . . I know what Christian Scientists stand for, and I sympathize with them; I understand what the osteopaths stand for, and I think they serve a good and useful purpose. They have been misled by the agents of the patent medicine association in this country, that are actually engaged in promoting the drug habit in our citizens. . . ."

Continuing, the editorial asserted:

"The proposed department of health would have just as

much authority to determine 'what kind of medical treatment' the people should employ as the Department of Agriculture has to dictate to the farmer regarding the implement company he should buy his plows of. Yet we are asked to believe, apparently, that the national department of health would mean that the freeborn American citizen who wanted to have a purulent appendix cured by the 'spinal adjustment' rote would have to patronize a surgeon, even though he were a 'conscientious objector' to surgery. It would mean, it seems, that the individual suffering from malaria who wished to be freed from this 'moral error' by 'absent treatment' would be ignominiously dragged to the internist and dosed with quinine. . . ."

John D. Works, United States senator from California, and a Christian Scientist, spoke out on the floor of the Senate:

"The first thing to which I desire to address myself is the claim made in the articles that have been read in the *Record* by the Senator from Oklahoma (Mr. Owen) that the League for Medical Freedom is, if not made up by, actually influenced and controlled by selfish interests, by the vendors and manufacturers of patent medicines.

"I want right at the beginning to deny that assertion emphatically and without qualification. I know something about the composition of the League for Medical Freedom. I know that the people who are standing behind that league and undertaking to prevent the kind of legislation that is sought here in Congress and throughout the States are people who are simply standing for the principle that every sort of healing medium, whether it be the doctors of this profession, or that profession, this school or that school, or whatever it may be, shall have the right and freedom to exercise their rights as American citizens in that direction as well as in all others.

"It is for this very reason that the American Medical Association has for the past 20 years been seeking legislation in the various States of this country that would shut out and prevent the exercise of the power of healing disease on the part of others that the opposition has arisen, and for no other reason.

"I have some personal knowledge of the efforts that have been made in my own State to bring about just such legislation as this. We have been compelled to meet it at every session of the legislature of our State for years past. It has not stopped at the effort to elevate and make efficient the medical profession to which no one has ever objected. It has gone further than that and attempted, by legislation, to exclude everybody else from practicing at all.

"For a long time it was directed at the Homeopathic School of Medicine, until that school became so strong that it was useless to attempt longer anything of that sort. Then it followed in the case of others and, finally, came to the Christian Scientists, and for the past 8 or 10 years the effort of the American Medical Association has been to secure some sort of legislation that would absolutely bar the Christian Scientists from all opportunity to exercise their right of healing disease. . . .

"We have had to keep vigilant watch constantly in my State. I know it is just as true with respect to other States; and back of all this effort to keep everybody else out of the practice of healing disease has been the American Medical Association, not always openly, sometimes they pushed somebody else to the front, but you will always find behind it the force and power of the American Medical Association.

"That is exactly the condition that exists with respect to the bill now before the Senate. . . ."

The charge that Christian Scientists opposed laws providing for sanitation and pure food was not true; nor was it true, as the American Medical Association inferred, that Christian Scientists, as a group, were endorsing the League for Medical Freedom. As individuals, Christian Scientists were members, with membership being an individual act, not representing any Christian Science church. Individual doctors were members, too, but not as representatives of the American Medical Association.

Also, it was not true that Christian Scientists sought to destroy public confidence in the medical profession. To have done so would have been to violate their Leader's teachings. In *Miscellaneous Writings* (pp. 79-80), Mrs. Eddy advised her followers to

> beware of joining any medical league which in any way obligates you to assist—because they chance to be under arrest—vendors of patent pills, mesmerists, occultists, sellers of impure literature, and authors of spurious works on mental healing. By rendering error such a service, you lose much more than can be gained by mere unity on the single issue of opposition to unjust medical laws.

In Mrs. Eddy's teachings there is complete willingness to abide by the test proposed by Gamaliel so long ago.

Pausing at the gate to the temple, the disciples looked down and, expecting alms, the lame man looked up; but, instead of seeing an open purse, the alms-seeker heard Peter say, "Silver and gold have I none; but such as I have I give thee: In the name of Jesus Christ of Nazareth rise up and walk."

Toward evening of the same day Peter and John were come upon by the priests, and by the captain of the temple, and by the Sadducees, were arrested, and were taken away. The following day Annas, the high priest who questioned Jesus on the night of Gethsemane, questioned them, seeking to learn by what means the man who had been lame from birth was made well; and he resented Peter's answer:

> Be it known unto you all, and to all the people of Israel, that by the name of Jesus Christ of Nazareth, whom ye crucified, whom God raised from the dead, *even* by him does this man stand before you whole.

Ordering Peter and John to teach no more in the name of the crucified One, the high priest let them go; but arrested them once more and cast them into the common prison because, in the name of Jesus, they again healed the sick in the streets of Jerusalem.

That night the angel of the Lord opened the prison doors and told the disciples to go to the temple and speak there to the people. In the morning when the high priest and the chief priests heard of the deliverance, and of the continued disobedience, they had the disciples brought before them; they talked among themselves of killing Peter and John who, in defending their disobedience, said, "We ought to obey God rather than men."

It was while the high priest and the chief priests were agreeing to put to death these whose teachings were certified in their deeds that there stood forth a Pharisee, a doctor of the law, named Gamaliel. Gamaliel then advised the high priest and the chief priests, saying: "Refrain from these men, and let them alone; for if this counsel or this work be of men, it will come to nought: But if it be of God, ye cannot overthrow it."

CHAPTER THREE

To Ask God to Heal the Sick
Is against the Law

THE office consisted of two rooms and was on the ninth floor of a building located at Fifth Avenue and 26th Street, in New York City.

The inner of the two rooms contained a desk, two chairs, and on the desk was a telephone and two books: one the Bible, the other *Science and Health*. The outer room was a reception room containing several chairs and a table, on which was a selection of Christian Science literature. On the glass panel of the door opening into the corridor were printed the words, WILLIS VERNON COLE, Christian Scientist.

In the reception room were several people, and in the inner office behind the desk was a man. Opposite him, sitting on a chair in front of the desk, was a woman. The man was Willis Vernon Cole; the woman was Mrs. Isabelle Goodwin and she had come because, as she said, she was sick and she had read in the newspapers that he healed the sick.

He talked to her, not about sickness but about God, of her relationship to God; in her presence he prayed that she might find the health she said she was seeking. She did not tell him she was a police matron and that she was gathering evidence for the purpose of having him arrested.

It was shortly before noon on Saturday when the police

matron left Cole's office. She hurried back to Central Police Station where she wrote a detailed account of her visit with the Christian Science practitioner. She told of questioning him about Christian Science, of hearing him say that in Christian Science prayer is the treatment that destroys human ills; she reported that his charge for the first treatment was two dollars, and one dollar for each succeeding treatment, that she had paid him two dollars and he had accepted the money.

Completing her affidavit, she left it for the attention of her superiors in the police department.

The date was January 7, 1911.

A week later, in the afternoon of Saturday, January 14, two police detectives went to Cole's office, charged him with practicing medicine without a license, and arrested him. The practitioner was escorted to the Central Police Station, booked, advised to get a lawyer, and was taken to night police court. Here he was arraigned. At the request of his counsel,[1] the magistrate postponed hearing the case until January 26 and set bail at $500.

On January 26, it was disclosed that the police matron had failed to sign the affidavit upon which the warrant was issued and, to cover her failure, a police magistrate had signed it. Taking advantage of this legal technicality, Cole's attorney demanded dismissal of the case.

His argument was allowed, but Cole was rearrested on a new warrant issued at the instance of the district attorney, who was displaying a lively interest in what was being treated by the newspapers as a routine police incident. Actively supporting the action of the district attorney was the New York County Medical Society; lawyers representing the So-

---

[1] William Travers Jerome, already famous as the prosecutor of Harry K. Thaw who shot and killed Stanford White.

ciety were advising him on the prosecution of the Christian
Science practitioner.

On February 11, Cole was in Jefferson Market Court. The
noise of the elevated trains on Sixth Avenue, just outside
the closed windows of the courtroom, did not keep Cole
from hearing himself, and his work as a Christian Science
practitioner, castigated by the district attorney.

"The practice of belief in Almighty God and in the religious tenets of the church has never been construed by
any court in America to be a business, a vocation, a profession; nor has any court in America ever countenanced
pseudo-religious practices in defiance of established law.
The defendant was neither conducting an eleemosynary institution nor a church; he was neither preaching nor teaching; he was not in the sanctuary of the faith.

"On the contrary, he was in a suite of offices in an office
building, with his name on the door, conducting a business
of receiving all comers, and selling them an intangible something for tangible specie. This was not religion. It was business. Similar business might be carried on by anyone under
the pretense of carrying out the tenets of a religious faith."

In reply, Cole's attorney observed, "There is something
of cant and hypocrisy in that objection [accepting money
for treatment] though we doubt not it is heartfelt enough on
the part of physicians. The practitioner, as well as the minister, must earn a living; and so must the doctor."

Sardonically, the district attorney sought to learn from the
practitioner how he prayed, what he said when he prayed,
and if he fitted his prayer to meet the occasion. Cole's attorney instructed his client not to answer these, or like,
questions. Then, going directly to the issue involved, the
lawyer pointed out that Cole's arrest, detention, and trial
did violence to the freedom of religion which was guaran-

teed the individual citizen by the Constitution of the State of New York and by the Constitution of the United States, with its Bill of Rights.

Supporting him were documents reminding the magistrate of the provision in the Charter of Liberty and Privileges adopted by the first legislature in New York in October, 1683:

"THAT Noe person or persons which profess ffaith in God by Jesus Christ Shall at any time by any wayes molested punished disquieted or called in Question for any Difference in opinion or Matter of Religious Concernment, who do not actually disturb the Civill peace of the province, but that all and every such person or persons may from time to time and at all times freely have and fully enjoy his or their Judgments or Consciencyes in matters of Religion throughout the province, they behaveing themselves peaceably and quietly and not using this Liberty to Lycentiousnesse nor to the Civill Injury or outward disturbance of others. . . ."

The lawyer pointed out that the First Constitution of the State of New York, as ratified in April, 1777, "did ORDAIN, DETERMINE, AND DECLARE That the free exercise and enjoyment of religious profession and worship, with discrimination or preference, shall forever hereafter be allowed within this state to all mankind; Provided, That the liberty of conscience hereby granted shall not be so construed as to excuse acts of licentiousness, or to justify practices inconsistent with the peace or safety of this state."

And as provided in October, 1683, and again in April, 1777, so in March, 1789, when the Constitution of the United States was declared in effect, that Constitution guaranteed, in Article I of its Bill of Rights (First Amendment):

"Congress shall make no law respecting an establishment of religion, or prohibiting the free exercise thereof. . . ."

Also, there was the New York Public Health Law of 1907 which pertained to the practice of medicine, and which contained the words: "This article shall not be construed to affect . . . the practice of the religious tenets of any church."

Having emphasized these guarantees, Cole's attorney referred to the implied contention of the district attorney that, under the laws of the State of New York, "no one has the right to heal sickness by prayer"; and then he commented, with a show of asperity: "The prayer of faith that heals the sick, as recommended by St. James, is against the law unless the supplicant is a licensed administrator of drugs, the supposed beneficence of such law being that the patient should trust primarily to a bolus of some kind—and inadvertently and contingently, but only in extremis, to God Himself."

The magistrate was not persuaded. In a decision covering some twenty typewritten pages, he found Cole guilty and, in so doing, said:

"The establishment and the teaching of the religion in which the defendant is an ardent believer contravenes no law. Prohibiting the free exercise thereof would clearly be unconstitutional. But the freedom of religion cannot be extended to prevent the punishment of crime. The field of personal opinion is inviolable. The Church and the State must be independent. The inviolability of the freedom of religious profession and worship must, however, in no wise impair or menace the safety of the State, or the security of its people in their health.

"The Christian Scientist has the right to believe he can heal by prayer, but I am of the opinion that if he carries and puts that belief into practice for hire, and solicits patronage by advertising then he exceeds his rights as an individual under the law, and comes directly within the prohibition contained in the Constitution of the State of New York."

Cole was fined $100, which he paid under protest.

Here, for the time being, the case rested, although, after he had imposed the fine, the magistrate was reported as having said, "Did I not know the case would be taken to a higher court, I would have sentenced Cole to jail, in addition to fining him," so strongly did the magistrate seem to feel the menace of Christian Science to the "safety of the State, and the health of its people."

With the decision, the members of the ten Churches of Christ, Scientist, in the City of New York, in accordance with Cole's wishes, employed Samuel Untermyer and Henry D. Estabrook as legal counsel for the practitioner.

What was involved here was not the freedom, or the good repute, of one individual, nor the freedom, or good repute, of one group. Involved here was the freedom, and good repute, of all mankind, whether Jew or Gentile, Roman Catholic or Protestant, Christian Scientist, Buddhist, Hindu, Mohammedan, Mormon, or Taoist. Involved was a principle which, if denied to a Christian Scientist, could be denied to the Jew in his ancient ceremony of circumcision, with its attendance of the Mohl; a principle which, if denied to a Jew, would deny to the Roman Catholic the candles of his devotion to the saints of his church:

The free exercise and enjoyment of religious profession and worship, without discrimination or preference, shall forever be allowed in this state to all mankind. . . . Congress shall make no laws respecting an establishment of religion, or prohibiting the free exercise thereof. . . .

These were guarantees of state and of nation.

The validity of these guarantees was involved—solely their validity, nothing else.

One of the first things Untermyer and Estabrook did was to meet with the attorneys for the Medical Society and agree that the Cole case would be a test case. There would be no more arrests of Christian Science practitioners until the case was decided in the courts.

The agreement was not kept.

A number of practitioners were arrested, among them Wentworth Byron Winslow. The newspapers were informed that, fifteen years before, Winslow was sent to jail as "a common drunkard." What the attorneys for the Medical Society, and the district attorney, did not tell the newspapers was that Winslow had been healed of alcoholism by a Christian Science practitioner and, in gratitude, had become a student of Mrs. Eddy's teachings.

Untermyer and Estabrook protested the arrests as an attempt by the Medical Society to compel them to agree to the trying of the case in the Court of Special Sessions where there were three judges and no jury, instead of in the Court of General Sessions where there was a jury and one judge. They appealed to the chief magistrate to compel the attorneys for the Medical Society to keep their agreement:

"In answer to our appeal to the counsel for the Medical Society to cease making these arrests until a test of the law and its application to practitioners of the Christian Science church can be held in accordance with the expressed wish of the Society, we are told (1) that it is not willing to have a test of the law in the Cole case now pending in General Sessions, and (2) that it will continue making these arrests until some court can be found that will not grant the defendant a jury trial.

"While the New York County Medical Society includes

in its membership many of the best and most public-spirited men in the community, its action in this case in attempting to interfere with religious liberty adds another to the many illustrations of the unwisdom of permitting private individuals or associations to act as prosecutors in the enforcement of the criminal laws of the State. Such private prosecutors are likely to become unconsciously fanatics and persecutors.

"We herewith appeal and protest to you and through you to the Magistrates in the First and Second Divisions against the proposed test of this law being used as an instrument of persecution. We accordingly ask that the Magistrates be requested to issue no further warrants in these cases until such a test is made. The idea of attempting to force us to waive a jury trial is intolerable."

The request was granted by the chief magistrate.

Meanwhile, Cole was continuing his work as a Christian Science practitioner and among those who came to see him was Mrs. Frances Benzecry, an investigator for the New York County Medical Society, although Cole did not know it.

Sitting in the same chair where the police matron had sat, the investigator said she, too, was sick; and, as he had with the policewoman, Cole talked about God, saying, substantially [as later testified] that "Christian Science is the truth about God, and the truth about man, and the truth about man's relationship to God, and the truth of his birthright as a result of this relationship ... and disease was not a part of this birthright."

The investigator made five visits to Cole's office, paying two dollars for the first visit, and one dollar for each of the four subsequent visits. On January 19, which was the day she first saw Cole, she said she was suffering from "eye trouble"; on January 20, she had "pains in her back"; on January 23, she complained because eating bread and potatoes gave her "a distressed stomach"; on January 25, she did not "feel good"; on January 27, she brought along her small daughter, and asked that the child be healed of the need for wearing glasses—and, also, she came to inquire about "a delicate condition."

Determined to deny Cole a jury trial, and knowing that a Grand Jury indictment was necessary if the case was to be presented to the three judges in the Court of Special Sessions, the lawyers for the Medical Society handed the reports of the investigator to the district attorney and asked that they be presented to the grand jury.

This was done and, on March 21, 1911, the grand jury returned an indictment [2] charging Cole with "the crime of practicing medicine without lawful authorization and registration committed as follows: January 19, 1911, thence continually to the 28th of January 1911."

Untermyer and Estabrook were twitted by the Medical Society lawyers about their public stand that "the great question to be decided is whether the court has a right to interfere with prayer," and were told, if it was law they wanted, "three learned judges could decide that question better than twelve laymen sitting in a jury box." The Medical Society lawyers were reminded that they had charged Cole with committing a crime, had branded him a criminal and that, being so charged, their victim was entitled to a jury trial.

After weeks of legalistic sparring, the case opened for trial before a jury in the Court of General Sessions.

There was no verdict. The jury was divided, eight for acquittal, and four for conviction, and was discharged. An-

[2] The grand jury refused to indict other Christian Science practitioners.

other trial was ordered in the same courtroom, and before the same judge.

The second trial opened March 28, 1912, with Untermyer protesting the action of the judge and his delay of the trial in calling for a special jury panel, instead of using "an ordinary petit jury." The protest was not allowed and the first day was spent in selecting a jury from the special panel. The following morning the district attorney opened for the prosecution by telling the jury: "This case is a case of great importance. You gentlemen may have thought it was strange that a jury be ordered from a special panel to try a man merely for a misdemeanor. But you can easily see now that it is a case of great importance."

After explaining the issue as one that concerned the right of a Christian Science practitioner to practice medicine, the district attorney continued: "I do not know how large the church is. But I take it there is a considerable number of people in it. And if those people are the only class of people in the State of New York that can treat physical disease without a license, telling those that come to them to dispense with the services of a doctor, and they are entitled to do it without danger of arrest—if they are doing that lawfully, they ought to know it so they can go ahead without thinking that the people that come in there are going to procure their arrest.

"On the other hand, if they are not entitled to it, if it is, as the People allege, a great danger and menace, that those people without any medical training of any description, can hold themselves out as people to treat any disease of any kind, of any nature, preventing people from resorting to medical help and assistance—if that can be done, we want to know that.

"And, therefore, you will see that it is of great importance in this case, as it is in every case, that the verdict of the jury should simply declare the facts in the light of the law as the court lays down to you, so that we may have a valid and logical basis to go on whatever future action either side may be forced to take in this case; and that the verdict of this jury should not reflect any sentimentality, sympathy or speculation on matters outside the evidence; that it may be a solid and firm and logical foundation for the action that ought to be necessary one way or the other in this case."

In the second trial, as in the first, the district attorney sought to prove that the treatment of disease through prayer was within the language of the Public Health Law which provided that a person practices medicine when he "holds himself out as being able to diagnose, treat, operate or prescribe for any human disease, pain, injury, deformity or physical condition, and who shall either offer, or undertake, by any means or method, to diagnose, treat, operate, or prescribe for any human disease, pain, injury, deformity or physical condition"—and he also sought to prove that the exception to the Public Law which denied the right of interference with "the religious tenets of any church" did not apply to Christian Science, indicating his own opinion that Christian Science could not be considered a religion.

The investigator for the Medical Society was questioned about her five visits to the office of the practitioner. She testified that on the day of her first visit she asked, " 'Are you Dr. Cole?' and he said, 'I am Mr. Cole, and I am a Christian Science healer.'

"I said I had read about him in the newspapers, and that I came to see if he could cure my eyes and he said, 'How long have you been wearing glasses?' and I said, 'Ten years,' and he said, 'You understand I do not give medicine, I give only Christian Science treatment.'

" 'What is Christian Science treatment?' I asked. He said

you must have faith in God; that God don't make us have any diseases; that we must be all love and all kindness and that God would cure the infidel as well as the confirmed believer in His Divine power. And I said, 'What would be the fee?' and he said, 'Two dollars for the first treatment, and all subsequent treatments one dollar.' "

"Did you ask him to treat you?" questioned the district attorney.

"Yes."

"And then?"

"So Mr. Cole had his chair facing mine, and he closed his eyes and raised his hands up to his face, and remained in perfect silence for fifteen or twenty minutes. He said, 'That will do for today's treatment.' "

On the second visit the investigator for the Medical Society testified that she told Cole, "I have a pain in my back," that she was wearing a porous plaster, and asked him to diagnose her condition. This he did not do, but did say if he was to help her she must remove the porous plaster, and explained that doing this would manifest her "reliance upon God to heal her of disease." On the possibility she might be suffering from "locomotor ataxia," she asked if this disease could be healed in Christian Science. He assured her it could be healed "by prayer, and by having faith in God."

Three days afterwards she was back. She testified she told Cole she had "removed the porous plaster," and he had said, "I want you also to remove the glasses." This she did not do, explaining her immediate problem as being the eating of bread and potatoes because "they distress my stomach very much." She paid for her third treatment, and heard Cole say: "Leave your stomach alone. You go home, and eat anything you want."

Because she did not "feel very good, all over," she was back in Cole's office on January 23, or two days after her third visit. On January 27, she was there again, and with her was her ten-year-old daughter. The little girl was suffering from a cold, and the mother inquired: "Can you cure her by Christian Science?"

"Absolutely," Cole replied.

The investigator testified that she told Cole the child liked to roller skate "and, wearing glasses, if she should fall she would injure herself." In reply, so she said, Cole told her "not to put such fears into the child's mind, but take the glasses off and let the child romp and play like other children."

Under cross-examination by Untermyer, Mrs. Benzecry disclosed another reason for her fifth visit.

"How many Christian Scientists have you investigated since Mr. Cole?" asked Untermyer.

"Only one besides Mr. Cole."

"You were told to represent to them [the practitioners] that you were in delicate condition, and see if they would perform an abortion?"

"Oh no, not an abortion."

"Well, to get rid of pregnancy?"

"I wanted to see what position they would take on it."

"You were instructed to see what position they would take on it?"

Before the witness could answer the district attorney was on his feet, protesting further questioning on this subject. The court sustained the protest.

Untermyer sought to learn from the witness whether "Mr. Cole did have anything to say about it." Again the district attorney objected, arguing that any answer the witness would give "would be irrelevant." Again he was sustained.

Untermyer persisted. He began a question, "they refused," and was interrupted by the district attorney. Appealing to the judge for permission to complete his question, and receiving it, Cole's attorney said to the witness: "Weren't you told that Christian Science does not talk about such things?"

Again the court agreed with the district attorney that the witness need not answer. Untermyer took an exception to the ruling, and relinquished the witness to his associate, Henry D. Estabrook.

Under Estabrook's questioning, Mrs. Benzecry was taken over the familiar ground of her experience as an investigator. Using the name of Belle Holmes, she said she had been active in police raids on the offices of palmists and astrologers, that she wrote for magazines and newspapers, and that she had been in the employ of the New York County Medical Society for seven years. She had gone to see Cole under instructions from attorneys for the Medical Society.

"Did you know what Christian Science was?" asked Estabrook.

"No, I did not."

"Or what it pretended to be?"

"Only by hearsay."

"Did not you know in a general way that it pretended to be founded on the teachings of the Bible?"

"I knew something about Mrs. Eddy. That is all."

"You had not found out that it pretended to be founded on the Bible teachings?"

"No, I did not."

"You had heard of it as a church here in town?"

"Yes sir."

"As a religious denomination?"

"Yes."

"As a matter of fact, when you went out to investigate this religion, as you say you knew it was, or this church and its practitioners, had you ever heard of the Bible?"

"Yes."

"Had you ever read it, or studied it?"

"No, I never studied it. I read a couple of pages in it years ago."

"A couple of pages? When?"

"When I was a young child."

"And that was the extent of your equipment in the knowledge of the Scriptures when you went out to investigate this religion, was it?"

"Yes."

Sworn as a witness, Cole denied that in practicing Christian Science he was engaged in the practice of medicine as defined by the prosecution.

He testified that at no time did he attempt to make a diagnosis, saying "one disease is no more real than another," [3] and testified further that he told the investigator for the Medical Society: "I cannot cure you. I have no more power to cure you than anyone else. God is the only power, and the only healer. You can cure yourself if you will study and purify your life and your thoughts and cleanse from your consciousness fear and inharmony and false thoughts. By studying and gaining an understanding, you can apply the principle of Christian Science as well as I can."

The court record also disclosed that, during a discussion about Christian Science, Cole picked up the copy of *Science and Health* that was on his desk, opened it, and read from

[3] *Science and Health*, p. 176.

Mrs. Eddy's teachings. The practitioner was asked by Untermyer to identify the paragraphs he had read, whereupon
the district attorney voiced an objection.

The district attorney objected to "using a courtroom for
the dissemination of Christian Science propaganda." The
court agreed, but did allow the particular paragraphs to be
submitted to Mrs. Benzecry for identification and inclusion
in the record.

The investigator for the Medical Society identified four
paragraphs as having been read to her. The first three were:

> To be "present with the Lord" is to have, not
> mere emotional ecstasy or faith, but the actual
> demonstration and understanding of Life as re-
> vealed in Christian Science. To be "with the
> Lord" is to be in obedience to the law of God,
> to be absolutely governed by divine Love,—by
> Spirit, not by matter.
>
> Become conscious for a single moment that Life
> and intelligence are purely spiritual,—neither in
> nor of matter,—and the body will then utter no
> complaints. If suffering from a belief in sickness,
> you will find yourself suddenly well. Sorrow is
> turned into joy when the body is controlled by
> spiritual Life, Truth, and Love.
>
> Entirely separate from the belief and dream of
> material living, is the Life divine, revealing spir-
> itual understanding and the consciousness of man's
> dominion over the whole earth. This understand-
> ing casts out error and heals the sick, and with it
> you can speak as "one having authority." [4]

[4] *Science and Health*, p. 14.

Finally, this paragraph:

> There is no life, truth, intelligence, nor substance in matter. All is infinite Mind and its infinite manifestation, for God is All-in-all. Spirit is immortal Truth; matter is mortal error. Spirit is the real and eternal; matter is the unreal and temporal. Spirit is God, and man is His image and likeness. Therefore man is not material; he is spiritual.[5]

Cole was sharply questioned about his charges for treatment, about the inclusion of his name among the practitioners listed in the *Christian Science Journal,* and about the charges for such listing. He was asked if he had told Mrs. Benzecry that "locomotor ataxia can be healed in Christian Science." He agreed he had said substantially what he was charged with saying and was questioned by a disbelieving district attorney, and by a disbelieving court. The questioning widened to include contagious diseases, such as diphtheria.

Cole said he had treated sufferers from contagious diseases, including diphtheria, and they were healed. The district attorney wanted to know how Cole could know they were contagious diseases if, in Christian Science, all disease was unreal. Cole explained that in cases where communicable diseases were suspected, the patients were sent to medical doctors, or to local or state health departments for examination, and added that under the rules of the Church, all Christian Science practitioners were required to obey all state and local laws pertaining to the reporting of communicable diseases.

[5] *Science and Health,* p. 468.

The district attorney then wanted to know if, when sent to doctors for medical examination, patients were given medical treatment if found to be suffering from contagious, or communicable, diseases.

"Only if they ask for medical treatment."

The district attorney wanted to know if, as a Christian Science practitioner, Cole could, or would, prevent patients from seeking medical treatment. Cole explained that such a patient was not denied medical treatment, "but could not have both Christian Science treatment and medical treatment at the same time"; he went on to say that all patients suffering from contagious diseases, who were under Christian Science treatment, were kept under quarantine and isolated, in accordance with the health laws of the community.

After this long interrogation by the district attorney, and by the court, as to the efficacy of Christian Science treatment in cases of contagious diseases, Untermyer interrupted the questioning by offering to produce, and to place under oath, individuals who would testify to such healings. The district attorney declined the offer, saying it was irrelevant (which it was under the specifications of the indictment) and was sustained by the court.

Soon afterwards, Cole was excused as a witness. Untermyer moved to have the case dismissed, contending that the defendant "did not either offer or undertake by any means, or methods, to diagnose, treat, operate or prescribe therefor," and "it would be absurd for the defendant, who does not believe in medicine, to take a course in it to practice his religion."

The motion was denied and, in summing up, the district attorney argued, "Absurd it is to claim that a Presbyterian has got to get a license, or a Catholic, or Episcopalian, before they can practice medicine, and yet a man because he belongs to the Christian Science church can go and practice healing without any license at all. . . . It is not a question of his [Cole's] convenience, or what is expensive to him, or what he does not believe in. It is a question of what is faith to the State. The State has said that before a man shall assume to treat disease, he has got to go and submit to this examination."

In presenting the case to the jury, the court reviewed the testimony and the evidence and charged the jury that in deciding "whether or not the defendant was engaged in practicing medicine, you will first determine as to what the defendant did. Having determined the acts which the defendant did, it is for you to say whether or not these acts fall within the definition" of the Public Health Law of the State of New York.

Instructing the jury further, the court told it "when a person claims to be practicing the religious tenets of any church, particularly when compensation is taken therefor and the practice is apart from a church edifice or the sanctity of the home of the applicant, the question whether such person is within [the Public Health Law] should be left to a jury as a question of fact. . . .

"If you find from the evidence in this case that this defendant did engage in the practice of medicine as alleged in the indictment, within the definition I have given you, it is no defense that he did what he did from any sense of duty, or that he did these acts in the practice of the religious tenets of the Christian Science church."

Soon thereafter, the court closed its instructions to the jury:

"In reaching a conclusion upon this matter, it is proper for you to inquire:

"First: Did the defendant hold himself out by sign, card, or published advertisement as being able to cure, treat or prescribe for any human disease, pain or injury, or physical condition; and

"Second: Did he maintain an office to which the public was invited to come for such treatment; and

"Third: Did Mrs. Benzecry come to his office asking treatment for disease, pain, injury or physical condition; and

"Fourth: If she did, did the defendant offer or undertake by any means or method to treat, operate, or prescribe for any human disease, pain, injury, deformity or physical condition?

"If you answer all these questions in the affirmative, then I charge that under the law of this State this defendant was engaged in the practice of medicine; and as it was conceded that he was not duly licensed to practice medicine, you should, under those circumstances, return him guilty."

Only forty-five minutes were needed for the jury to reach its verdict: Guilty.

Untermyer was standing as the foreman of the jury completed his announcement of the verdict, and was addressing the court:

"We except to the verdict, and move to set it aside, on the grounds provided by the statute, for a new trial."

Nodding his assent, the judge addressed Cole's attorneys and the district attorney:

"I am going to facilitate you gentlemen in taking this matter up, and for the sake of doing that I am going to impose a fine in this case, and, as I say, facilitate you, so that you can take it up and review the question and get an authoritative construction of this statute. And if you want to waive the time?"

"Yes, I will waive the time," agreed Untermyer, "and ask your Honor to impose the sentence now."

The court imposed a fine of $100. It was paid under protest.

Being a community more concerned with its gossip than with its covenant of freedom, New York took little note of the fact that in the Court of General Sessions, and by command from a judge, a jury rendered a verdict which made it a crime to ask God to heal the sick.

Public interest—what there was—was in Cole, but, as a defendant, he was not a good advocate for his cause. As a litigant, he was cross-grained; as a witness, he was too often discursive; as an exponent of Christian Science, he did injury to his church, if not to its teachings, by his eagerness to be noticed in the newspapers. Yet, even with his poor help, it is altogether likely that the finding of the jury would not have been different had he been different.

Throughout the trial, it was apparent the judge was determined there would be no recurrence of a divided jury. Equally apparent was his small knowledge of the subject on which he was sitting in judgment, as was illustrated in his summation to the jury when he directed its attention to the inclusion of Cole's name among the practitioners listed in the *Christian Science Journal,* and said: "From his testimony, it appears that his authority to treat was derived from the publication of an advertisement in the *Christian Science Journal,* that was paid for at advertising rates."

It was not true that "authority to treat was derived from the publication of an advertisement in the *Christian Science*

Journal." [6] Nor, in the sense the court was using the word, was there "an advertisement." There was the inclusion of a name in a directory. Also, had it been an advertisement, it would have had nothing to do with the issue in dispute.

That issue was: Does the court have the right to interfere with prayer?

Yet, even though this was the issue, there were clergymen who found savoriness in the verdict, as there were medical men who were pleased because, as one wrote in the *New York Sun,* "they [practitioners] are interfering with our bread and butter." In their animosity for Christian Science, the clergymen were oblivious to moral rights. In their zeal to be partners in a prosecution, the medical men were reckless with legal rights.

In view again, now that it was a crime to be a Christian Scientist, was the dark struggle of whether men should be supplicants for the favors of a judge or seekers of the laws of God.

In Boston, The Christian Science Board of Directors sent Judge Clifford P. Smith, a member of The Mother Church and one of the fine legal minds of New England, to New York to meet with Untermyer and Estabrook.

Untermyer and Estabrook were of the opinion that it would be necessary to carry the case beyond the Appellate Division of the Supreme Court of the State of New York, to which it had been appealed, and to the highest tribunal in the state, the Court of Appeals, before there would be a legal victory. Estabrook told Smith the calendar of the

---

[6] The listing of the names of practitioners in the *Christian Science Journal* is designed as a service to the public as well as to the practitioner. Every student of Christian Science, whether listed as a practitioner, or not listed, accepts the leadership of Mary Baker Eddy and, under that leadership, has the individual responsibility of bringing healing to all who seek it, everywhere in the world.

Appellate Division was crowded, and the justices over-worked. "In fact," he said, "my own firm has won reversals in eleven out of thirteen cases we have taken to the Court of Appeals." To this Untermyer added, "There are so many weaknesses in the medical case that I am satisfied it will not stand up."

Saying he was speaking for the Directors and for himself, all as Christian Scientists, Smith told the two lawyers he was not interested in any weakness in the medical case. "Our only concern," he said, "is the moral and legal position of Christian Science, and the correctness of that position must be established if we have to carry our arguments beyond the Court of Appeals and before the United States Supreme Court."

With one justice dissenting, the Appellate Division of the Supreme Court, on January 10, 1914, upheld the verdict of the lower courts and declared the practice of Christian Science "is the commercialized use of prayer"—decreeing that, to serve those who came to him for healing, a Christian Science practitioner "must be duly licensed as a medical doctor."

In announcing their decision, the justices said they had agreed to hold up the issuance of any order closing the offices of Christian Science practitioners in the State of New York until the Court of Appeals had heard the arguments and rendered its verdict.

With publication of the decision, and with the approval of the New York County Medical Society, practitioners were informed in the newspapers:

"The statutes under which licenses to practice medicine may be obtained require that an examination shall be con-ducted by a board of medical examiners appointed by the Board of Regents. The Regents shall admit to the examination any person who is more than 21 years of age, is of a good moral character, and has studied medicine not less than four school years, including four satisfactory courses of at least seven months each in four different calendar years in a medical school registered as maintaining a standing satisfactory to the Regents."

By way of additional information, the practitioners were told that "examinations are held four times yearly in four convenient places in the state."

Newspaper editors were divided in their opinions. The *New York Times* was in agreement with the decision and proposed a way to put an end to the practice of Christian Science:

"The decision will be a stunning blow to the exploiters of the particular form of suggestion to which Mrs. Eddy gave vogue among the credulous and erratic. . . . A persistent infliction of fines . . . would make 'healing' an unprofitable business and soon put an end to it. . . .

"As always when Christian Scientists are indicted, the defense rests on the claim that Christian Science is a religion, and that its cures, being effected by prayer, come in the same category, so far as the law is concerned, as do the ministrations of the sick by clergymen. It seems strange that the learned Justices did not question the defendant, or his counsel, on the place that prayer, as commonly understood—an appeal, that is, for aid to a divine personality—has in Eddyism.

"They would have discovered that the 'healers' do not pray at all, but simply make affirmations, silent or audible, of the non-existence of disease, addressed to nobody in particular and depending wholly for efficiency on the suggestibility of the patient and the nature of his, or her, malady."

The *Buffalo News* declared the case to be "one that illustrates the necessity of having laws which courts shall interpret as nearly as possible in accordance with their terms," and advised Christian Scientists to seek relief in the state legislature if the Court of Appeals failed to reverse the decision.

Two years afterwards there was another court, and another verdict.

On October 3, 1916, in the Court of Appeals, the decisions of the lower courts were rejected, with the chief justice writing: "I deny the power of the legislature to make it a crime to treat disease by prayer."

In its momentous decision, the Court of Appeals declared:

"The Christian Science church is in terms expressly excepted from the prohibition contained in the medical practice acts of many of the states. It is so expressly excepted in the statutes of Maine, New Hampshire, Massachusetts, Connecticut, North Carolina, North and South Dakota, Kentucky, Tennessee and Wisconsin.[7]

"We think the exception in the statutes of this state is broad enough to permit offering prayer for the healing of disease in accordance with the recognized tenets of the Christian Science church. It may be said that if the exception is so construed, it will lead to numberless persons assuming to cure diseases in the name of a church for the purpose of thereby maintaining a business and securing a livelihood. The religious tenets of a church must be practiced in good faith to come within the exception.

"When such practice is a fraud or pretense it is not excepted from the general prohibition. When wrong is practiced in the name of religion it is not protected by Constitution or statute. . . . Many of the decisions referred to by

---

[7] This exception is now written into the laws of all states.

counsel may be explained by the fact that the persons therein severally considered were frauds and shams. . . .

"A person should not be allowed to assume to practice the tenets of the Christian Science church or any church as a shield to cover a business undertaking. When a person claims to be practicing the religious tenets of any church, particularly where compensation is taken therefor and the practice is apart from a church edifice or the sanctity of the home of the applicant, the question whether such person is within the exception should be left to a jury as a question of fact.

"In this case the court charged the jury: 'If you find from the evidence in this case that this defendant did engage in the practice of medicine as alleged in the indictment, within the definition which I have given to you, it is no defense that he did what he did from any sense of duty, or that he did those acts in the practice of the religious tenets of the Christian Science church.'

"We are of the opinion that the court was in error in so charging the jury. The exception was intended by the legislature to exclude from the prohibition the practice of the religious tenets of the Christian Science church and other churches. It was necessary, as we have seen, that the practice be of the tenets of a recognized church and the court, instead of charging the jury as stated, should have left to the jury the question of whether the defendant was in good faith practicing the tenets of such a church within the meaning of the statutory exceptions." [8]

As with the decision of the Appellate Division, there were divided views regarding the decision of the Court of Appeals.

The *Syracuse* (N.Y.) *Journal* called it "a judicial triumph

[8] For full text, see Appendix 1.

for freedom of religious belief." The *Brooklyn Eagle* thought it good because "our Court of Appeals is unanimous in the opinion . . . that man cannot limit God." The *Christian Intelligencer* (N.Y.) said "the Court of Appeals would seem to a layman to have made another of those hair-splitting distinctions which so long have made our courts ridiculous."

Unyielding in its attitude toward Christian Science, the *New York Times* said "the Court of Appeals was obliged to decide as it did, and the responsibility rests—and in the opinion of all sane people rests very heavily—on the legislature for specifically excerpting from the provisions of the Act 'those who in the treatment of human ills follow the tenets of any religion'. . . . The truth is, and nobody who has read their books or heard their talks can doubt it, that the followers of Mrs. Eddy make no use whatever of prayer."

Siding with the *Times,* and discounting the clear words of the chief justice of the Court of Appeals, attorneys for the New York County Medical Society recommended the introduction into the state legislature of a bill "forbidding healing without a physician's license."

Bench and Bar, a magazine for lawyers, was particularly interested in the denial by the chief justice of the "power of any legislature to make it a crime to treat disease by prayer."

"This suggestion," stated the publication, "raises perhaps the most interesting feature of the case. Can the attempted cure of disease by prayer be constitutionally inhibited? That the treatment of disease so closely concerns the public health as to come within the police power of the State is, of course, too plain for serious argument. The licensing of physicians and surgeons is manifestly a valid police measure. Both operate directly upon the body. The one administers drugs; the other wields the knife. If the doctor knows nothing of the effect of his medicine upon the human body, or the surgeon has no knowledge of anatomy, the results are likely to be disastrous. Knowledge on these points is essential, and the State has a right to require it.

"The case of the Christian Scientist is radically different. He does not operate upon the body at all. He even denies its existence. His theory is, that disease originates in the mind; and that even the mental concepts resulting in what is called disease are false and unreal, and can be dispelled by the apprehension of truth. A treatment based upon such theories cannot result in malpractice upon the body; and to a great extent the reasons which necessitate the licensing of the ordinary medical practitioner disappear.

"There remains, however, the argument of neglect—that the patient may resort to the Christian Science practitioner, without benefit, whereas his case, if taken in time, might have been cured by more familiar methods. But how could the patient be forced to resort to the established school of medicine? Again the distinction in method is of vital importance.

"A believer in the use of drugs might resort to some unlicensed quack or harmful nostrum, and receive serious injury. In his case, there might have been protection in a law forbidding the quack to practice, or preventing the sale of the nostrum. Christian Science, however, holds no hope for such a person. His belief that the seat of the disease is in the body, and beyond the control of the mind, would prevent his resorting to it.

"On the other hand, if the patient did believe in the healing power of the mind, and disbelieved in material methods, it is difficult to see how the legislature would protect him in forbidding the Christian Scientist to practice. He could not then resort to such a practitioner, but neither would he apply to the established school of medicine."

For Christian Scientists, the decision of the Court of Appeals and the words of its chief justice recalled the words and the assurance of Mary Baker Eddy. In 1899, a question came to Mrs. Eddy, and she considered it of such importance that she used the *Christian Science Sentinel* (January 26) to publish her answer:

> The question: Is a righteous prayer, voluntarily sought for the sick, and used as a means for healing, capable of becoming a crime?
>
> Mrs. Eddy's answer: Under the Constitution of the United States, we answer: No! If the Scriptures are valid and their requirements just, importunate prayer, to preserve human life, has the sanction of Christianity, and in no sense is criminal. The higher courts of our land will never construe prayer a crime. This I said over thirty years ago; and every case of persecution and prosecution of Christian Scientists for this pathological practice has, by appealing from the lower to the higher court, proved this saying true. Our superior courts have always sustained these cases as belonging to the individual rights guaranteed by the constitutions of the nation and states.

To Archibald McLellan, editor of the *Christian Science Sentinel,* the decision not only established "the treating and healing of the sick by prayer [to be] a tenet of the Church of Christ, Scientist," but gave an opportunity for hope that "those critics who have been loath to admit either the Christianity of Christian Science, or its right to be called a religion, and its organization to be called a church, will also consider these questions settled."

To this hope, McLellan added another, it being "that this decision of a court of last resort will largely put an end to the contention of interested parties that the healing of the sick, irrespective of the means employed, is *per se* the practice of medicine."

The hope was within realization, although the way of its coming was not expected.

In Buffalo, on April 11, 1916, Theodore J. Vogelgesang, a Spiritualist, was found guilty of practicing medicine without a license and was sentenced to prison for six months. Maintaining that in treating the sick he was putting into practice the tenets of his church, was doing it under the authority of his church, and was acting within his right, Vogelgesang carried his case to the Appellate Division of the Supreme Court. It confirmed the decision of the lower court.

On June 13, 1917, his case was argued before the seven justices of the Court of Appeals. On July 11, 1917, its decision was published.

In reaching its decision, the Court of Appeals had before it the testimony. In the testimony it was disclosed that when Vogelgesang was a boy "he would get herbs and give them to sick people, for he seemed to know what would be good for them." As an adult, he continued to gather herbs, and prescribe them for the sick. He was arrested and fined for practicing medicine without a license.

Following this conviction he joined the New York State Association of Spiritualists, and continued to treat the sick, and was arrested again.

In court, he described himself as a therapeutic, a dispenser of patent medicines, and a spiritualist healer. In treating disease he used external and internal remedies of his own patent. He had a liniment which he used when massaging a patient and, while so doing, he gave mental treatment in the form of spiritualistic healing. The liniment was "compounded of angle worms, turpentine, sweet oil and benzine." For internal disorders, he gave "a medicine compounded of wine, beef tea and citrate of iron." He testified he used the same medicines for all ailments.

In examining Vogelgesang's defense, the Court of Appeals reasoned:

"The statute prohibits the practice of medicine without a license, but excepts from its prohibition 'the practice of the religious tenets of any church.' We held in the *People v. Cole* that the exception protected the practitioners of Christian Science, who taught as part of their religion the healing power of mind. . . .

"But things were done by this defendant which no good faith could justify. He combined faith with patent medicine. If he invoked the power of spirit, he did not forget to prescribe his drugs. 'It is beyond all question of dispute,' said Voltaire, 'that magic words and ceremonies are quite capable of most effectually destroying a whole flock of sheep, if the words be accompanied by a sufficient quantity of arsenic.'

"The law, in its protection of believers, has other cures in mind. The tenets to which it accords freedom, alike of practice and of profession, are not merely the tenets, but the *religious* tenets of a church. The profession and practice of the religion must be itself the cure.

"The sufferer's mind must be brought into submission to the infinite mind, and in this must be the healing. The operation of the power of spirit must not be indirect and remote, but direct and immediate.

"If that were not so, a body of men who claimed divine inspiration might prescribe drugs and perform surgical

operations under cover of the law. While the healer inculcates the faith of his church as a method of healing, he is
immune. When he goes beyond that, puts his spiritual agencies aside and takes up the agencies of the flesh, his immunity
ceases. He is then competing with physicians on their own
ground, using the same instrumentalities, and arrogating to
himself the right to pursue the same methods without the
same training."

After reviewing pertinent legislation in other states, the
decision continued:

"Through all this legislation there runs a common purpose. The law exacts no license for the ministration by
prayer or by the power of religion. But one who heals
by other agencies must have the training of the expert.

"If that is the true view of the meaning of the statute . . .
the defendant was justly convicted, and the judgment should
be affirmed." [9]

The decision was written by Benjamin N. Cardozo who
was elevated to the United States Supreme Court in 1932.
His was one of the great minds in the history of American
jurisprudence; and his statement of the position of the law
as it relates to religion has become a legal classic: *The law
exacts no license for the ministration by prayer, or by the
power of religion.*

It is a decision which makes secure the right of Christian
Scientists to practice spiritual healing under the New York
constitution free from the New York Medical Practice Act.

It was an historic decision.

[9] For full text, see Appendix 2.

CHAPTER FOUR

A King Interferes

T HE decision of the Court of Appeals in the Cole case did more than sustain the right of Christian Scientists to practice their own religion. By denying to the medical profession a monopoly in the treatment of disease, it kept that profession from destroying itself.

In its effort to suppress Christian Science, the New York County Medical Society had defended a lower court opinion which made it a crime to pray to God to heal the sick unless prayer was offered "in a church edifice, or in the sanctity of the home." This attempt to proscribe the places where man may speak to God, or where God may speak to man, could not have failed to react disastrously upon the medical profession.

As a judge, the court seemed not to know that God is not a prisoner of places; as a group, the Medical Society seemed not to understand that freedom cannot be denied to a Christian Scientist without being denied to members of all religions; and to all other, including medical, men.

In charging the jury as it did, the court did not recognize that, in Christian Science, there is only one place, and it is "the secret place of the most High." This place is a mental habitation, is found only when God is found, is divine Mind, and embraces infinity.

Because Cole, the practitioner, had his name on an office door, in an office building, in a business district in New

York, the judge was persuaded to the medical view that the Christian Scientist was practicing medicine—not perceiving that a name on an office door could not alter the eternal fact that the sanctuary of prayer is wherever man *is*.

As Ruskin said, "Men say the pinnacles of churches point to heaven, so does every tree that buds; and every bird that rises and sings—they say their aisles are good for worship; so is every rough seashore and mountain glen. . . ."

It may have been that the simplicity of Mrs. Eddy's teachings made them incomprehensible to the judge. Accepted in them is the testimony that "God created man in his *own* image"; taught in them is that "the prayer that reforms the sinner and heals the sick is an absolute faith that all things are possible to God,—a spiritual understanding of Him, an unselfed love." [1]

These are simple teachings. The choice between Spirit and matter—one, but not both, is offered; the assurance that we are immortal not in matter, but in Spirit, is explained; to believe in God is the only requirement.

Yet, simple as these teachings are, it still is difficult for a world grown accustomed to pomp and ceremony to find no candles between it and God, to hear no formulas in prayer, to accept the precept that redemption is an individual responsibility—or to agree that, in his spiritual progress, the individual is in competition with no one but himself.

In this precept is found the admonition that, being spiritual, life is complete in itself and, being complete, it permits no intrusion into its unity with God—heard, too, is the reminder "if God *be* for us, who *can be* against us?"

There were those who saw that nothing was hidden in the teachings, nothing asked beyond the ability of the in-

[1] *Science and Health,* p. 1.

dividual to understand. As a result, and despite the burden of the Cole case which gave its enemies more than four years in which to harm it, the Christian Science movement grew substantially in those same years.

In 1911, the year Cole was arrested, the total number of Christian Science practitioners was less than 5,000; in 1916, when Justice Cardozo wrote his opinion confirming freedom of religion, more than 6,000 persons were devoting their full efforts to Christian Science healings. In 1906, when the extension to The Mother Church was dedicated, there were 949 Christian Science organizations in the world; in 1916, there were 1,616 such organizations and, in addition, more than 3,000 unorganized groups were holding services.

Through the ten years there was an average of one new Christian Science church, or Christian Science society, every five and one-half days. In 1916, there was a new organization every three and one-half days. Christian Science lecturers were traveling the world and speaking in crowded halls.

In 1912, lectures were given in German for the first time. Approximately 1,800 persons gathered for the first such lecture, which was given in Hannover, and when the lecturer [2] arrived, it was to find a lieutenant of police waiting. With the police officer was a stenographer. The lecturer was told that everything he said would be taken down; he was threatened with arrest if he "said anything illegal." The police lieutenant heard nothing illegal.

In this same year, *Science and Health* was published in German [3] and, according to reports made to the Clerk of

[2] Hermann S. Hering, C. S. B.

[3] The typographic plan called for each page in German to face its corresponding page in English. Inasmuch as more space is needed to say in German what is said in English, the problem was immediate. Complicating the problem was the fact that each page in *Science and Health* has num-

The Mother Church, the sales in Germany, in Switzerland, and in Sweden, were "most gratifying." In Sweden, Christian Scientists had petitioned for recognition as a church. Accompanied by copies of *Science and Health* and Christian Science periodicals, the petitions were sent to the government and to the synod of ministers of the Lutheran Church by Christian Scientists living in Stockholm.

At its quarterly meetings, and for more than a year, the Lutheran ministers discussed the request, and then rejected it; but, as representatives of the state (the Lutheran Church is the state religion), they permitted an appeal to be made to a higher church body. This body, consisting of four ministers, also denied the petition. Under Swedish law, it was permissible to make a final appeal to the king. This final appeal was made.

A group of Stockholm Christian Scientists met with the prime minister, who made a personal investigation into the testimony of healing that was given before him. Impressed by his own findings, the prime minister reported them to the king. A month later, by order of Gustav V the practice of Christian Science was "legalized" in Sweden.

Among the reasons for the growth overseas, as well as within the United States, was Mrs. Eddy's insistence on self-government within the Christian Science movement and her requirement that each Christian Scientist group must

---

bered lines. The problem was solved by using slightly smaller type and larger leading so as to print on each page the same subject matter.

A second problem was encountered in the running heads at the top of each page. Ordinarily the title of the book is placed at the top of the left page and the chapter title at the top of the right page. In the German translation, both book title and chapter title are on each page. Because of these double running heads, *Wissenschaft und Gesundheit,* the German translation of *Science and Health,* is a rarity in book manufacture.

"Fruitage" was added to the German translation on July 17, 1937.

do its own work. She taught that individuals, singly or together, are governed exactly in accordance with the measure of truth they express—and for groups to rise to self-government they must rise to obedience and faith, in the understanding that self-government is the attribute of all who reflect God.

In *Miscellaneous Writings* (p. 317) she emphasized this teaching: "The hour has struck for Christian Scientists to do their own work; to appreciate the signs of the times; to demonstrate self-knowledge and self-government."

In the *Church Manual* she made clear her wishes for local self-government by the branch churches:

> *Local Self-Government.* Sect. 1. The Mother Church of Christ, Scientist, shall assume no general official control over other churches, and it shall be controlled by none other.
>
> Each Church of Christ, Scientist, shall have its own form of government. No conference of churches shall be held, unless it be when our churches, located in the same State, convene to confer on a statute of said State, or to confer harmoniously on individual unity and action of the churches of said State.
>
> [Article XXIII, Section 1.]

It has been said, many times, that Mary Baker Eddy was a wise woman, and surely it was wisdom that exacted obedience and faith and truth as the price of self-government.

The same wisdom that established local self-government for the branch churches wrote the By-laws which forbid, for publication, any numbering of the membership of The Mother Church or of the branch churches:

Numbering the People. Sect. 28. Christian Scientists shall not report for publication the number of members of The Mother Church, nor that of the branch churches. According to the Scripture they shall turn away from personality and numbering the people.

[*Church Manual,* Article VIII, SECTION 28.]

To Mrs. Eddy, as the founder of Christian Science, the Bible was important only in its spiritual meaning. She accepted the teachings of the Christ as infallible, but found in them no standing for numbers. In them, she found only "the healer of men, the Christ, the Truth." [4] As a Christian Scientist, she knew spiritual law contains no table of mathematics.

A student of its contents, she was aware that in the Bible are both perfection and imperfection, what is true and what is not true, what is real and what is not real, what is inspiration and what is not inspiration.

She believed, as did the ancient recorder of Chronicles, that God is pure and good, and that He deals only in what is pure and in what is good; she believed, as did the recorder, that God could not have commanded David, as set down in the Second Book of Samuel (24:1): "And again the anger of the LORD was kindled against Israel, and he moved against them, Go, number Israel and Judah."

Writing of this same event, the recorder of Chronicles (I Chronicles, 21:1) spoke of it this way: "And Satan stood up against Israel, and provoked David to number Israel."

In his sharply different recital of the temptation of David, the Chronicler discloses his rejection of a doctrine which

---

[4] *Miscellany,* p. 104.

was Persian in its origin, but which had infiltrated the Hebraic religion, even in the days of Elijah and Elisha.

This was a doctrine which spoke of God as both good and evil.[5]

The acknowledgment that God is without evil was an affirmation of the highest importance. It came into fullness in the teachings of Jesus some two hundred or three hundred years afterwards, and was echoed in the words of James, "Let no man say when he is tempted, I am tempted of God; for God cannot be tempted with evil, neither tempteth he any man"—and it found fullness again in the teachings of Mary Baker Eddy.

It is a conception of God that permits no reliance upon numbers—an understanding that knows that when faith is in numbers the way into the Presence is already lost.

Before her passing in 1910, Mrs. Eddy decided upon the title of a new book, and left an album containing manuscripts, letters, and addresses she had made to different groups. The title she chose was *The First Church of Christ, Scientist, and Miscellany*. The announcement of publication

[5] Because of their attention to the religious history of the tribes of Israel, the books of Chronicles, Ezra, and Nehemiah are often called "the second history of the world." In Ezra (7:10, 11, 12) is found the scribe, a priest whose duty it was to interpret the law of Moses; and in Nehemiah (8:17) is found the emancipation of the congregation from the authority of the priests: "And all the congregation of them were come again out of the captivity made booths and sat under the booths; for since the days of Jeshua the son of Nun unto that day had not the children of Israel done so. And there was very great gladness."

No longer was the law of Moses the exclusive property of the priests. Spiritual matters were now the individual responsibility of the individuals of the congregation. Much the same sort of relationship existed in the first century of the Christian church, presbyters and bishops being chosen by the people from among themselves, and acting for the congregation only in church matters. In spiritual affairs, the members of the congregation considered themselves the full equals of their church officers.

was made in the *Christian Science Sentinel* in its issue of November 1, 1913.[6]

It was an announcement which said "A volume of the later writings of Mrs. Eddy compiled from the files of the Christian Science Journal and Sentinel, together with historical matter pertaining thereto, as selected by her, is now in press, and orders will be received by the publishers."

Copyrighted by the Trustees under the Will of Mary Baker Eddy, published by the Christian Science Publishing Society, and containing more than three hundred and fifty pages, the book was in two parts. Part I was titled *The First Church of Christ, Scientist,* and contained, in 100 pages, two chapters, a foreword, and an appendix. Part II was titled *Miscellany,* and contained, in 266 pages, twenty chapters. It is the third largest of Mrs. Eddy's books. *Science and Health with Key to the Scriptures* contains 700 pages, not including *Preface and Index. Miscellaneous Writings* contains 471 pages.

Most of Mrs. Eddy's writings in the years 1897-1910 are in *The First Church of Christ, Scientist, and Miscellany;* as revised by her for book publication, the following writings appear on the indicated pages, and under the indicated titles:

103-8:   To The Christian World.
124-31: Communion, June 4, 1899.
131-33: Address at Annual Meeting, June 6, 1899.

[6] Announcement of publication also was made in the *Monitor* and the *Journal*. This publication released material that had waited the adjustment of Mrs. Eddy's estate. In Concord, New Hampshire, on October 18, 1913, and in accordance with a decision of the Supreme Court of New Hampshire on October 7, Judge Charles R. Corning appointed trustees to administer the trust created by Mrs. Eddy's will. Appointed were Archibald McLellan, Allison V. Stewart, John V. Dittemore, Adam H. Dickey, and James A. Neal, who comprised The Christian Science Board of Directors, and Josiah E. Fernald, the Administrator *de bonis non* of the estate.

148-51: Address to the Concord Church, February, 1899.

151-54: Message, April 19, 1899, Subject: "Not Matter, but Spirit."

184-91: Letters to branch churches in Toronto, Ont., White Mountain, N. H., Duluth, Minn., Salt Lake City, Utah, and Atlanta, Ga.

210: What Our Leader Says.

238: Will the Bible, if read and practised, heal as effectually as your book, "Science and Health with Key to the Scriptures?"

239: Must Mankind wait for the ultimate of the millennium—until every man and woman comes into the knowledge of Christ and all are taught of God and see their apparent identity as one man and one woman—for God to be represented by His idea or image and likeness?

244-46: Massachusetts Metaphysical College.

256: Early Chimes, December, 1898.

299-301: Christian Science and the Church.

338: To the Public.

339-41: Fast Day in New Hampshire, 1899.

The historical matter pertaining to the first two of the writings is of particular interest, both to Christian Scientists and to those who are not Christian Scientists.

To The Christian World: In London, England, in 1898, Harold Frederic, an American author, died. At an autopsy it was testified he had been under Christian Science treatment. Stigmatizing Mrs. Eddy's teachings as "a dangerous importation," London newspapers demanded the arrest of the practitioner. It was done. The charge was murder.

Throughout the British Isles, in Canada, and in the United States there was agitation for laws prohibiting the practice of Christian Science, and leading the agitation was the medical profession. In *The Journal of the American*

Medical Association (December 10, 1898) were these paragraphs:

"The case of Harold Frederic is at once maddening and
pathetic. All his years the man had lived and fought for the
realities, the sanities, and the honesties of life. Finally a cell,
or a duct in the over-worked brain gave way and left him
temporarily and partially incapable of distinguishing between the true and the false. . . . Nature, aided by science,
would have soon repaired the injury, but at a moment when
the clear eyes were darkened and the strong mind was helpless, a miserable creature appeared, stretching out rapacious
hands for the sick man's gold. She got it, and Harold Frederic is dead. . . .

"There is ground for hope, however, that this is not quite
the end of the tragic episode. The woman who killed Mr.
Frederic has confessed her utter lack of legal qualifications
to act as a doctor, and that she accepted fees for treatment.
Counsel for the executors warned her, while she was testify-
ing before a coroner's jury, that she was in 'a serious position.' If England has any justice, she will soon be in prison;
and stay there for a considerable period."

About a week after this attack in the official publication
of the American Medical Association, Mrs. Eddy wrote an
open letter to the *New York Sun*. This was the letter she
revised, and titled *To The Christian World*.

In part, it reads:

> . . . It is of the utmost concern to the world that
> men suspend judgment and sentence on the pi-
> oneers of Christianity till they know of what and
> of whom these pioneers speak. A person's igno-
> rance of Christian Science is a sufficient reason for

his silence on the subject, but what can atone for the vulgar denunciation of that of which a man knows absolutely nothing. . . .

In the ranks of the M.D.'s are noble men and women, and I love them; but they must refrain from persecuting and misrepresenting a system of medicine which from personal experience I have proved to be more certain and curative in functional and organic diseases than any material method. I admonish Christian Scientists either to speak charitably of all mankind or to keep silent, for love fulfills divine law and without this proof of love mental practice were profitless. . . .

Our great Exemplar, the Nazarene Prophet, healed through Mind, and commanded his followers to do likewise. The prophets and apostles and the Christians in the first century healed the sick as a token of their Christianity. Has Christianity improved upon its earlier records, or has it retrograded? Compare the lives of its professors with those of its followers at the beginning of the Christian era, and you have the correct answer. . . .

Ignorance, slang, and malice touch not the hem of the garment of Christian Scientists, for if they did once touch it, they would be destroyed. To be stoned for that which our Master designated as his best work, saying, "For which of those works do ye stone me," is to make known the best work of a Christian Scientist.

Finally, beloved brethren in Christ, the words of the New York press—"Mrs. Eddy not shaken"—are valid. I remain steadfast in St. Paul's faith, and will close with his own words: "Christ is the head of the church: and he is the saviour of the body." [7]

Mrs. Eddy's suggestion that "it is of the utmost concern to the world that men suspend judgment and sentence on the pioneers of Christianity till they know of what and of whom these pioneers speak," was not well received in much of the press and in many pulpits. There was much prejudgment of the practitioner and general demand that she be jailed. But she was acquitted.

In the trial it was proved that Frederic was under medical treatment and was told by his doctors that his case was hopeless. In despair, he turned to Christian Science, listened to a practitioner but briefly, returned to the care of the medical men, and was under their care when he died.

Communion, June 4, 1899: The historical event associated with Mrs. Eddy's Communion message of June 4, 1899, concerns a lawsuit brought by Mrs. Josephine Woodbury who was expelled from membership in The Mother Church by the First Members and The Board of Directors.[8] Mrs. Woodbury became a violent critic of Mrs. Eddy and a vicious enemy. In her lawsuit, she charged her former teacher with libel, saying the Communion message was a personal attack upon her.

---

[7] For complete text see *Miscellany,* pp. 103-108. First published in the *New York Sun* on December 16, 1898, the letter was reprinted in the *Concord* (N.H.) *Monitor* the following day. Mrs. Eddy revised it and, in its revised form, it was published in the *Independent Statesman,* of Concord, N. H., on December 22, 1898, in the *Christian Science Sentinel* on December 29, 1898, and in the *Christian Science Journal* in January, 1899.

[8] Mrs. Woodbury was excommunicated on April 4, 1896, for indiscretions as a Christian Scientist. It was her second excommunication, the first being in 1890. At Mrs. Eddy's request, the First Members and the Directors gave the woman a second opportunity "to stop falsifying, and living impurely in thought, in vile schemes, in fraudulent money-getting, etc."

In the Communion message, Mrs. Eddy spoke of the
duties of a Christian Scientist and of her own gratitude
"that the church militant is looking into the subject of
Christian Science"; she said "the doom of the Babylonish
woman referred to in Revelation is being fulfilled. . . . The
Babylonish woman is fallen, and who should mourn over
the widowhood of lust, of her that 'is become the habitation
of devils and the hold of every foul spirit, and the cage of
every unclean . . . bird?' " She instructed all Christian Scientists to "Trust God to direct your steps," advised them to
accept her "counsel and teaching, only as they include the
spirit and the letter of the Ten Commandments, the Beati-
tudes, and the teachings and example of Christ Jesus," and
instructed them further: "Refrain from public controversy;
correct the false with the true—then leave the latter to propagate." She assured them:

> The effort of disloyal students to blacken me
> and to keep my works from public recognition—
> students seeking only public notoriety, whom I
> have assisted pecuniarily and striven to uplift mor-
> ally—has been made too many times and has failed
> too often for me to fear it. The spirit of Truth is
> the lever which elevates mankind. . . .
>
> Beloved, that which purifies the affections also
> strengthens them, removes fear, subdues sin, and
> endues with divine power; that which refines char-
> acter at the same time humbles, exalts, and com-
> mands a man, and obedience gives him courage,
> devotion, and attainment. For this hour, for this
> period, for spiritual sacrament, sacrifice, and ascen-
> sion, we unite in giving thanks.[9]

[9] For complete text, see *Miscellany*, pp. 124-31.

Alleging that when speaking of "the Babylonish woman," Mrs. Eddy was referring to her, Mrs. Woodbury assailed her former teacher from public platforms throughout New England and in the press. Attracting international attention, the case aroused so much argument that a message to all Christian Scientists was carried on the editorial page of the *Sentinel* in its issues of August 3, and August 10, 1899: "Peace be still! Our Father is at the helm. Mary Baker Eddy."

In court, the testimony began and ended with the claims of Mrs. Woodbury. As her attorneys concluded, the judge inquired if they had introduced all their evidence. They said they had. The court directed a verdict for Mrs. Eddy without further testimony.

The importance of the events Mrs. Eddy selected for the permanence of her last book was not understood, at first, by the field. The field was puzzled, not knowing that for some time before her passing, Mrs. Eddy had been discussing the book with the Directors, had been selecting material for it, and had given the Directors some leeway in choosing other material.

Letters began coming in to the periodicals and to The Board of Directors in such volume that in the *Sentinel,* December 6, 1913, Archibald McLellan used his editorial column to assure Christian Scientists, and all others, that the new book was in full keeping with Mrs. Eddy's plans and wishes. He called attention to their Leader's instructions as published in *Miscellany* (pp. 223-25), and to a particular paragraph:

> My books state Christian Science correctly. They
> may not be as taking to those ignorant of this
> Science as some books less correct and therefore

less profound. But it is not safe to accept the latter as standards. We would not deny their authors a hearing, since the Scripture declares, "He that is not against us is on our part." And we should also speak in loving terms of their efforts, but we cannot afford to recommend any literature as wholly Christian Science which is not absolutely genuine.

Publication of the editorial had an immediate effect. Opposition subsided, then disappeared.

In the same year of 1913, Albert F. Conant completed the compilation of the *Concordance to Other Writings.* The compilation was on 3,910 cards and work was hardly completed when it was decided there should be a new concordance to *Science and Health.* In 1903, at Mrs. Eddy's request, Conant prepared the copy for the first real concordance to the textbook. Now, with Mrs. Eddy gone, Conant was able to make changes that would give the new concordance a degree of permanence.

In his preface to the new edition, Conant spoke of the many changes that were made:

"About five thousand new references have been inserted. Of these, nearly sixteen hundred were needed for new words not hitherto indexed; and more than thirty-four hundred were required to index the changes in Science and Health which have been made by its author since the first Concordance was printed.

"Mrs. Eddy has said, 'I have revised Science and Health only to give clearer and fuller expression of its original meaning.' (Science and Health, 361-21). Some idea of the extent of her recent revisions may be gained from the above figures, which thus serve to enhance an appreciative recognition of the indefatigable labors of our Leader in the interests of humanity."

The final concordance to *Science and Health* was published in 1916. It was compiled to include the 1910 edition of *Science and Health* "as finally revised by its author." At about the same time, the two concordances were published on Bible paper, and in a somewhat smaller format.

By 1914, so many were the questions requiring the attention of the Directors that regular meetings were held, several times a week. This was quite a change from earlier years when only an occasional meeting was needed, or from a few years before when one afternoon a week was sufficient to deal with matters concerning The Mother Church.

There were the many questions involving the activities of unnumbered church workers and laymen in all parts of the world. At least once weekly, there were meetings with the Board of Trustees of The Christian Science Publishing Society for the purpose of discussing and giving decisions on matters affecting the periodicals.

Being responsible, under the *Church Manual,* for the editing of all Christian Science periodicals, the Directors held weekly meetings with the editors of the *Journal*, the *Sentinel,* the German and French *Heralds,* and the *Monitor*. Questions pertaining to The Christian Science Benevolent Association, an expression of helpfulness which began manifesting itself in Mrs. Eddy's home in Lynn, Massachusetts, in 1888, were beginning to require attention.

There were regular meetings with the members of the Board of Lectureship, the Treasurer of The Mother Church, the Clerk of The Mother Church, the Manager of the Committees on Publication, and with officials who were in charge of other activities of The Mother Church. There were meetings with Christian Scientists, many coming from far places; there was a growing volume of official, and personal, correspondence.

These were some of the duties of five people who, as when Mrs. Eddy was here, in person, opened each meeting in silent prayer, followed by the audible repetition of the *Daily Prayer,* as provided in the *Church Manual* (Article VIII, SECTION 4) for all members of The Mother Church.

It is a simple prayer; and these are its words:

> *"Thy kingdom come;" let the reign of divine Truth, Life and Love be established in me, and rule out of me all sin; and may Thy Word enrich the affections of all mankind, and govern them!*

In 1917, *Science and Health* was translated into French and published under the title, *Science et Santé.* Also, in 1917, the Trustees under the Will of Mary Baker Eddy signed a contract with the Board of Trustees of The Christian Science Publishing Society to print and distribute Mrs. Eddy's writings.

In entering into the contract, it was assumed by the Trustees under the Will that the printing and distribution methods would remain unchanged. These methods had been in effect for years. They carried out Mrs. Eddy's intentions. They had her approval. It was not long before it was clear that they did not have the approval of the Trustees of the Publishing Society, two of whom were new members. These two were David B. Ogden and Lamont Rowlands, who were appointed on August 1, 1917. The third member was Herbert W. Eustace, who was appointed on December 2, 1912.

Realizing that the Board of Trustees of the Publishing Society did not agree with policies that carried out Mrs.

Eddy's intentions and had her approval, the Trustees under
the Will sought to cancel the contract. They met resistance
and almost five years went by before the contract was ter-
minated. These were years of contention in the courts and
unhappiness within the movement.

CHAPTER FIVE

"Whose Neighbour Am I?"

T HE day came when the door opened wide to the jungle ideas of the world. This was the day of war in 1914.

Soon messages of suffering were being received in Boston, and just as soon a War Relief Fund was set up by The Christian Science Board of Directors. Preparations were made to send a member of the Board of Lectureship familiar with conditions in Europe to organize relief in different countries, and, in the *Sentinel* (October 24, 1914) was an announcement:

A RELIEF FUND

The many Christian Scientists who have desired to contribute to the relief of those of our people who are enduring the hardships which war entails, will welcome the opportunity afforded by the following letter, a copy of which has been mailed to all branch churches and societies in the United States:

To the Christian Science Churches and Societies in the United States.

DEAR FRIENDS:

This Board has been informed that, as a consequence of the war in Europe, Christian Scientists in the countries affected are in great distress. As a means of relieving this distress, The Mother Church will take a collection at both of its services on Sunday, October 25. If your organization should desire to take similar action this Board will be glad to forward to reliable committees of Christian Scientists whatever amounts you may send for this purpose.

Remittances may be sent to Adam H. Dickey, Treasurer, 103 Falmouth Street, Boston, Massachusetts.

Very Sincerely
THE CHRISTIAN SCIENCE BOARD OF DIRECTORS.
By John V. Dittemore, Secretary.

Two weeks later, in the *Sentinel* of November 7, there was an announcement by the Directors that William D. McCrackan of the Board of Lectureship had been given the assignment to head the relief activities in Europe. He sailed from New York on November 16, taking credentials from The Mother Church and a commendation from the Secretary of State in Washington.

Meanwhile, although churches and societies were responding to the request for contributions, more help was needed. On December 5, 1914, the Fund was opened to non-Scientists and in a statement made to the field it was said, "There is great need for funds for the relief of hundreds of thousands of others besides our own people who are in poverty and distress by reason of the war, and a collection for their benefit will be taken in The Mother Church at both services on Sunday, December 6."

In the same announcement it was disclosed that $80,413.90 had been received from the call that was made on October 24 and "it is believed that the amount of money now in hand will be sufficient for the needs of Christian Scientists, and for the present at least, the fund will be closed."

In London, McCrackan was not long in learning that, under the Defense of the Realm Act, contributions by Christian Scientists in England and in her dominions could not be used to relieve distress in countries with which England and her dominions were at war. Informing the Directors of this restriction, McCrackan was told that The Mother Church would assume the responsibility for gathering and dispensing funds for those in need in Germany and in Austria-Hungary [1] and was instructed to continue his work of organizing relief committees in the British Isles, and other European countries.

Working through the Committee on Publication for Great Britain and Ireland, McCrackan formed relief committees throughout the British Isles, and the plan worked so well that it served as a model for other nations, particularly France, Switzerland, Holland, and Italy. Switzerland was crowded with the distressed of Germany and France—so crowded that there were two relief headquarters, one in Zürich for the Germans, and one in Geneva for the French.

Food and clothing and money were distributed from these cities and among the recipients, in addition to French and German citizens, were soldiers who had been captured, or interned, in Switzerland. In Holland, as in Switzerland, there were many calls upon the Relief Fund from nationals of the warring countries; in France and in Italy the need for the Fund did not lessen.

There was a Jewish girl from Algiers. She was young, but there were children, and a blind husband, and poverty. . . . A home in Rheims was destroyed, and its Russian occupants were without shelter. . . . An old German couple had lived in France for thirty years; they had no funds, and no friends, as they awaited deportation to Germany. . . . Except for the rags that served as clothing, the only other material possession of a starving Spanish family was a broken cup. . . . Mutilated soldiers, not able to work, nor find charity. . . . From Boston began the shipments that were not to end until the war was ended and there was representation of peace.

[1] In Germany, there were churches in Berlin, Frankfort-on-Main, Hannover, Stuttgart and Hamburg; there were societies in Braunschweig, Breslau, Dresden, and Mecklenburg-Schwerin; there were thirty practitioners in twelve cities.

The War Relief Fund became a long effort; and its changed status was announced in the *Sentinel* on April 3, 1915:

In response to the call for contributions for the relief of Christian Scientists in distress by reason of the present war in Europe, the sum of $82,104.02 has been received by the Treasurer of The Mother Church. Of this amount $77,595.51 has been disbursed to the relief committees organized by Mr. McCrackan in England, Germany, France and Switzerland, as called for by them. Much gratitude has been expressed by the Christian Scientists in these countries for the help extended to them by their brethren in America.

In addition to the $82,104.02 collected for the relief of Christian Scientists, there has also been collected the sum of $29,154.90 for the relief of war sufferers other than Christian Scientists. This entire amount has been disbursed to relief committees of Christian Scientists in Holland, England, and France, and Switzerland. The total amount received to date for these two funds is $111,258.92, of which but $4,508.51 remains unexpended. As the need for help still continues, this small balance will not last long; therefore, Christian Scientists are given the opportunity to continue to send contributions to the Treasurer of The Mother Church for this relief work. For the future it is proposed to maintain but one fund, and from this both Christian Scientists and others will be assisted.

From April 3, 1915, and into a period well beyond the Armistice on November 11, 1918, voluntary offerings flowed into the office of the Treasurer of The Mother Church. With the entrance of the United States into the war in 1917, the problems multiplied and came closer. The need for funds became greater; and it was with these things in mind that Archibald McLellan wrote in the *Sentinel:*

Christian Scientists stand for present and permanent peace. Indeed, no one at all conversant with prevailing conditions in the war-swept countries of the eastern hemisphere could but shrink from any step which would involve a peaceful and peace-seeking nation in strife, against its deepest and most earnest convictions; but on the other hand, they largely realize that, much as they abhor war, there are other and far worse things than war which could happen to humanity in its present state of material belief, not the least of which might well be the loss of that civil and religious liberty which has borne its greatest fruitage. . . .

In the titanic struggle now going on, Christian Scientists the world over have followed their Leader in basing their hopes and efforts for peace in unwavering reliance upon "the God of Hosts" so eloquently invoked by the patriot statesmen of colonial days. Nor are they to be condemned if, when the call of duty came, they remembered their Leader's counsel, "If our nation's rights or honor were seized, every citizen would be a soldier and woman would be armed with power girt for the hour" (*Miscellany*, p. 277) and felt themselves privileged to obey the call.[2]

With the declaration of war by the United States, a policy was established in Washington under which all religious and benevolent organizations except the Young Men's Christian Association and the Knights of Columbus were excluded from welfare activities in Army camps. Later this ruling was greatly relaxed. While it was in effect, it brought difficulties.

At the time, it was hoped that branch churches would be able to erect buildings containing facilities for recreation and study in the different camps and to have constantly available, in each camp, a Christian Science practitioner serving as chaplain. Comparatively speaking, Christian Science was new as a denominational religion, and the argument was made that, because they were fewer, Christian Scientists and other smaller groups could pocket their differences and join with larger denominations in religious and

[2] *Christian Science Sentinel*, April 14, 1917.

welfare work. The argument was not honest, but it prevailed.

However, the year was not over when the unfairness of the policy was to be recognized in Congress.

On October 26, 1917, Woodrow Wilson signed what was called a chaplains-at-large bill under which the President was authorized to commission twenty chaplains to represent denominations not included in existing law. The bill got its name because in it was a recommendation by a committee of the House of Representatives that all twenty chaplains be given roving assignments. As presented for signature by the President, the concluding paragraph in the bill read: "Division commanders may apply to the Adjutant General of the Army for the services of Chaplains-at-large of the Jewish, Christian Science, Eastern Catholic, Mormon, and Salvation Army denominations if they deem that there are sufficient members of the adherents of such faiths in their divisions to render Chaplains-at-large necessary."

Prior to this legislation, the applicant for a chaplain's commission (first lieutenant) had to be (1) a citizen of the United States between the ages of 21 and 45 years; (2) a graduate of a recognized college or university; (3) from the membership of the Federated Churches of Christ of America, or from the Roman Catholic Church; (4) an ordained clergyman; (5) recommended by the authorities of the denomination of which he is a member; and (6) had to pass an examination in subjects selected by the Adjutant General; and (7) had to pass a complete physical examination in the presence of an Army medical officer.

In commissioning the twenty Chaplains-at-large, the third and fourth requirements were waived, and of the twenty appointments two were Christian Scientists. They were Edward W. Dickey, of Los Angeles, California, and Martin

F. Jackson, of New York City. After endorsement by The Christian Science Board of Directors, the two men were given their commissions in November, 1917.

In 1918, eight more were commissioned, namely, Walter S. Cross, Baltimore, Maryland; Gustavus S. Paine, Reno, Nevada; Arthur C. Whitney and George R. Bonner, both of Boston, Massachusetts; William M. Bartlett, Concord, Massachusetts; Harry K. Filler, Youngstown, Ohio; Herbert W. Beck, Oakland, California; and Don C. Gilman, San Francisco, California.

Also contributing to better understanding by the public of Christian Science and its teachings was the action of the Directors when hearing a cry for help from the people of Halifax, Nova Scotia, on December 6, 1917. On that day disaster struck the Canadian city when two ammunition ships collided in Halifax harbor. In the explosion and fire that followed, more than 3,000 houses were destroyed and more than 1,300 people were killed.

As soon as the appeal was made, the Directors appointed a committee to gather supplies and, two days later, when the committee was ready, a special train was chartered. It left Boston the evening of December 8. On board, in addition to Christian Scientists, were newspaper reporters, nurses, doctors, and Red Cross workers who had no other way of reaching Halifax.

This was the third relief train to start for Halifax, and the first to reach the city, on Monday, December 10, since obstacles of various kinds had delayed the others. Of this errand, the *Daily Times Journal* of Fort William, Ontario, on December 17, carried these paragraphs:

"The Christian Scientists of Boston, Mass., magnificently came to the assistance of the stricken people of Halifax, when they sent a special train from the Massachusetts capital

bearing relief of all kinds in clothing, provisions and supplies for the suffering, homeless and destitute. . . .

"Accompanying this splendid donation was the sum of
$10,000 in cash. Hearing of the departure of the relief spe-
cial, thirty or forty Red Cross officials asked permission to
accompany the train, and leave was willingly granted. It was
an unusual spectacle—a train of relief from the mother
Christian Scientist church in Boston, with leading church
officials in charge, and Red Cross officers with them, all bent
on the one errand of mercy—the relief of suffering."

In November, 1917, after having given thought to the
policy that denied to Christian Scientists the opportunity
to establish their own centers in Army camps, The Christian
Science Board of Directors appointed a Christian Science
Camp Welfare Committee to cooperate with the War Department in working out a solution. Permission was given
by the War Department for the committee to visit a number
of the larger camps for the purpose of studying requirements and making recommendations.

The plan arrived at by the committee and the Directors
aimed essentially at rendering continuous service to all men
in the Army, including "healing by Christian Science methods and the supply of Christian Science books and literature
to whatever extent might be justified by the circumstances."
It was hoped that without too much delay workers would
be stationed in the camps, and on a permanent basis.

Temporarily, the plan provided for daily visits by workers, and it was stipulated that they were to remain within
the camps only so long as their services were required.
In the plan, and in each state, Christian Science churches
and Christian Science societies were expected to appoint a
War Relief Committee to supervise the work and to serve

as a link between camp activities and the Camp Welfare Committee of The Mother Church.

The plan was adopted and, before the end of January, 1918, the work was organized in more than thirty states. Before the Armistice, Army camps throughout the United States contained Christian Science centers, all built by branch churches. In some camps, Christian Science workers were on permanent duty. The centers were not large, but they were restful. In the centers was healing, so much healing that it attracted the attention of medical officers. To some extent, it broke the resistance of medical officers to the presence of Christian Science workers in Army hospitals.

Very early in the war, Mrs. Eddy's writings, together with other Christian Science literature, were supplied to the American Library Association for inclusion in portable overseas libraries. Also, on request, a Welfare Room was opened close by the Navy piers in Hoboken, New Jersey, one of the principal ports of embarkation.

This Welfare Room was so useful that the Navy authorities permitted the Camp Welfare Committee of The Mother Church to install duplicate facilities in other ports along the Atlantic seaboard and the Great Lakes, and to distribute *The Christian Science Monitor* and other Christian Science literature to ships and transports.

The only Christian Science chaplain to serve in the Navy was Richard J. Davis of Boston, Massachusetts. He was commissioned in January, 1918, was assigned to temporary duty in the Boston Navy Yard, and on Sunday, February 17, 1918, conducted on board the U.S.S. *Salem* the first official Christian Science services in the history of the United States Navy.

Of the two events, the appointment of a Christian Scientist as a Navy chaplain and the holding of Christian Science services on board an American warship, there are these accounts:

On February 5, 1918, in the *New York World:*

"The appointment by Secretary [Josephus] Daniels of a Christian Scientist as navy chaplain denotes a significant change in the public attitude toward the faith founded by Mrs. Eddy.

"Could such a selection of a spiritual adviser have been conceived of in Dewey's navy? Christian Science then and long after was anathema to the regular religious denominations of the country. Legislation was invoked to restrain it, medical societies prosecuted its practitioners and it was made to bear the brunt of a powerful opposition everywhere. Now the Government gives it full recognition and accords its readers an equal status with ministers of other creeds. Besides the navy chaplain, there are two Christian Science chaplains in the army.

"So have the old antagonisms subsided and the earlier intolerance given way under the spirit of religious freedom. History has repeated itself once more and the new kirk has fought its way to a place alongside the old kirk. It has been an interesting process, and the outcome is notable as an illustration of the liberalizing tendencies of modern opinion, whether religious or political."

On April 27, 1918, in the *Christian Science Sentinel:*

On Sunday, February 17, 1918, there took place on one of the battleships stationed at Boston Navy Yard, Charlestown, Massachusetts, the first official Christian Science service to be held in the United States Navy. The ship was rigged for church, and at a few minutes before half-past ten o'clock the bugle call for divine service was sounded. At the same time the church flag which bears the cross was raised, this flag being the only one which is ever hoisted above the Stars and Stripes. It remained flying throughout the duration of the service, to indicate that divine worship was in progress aboard the ship.

The reading desk consisted of two steel barrels, and several flat gratings covered with an American flag. A piano was available for hymns and solo, and chairs and benches were provided for the audience. Chaplain Richard J. Davis, U. S. N., acted as First Reader and Lieutenant Samuel W. Burgess as Second Reader. With the exception of a few guests the audience was composed of naval officers and seamen to the number of thirty or forty. All felt the deepest gratitude and joy that Christian Science services are now made possible for the men of the navy.

Soon afterwards, Chaplain Davis was transferred to the U.S.S. *Roanoke,* one of a fleet of ten mine-layers. The mine-layers were sent to Europe where they spent nine months seeding the North Sea with unpleasant news for enemy ships. Given leave from his ship for a short period, the chaplain assisted in establishing Welfare Rooms at different naval stations in the British Isles. Returning to the United States in December, 1918, he was transferred to the U.S.S. *Supply;* he closed his naval duties a few months later as chaplain of the U.S.S. *Columbia.*

As for the Army, eight of the ten Christian Science chaplains were in Europe soon after receiving their commissions. The experience of all was not greatly different from the experience of one:

Chaplain Whitney marched with me at the head of my company through heavy shell fire when we were marched into position for the attack. His calm and encouraging remarks helped materially to steady the men and, I am frank to say, caused me to feel a security and confidence that I had never felt before under shell fire. Later I was ordered to take my company across the Scheldte and relieve a certain French organization to our front. Chaplain Whitney insisted on being with the company even though I told him how dangerous our task was.

We passed through the French first line and, with the company deployed as skirmishers over a seven-hundred-yard front, advanced to a village (Hoorbeke-St-Corneille) eight hundred yards beyond. We took this village under heavy machine gun and shell fire and drove out fifty German machine gunners. Chaplain Whitney stayed with me throughout the engagement in the front line and I am glad to say my company did not suffer one single casualty. Divine Providence guided us safely to our positions and we received word that any further advance would be postponed. The following morning as we were forming for the attack, the armistice had been signed.[3]

Wherever Christian Scientists were, in camp, in the front lines, or at sea, there were services—"We held our first service, and it was a good one; we held it in a stable, just four of us." ... "I stood on a tank reading from *Science and Health,* with the Bible and *Quarterly* in my other hand, and men grouped about me." ... "Upon my arrival in camp, I made inquiries if there were any Scientists. I was told there were none. At the first opportunity, I had published a notice of a Christian Science meeting in a Y.M.C.A. hut. Can you imagine my feelings to have waiting for me on Sunday morn-

---

[3] Report of a company commander, 91st Division. With more than 1,200 students in its ranks, the 91st Division probably contained more Christian Scientists than any other U. S. Army division.

ing thirty-two men who had come through a drenching rain to attend services?" ... "We are meeting out of doors, in the finest-lighted and best-ventilated church in the world."

"I held a service all by myself yesterday on the banks of the St. John river [Florida] reading from the *Quarterly,* and singing the hymns from the *Hymnal.* I even took up a collection of thankfulness which I am sending to The Mother Church." ... "We choose Readers for each month, hoping they will be with us." ... "Every Christian Scientist comes to services prepared to be a Reader." ... "On request, we held services in the hospital, 110 came, every one a patient, in wheel chairs, and on crutches." ... "We have services right along. The last one was in a dug-out, six feet long and four feet high."

"The men went down to a clump of trees near a railroad track, piled railroad ties against two saplings to make a desk, the readers hung their hats in the trees, the congregation sat on the other ties, and the service began." ... "In a German prison camp, some forty prisoners of war [were] conducting a service in German." ... "We found a piano, and we had a boy who could play our hymns as well as I have ever heard them played." ... "We started a little service with six present, held in a tent. The following Sunday two were added." ... "We had a nice meeting today in a little village; went into the woods and read the lesson, and had prayer." ... "Workbenches for pews, and a soap box with a square board laid across the top for a desk; but the atmosphere was indeed worthy of The Mother Church."

Wherever there were troops, there were men giving testimony of God.

The supervising nurse asked the visitor to talk with the lad. "He will probably live but a few hours," she said, "and he's from your town." The boy who knew nothing of Christian Science had lost his Bible at Chateau Thierry. "I knew when I did," he gasped, "that it was all up with me, because I had carried the Bible with me everywhere."

"But you did not lose the Lord's Prayer," he was reminded, "and you could really use that prayer all day, actually use it for breathing. Just substitute it for breathing, if you're a little short of breath. Will you promise to say it all day?" And he promised.

Two weeks later the nurse who had him as her particular charge, almost shouted: "There's that lady who talked to you the day you were so bad. That was the day you got well."

Including $34,000 contributed for Halifax relief, the Christian Science War Relief Committee of The Mother Church [4] distributed more than $2,000,000 in relief work in the years of World War I. When the Fund was closed on June 2, 1919, contributions were $1,988,000. Added to this sum were receipts of approximately $16,000 identified in the report to the field as interest on daily bank balances and on United States Liberty Bonds. In addition, millions of garments were shipped to the stricken areas of Europe. [5]

There were other needs. One was for food. Another was for things to read and for things to study. Christian Science periodicals were on reading tables in the Y.M.C.A., the Red Cross, the Salvation Army, the Jewish Welfare Board. Copies

[4] Manager, Paul A. Harsch; assistant manager, Arthur J. Wallace.
[5] A total of 1,223,793 garments was shipped in the seventeen months between December 1, 1917, and May 1, 1919.

of *Science and Health* were in constant demand, some 40,000 copies of the "vest pocket" edition being distributed. This smaller size was for the use of military personnel particularly and was published in the autumn of 1917.

The Christian Science Monitor had its three most active months in 1918, the months and the distribution being: *September:* England, 159,255 copies; France, 45,689; United States and Canada, 936,840; *October:* England, 128,316; France, 65,250; United States and Canada, 1,088,541; *November:* England, 113,876; France, 67,855; United States and Canada, 864,008. Over-all total: 3,469,630.

In the British Isles, there were twenty-three Christian Science centers of distribution; in France, there were ten.

The lawyer acknowledged the commandment, "Thou shalt love thy neighbour as thyself" as a requirement of eternal life; but seeking justification for himself, asked "Who is my neighbour?"

The Teacher answered by telling of a man who was set upon by thieves, left half-dead by the roadside and neglected by one traveler and by a second traveler until a third traveler "came where he was; and when he saw him, he had compassion *on him.* And he went to *him,* and bound up his wounds, pouring in oil and wine, and set him on his own beast, and brought him to an inn, and took care of him."

Continuing, the Teacher told how, on the next day, when leaving, the good Samaritan gave money to the innkeeper for the continued care of the stranger, and the Teacher inquired of the lawyer, "Which now of these three, thinkest thou, was neighbour unto him that fell among thieves?"

Which now of these three, thinkest thou, was neighbour?

The Teacher's question was the Teacher's answer and,

because it was, the universe separated the questions. The Teacher did not ask, "Who is my neighbour?" He asked *which* of the three was *neighbour* to the man who was left half-dead by the roadside.

He asked, *Whose neighbour am I?*

CHAPTER SIX

Dedicated to Accomplishment

I N 1917, James F. Lord of Brookline, Massachusetts, acquired a piece of land in Bow, New Hampshire,[1] and on May 18, 1927, he gave the property to The Mother Church. The land was once the farm of Mark Baker, the father of Mary Baker Eddy. It was the place where she was born and where she lived until she was about fifteen years old.

In 1918, Lord built a Concord granite memorial on the site near where the farmhouse stood, and, in deeding the property to the Church made this acknowledgment: "In consideration of my most profound respect for Mary Baker Eddy and my deepest gratitude for the regenerating truth which she brought to the world through her discovery and teaching of Christian Science."

A letter accompanied the deed, in which Lord said to the Directors:

"Gentlemen:

"At your request I enclose herewith a brief statement of my connection with the Baker homestead at Bow, N. H.

"I also enclose a photograph of the letter from Mrs. Eddy to Rufus Baker [2] from which the inscription on the south side of the stone was taken. I think that the inscriptions on the four sides of the stone are all very appropriate.

[1] Lord's purchase consisted of 44.788 acres.
[2] Mrs. Eddy's cousin.

"I believe that in the future years hundreds of thousands will be interested in this place, and it has been some concern to me to provide for it the proper care and protection of it.

"I am grateful to have been the instrument used by Principle to rescue from oblivion, appropriately mark, and pass on to its proper ownership this piece of land where was born that one through whom the teachings of Christian Science were brought to a waiting world."

Once owned by Mary Baker Eddy's grandfather, the farm was close by the Merrimack River, whose shining waters run below the hill on which the farmhouse was built. In Mrs. Eddy's childhood, the farm, which spread across the infolding New Hampshire hills, was heavy with grain and fruit and wildflowers. But, for years before its purchase by Lord, no plow had turned its soil; abandoned to the elements, the farmhouse was gone; in place of grain and apple trees and pear trees and cherries and peaches stood scrub oak and pine and poplar.

Securing the property, Lord sought to restore its beauty and, while so doing, fixed the granite memorial in place. Chiseled into its four sides are four inscriptions. On the south side:

> Mary Baker Eddy, Discoverer of Christian Science. The Baker homestead around the memory thereof clusters the golden days of my childhood.
> Mary Baker Eddy.

The latter part of the above inscription is in Mrs. Eddy's handwriting, as is her signature.

The remaining three inscriptions are:

> Therefore thus saith the Lord, GOD, Behold, I lay in Zion for a foundation a stone, a precious corner

stone, a sure foundation: he that believeth shall not make haste.

Isaiah

This Truth is the rock which the builders rejected; but "the same is become the head of the corner." This is the chief corner-stone, the basis and support of creation, the interpreter of one God, the infinity and unity of good.

No and Yes, p. 38.

Novus Ordo Saeculorum
New Order of the Ages

With the property in the possession of The Mother Church, the Directors added to it,[3] landscaped it, planting shrubs and trees and flowers and wide lawns, leaving clear the summit, its marker, and the sweep of the view beyond the Merrimack and into the blue haze of the far places. As a girl, Mary Baker knew these hills, and as she grew older heard in them the cry of the Psalmist, finding in them, as did he, strength and help.

The homestead, the changing hills; the first frost on the corn standing in shock in the autumn of the year; the stars in the dark sky, and the snows of the lone winter lying deep in the valleys; the warm days of spring, the breaking up of the ice on the river, the first robin; the slim church steeples rising above the green leaves of summer—these were memories that were keepsakes of her childhood.

It was in these surroundings that, as a child of twelve, Mary Baker Eddy took her stand against the doctrine of eternal damnation for all who disagreed with clericalism.

---

[3] In December, 1935, The Mother Church bought four additional acres, and in May, 1944, it purchased an additional ten acres.

The times were not long removed from the years of compulsory taxation for the support of the clergy. This, of course, was taxation that was in disuse before the Revolutionary War, but there were fears of renewal and, as late as 1812, nine years before Mary Baker was born, householders in New Hampshire were writing to their selectmen:

"This may certify that I differ from Rev. Nathaniel Merrill's religion, and therefore refuse to pay him any ministerial tax, and shall not."

"Sir, for particular reasons I wish not to be taxed to Mr. Merrill again until I think different."

And, in protest to being taxed for a church stove requested by the minister, this letter:

"I have attended church these fifty years; I have fought the British seven years; I have slept in a tent on the frozen ground with nothing but a blanket to cover me; I have trod the snow path with bleeding feet nearly naked—and if Mr. Merrill needs a fire, let him go to a place where they keep one the year round." [4]

It was not until 1834, thirteen years after Mary Baker was born, that the Massachusetts legislature passed an act which nullified all previous state legislation and exempted the general public from paying taxes for the support of the clergy. The ministry accepted the change from compulsory to volunteer support, but continued to preach, as did William Adams in 1685:

"It is indeed wonderful condescension in the infinite GOD, thus to vouchsafe His Regard to such low worms as the *best* of the children of men are. That the Great God should look upon such nothings is a great stoop. . . . If the nations be as the drop of a bucket and as the small dust

[4] Ole Elizabeth Winslow, *Meetinghouse Hill: 1630-1783* (New York: copyright, The Macmillan Company, 1952).

which won't turn the Ballance, what then is a small handful of people, and what are single persons to Him?" [5]

Or, as Jonathan Edwards preached in the middle years of the eighteenth century: "The God that holds you over the pit of hell, much as one holds a spider, or some loathsome insect, over the fire, abhors you, and is dreadfully provoked."

To Mary Baker Eddy, as a child, these were utterances impossible to accept and, though her father, Mark Baker, believed, as she wrote in *Retrospection and Introspection* (p. 13), "in a final judgment day, in the danger of endless punishment, and in a Jehovah merciless towards unbelievers," she could not believe.

Described by Clifford P. Smith, in *Historical Sketches,* as "a positive man who formed individual opinions, and acted upon them," Mark Baker was deeply religious, a devoted Congregationalist. With his wife, he was a member of the Congregational church in Bow. After this church was closed in 1829, the Baker family attended services in Congregational churches in Pembroke and Concord and, after two years of such attendance, joined the First Congregational Church in Concord.

The Baker home in Bow was a stopping place for ministers of other denominations, and Baker was glad to have them as visitors because he enjoyed debating the punctuation marks of doctrine. Morning and evening prayers and Bible readings were daily events; each meal was blessed; Sunday was a day of strictness.

In the family were Mark Baker, his wife, Abigail, and their six children, three boys and three girls of whom Mary was the youngest.

[5] "God's Eye on the Contrite." Massachusetts Election Sermon, Boston, 1685.

Grieving over his one daughter's heresy, Baker pleaded with her to turn her back on wickedness; failing, he so frightened the young girl with his stern warnings of ever-lasting punishment in the fires of hell that she became ill. A doctor found her suffering from a high fever, left medi-cine, ordered quietness, and said he would come again. After the medical man was gone, her mother pressed cool fingers against her daughter's forehead, comforted her, and told her to seek God in prayer and ask His guidance.

She did and, as she recalled, "A soft glow of ineffable joy came over me. The fever was gone, and I rose and dressed myself, in a normal condition of health. Mother saw this, and was glad. The physician marvelled; and the 'horrible decree' of predestination—as John Calvin rightly called his own tenet—forever lost its power over me." [6]

Soon afterward Mary Baker was among the applicants for church membership. With the others, she listened to the reading of the church tenets, with their rigid dogma of pre-destination, and, alone, she informed the minister that she would not accept such a doctrine, even at the loss of church membership. She was questioned and, near the end of the questioning, she was asked for the moment when she "expe-rienced a change of heart."

This question she could not answer. The minister per-sisted, expressing the conviction that she had experienced a true regeneration, and inquired as to her emotions at the moment of change. To this question she had only one answer and the answer she gave was the words of the Psalmist: "Search me, O God, and know my heart: try me and know my thoughts: and see if *there* be any wicked way in me, and lead me in the way everlasting." [7]

---

[6] *Retrospection and Introspection,* pp. 13, 14.
[7] Psalms, 140:23, 24.

The earnestness in her voice so touched the minister that, despite her refusal to accept the full teachings, he accepted her at the communion table of church membership.[8]

This was 1833, and in 1836 Mark Baker moved his family from Bow to another farm, twenty-two miles away, in Sanbornton Bridge. Although she was only fifteen years old, there were mountains between the thoughts of Mary Baker and the thoughts of the others in her family, excepting her mother and Alfred, her brother.

Born in 1810, Alfred was her senior by eleven years. To pay for his college education, he taught school and tutored; he was graduated from Dartmouth College in 1834. After graduation, he studied law in the offices of Franklin Pierce in Hillsborough, New Hampshire, and with Richard Fletcher, in Boston. He returned to Hillsborough in 1837 to assume much of the legal practice of Pierce who became a United States senator in that same year and 14th President of the United States in 1853. Elected three times to the New Hampshire state legislature, Alfred Baker died on October 17, 1841, at the age of thirty-one.

Before he went to college, and while he was in college, and while he was in Hillsborough and Boston, Alfred Baker tutored his sister, introduced her to the wide field of literature, instructed her in Hebrew, Latin, and Greek, encouraged her versifying, talked long and eagerly with her on her favorite subjects of natural philosophy, logic, and moral science, poked gentle fun at her young habit of small argument, and fired her with his own aversion to tyranny and fraud.

Almost single-handed, he persuaded the New Hampshire legislature to abolish a law that punished debt by imprison-

---

[8] Until she formed the Church of Christ, Scientist, Mary Baker Eddy was a member of the Congregational Church.

ment—and, in so doing, his thoughts were not on the prison, but on the open fields. Like his sister, he was a searcher of truth; together, in their confidences, they walked over many lands—seeking, that they might heed; and listening, that they might understand.

Similarly, there was a strong bond between mother and daughter. Before her youngest child was born, Abigail Baker went to a neighbor and confided her wonderment because this child, she was sure, was dedicated to great accomplishment. Spiritually minded, Abigail must have turned her eyes many times toward the farmhouse window and must have seen, beyond the hills, what was beyond the gaze of her husband.

Nevertheless, while the child was yet small, Mark Baker did come to look upon his daughter as exceptional. Concerned over her health, he said her "brain was too large for her body," and he kept her out of school for long months at a time. Partly, at least, it was this decision by his father that caused Alfred Baker to assume a measure of responsibility for his sister's education.

It was in these new and sensitive years that Abigail Baker grew to know her daughter, and Mary Baker grew to know her mother. Doubtless, her mother was the first to hear poems [9] in which, even then, she was speaking of the temple that cannot be destroyed.

This stanza from a poem entitled "The Country-Seat" illustrates her early thought:

> Earth's beauty and glory delude as the shrine
> Or fount of real joy and of visions divine;
> But hope, as the eaglet that spurneth the sod,

[9] Among Mrs. Eddy's published poems are five that were written in her girlhood. They are on pages 18, 32, 58, 60, and 62 in her book *Poems*.

May soar above matter, to fasten on God,
And freely adore all His spirit hath made,
Where rapture and radiance and glory ne'er fade.[10]

Written, probably, when Mary Baker was eighteen years old, this verse is especially interesting to Christian Scientists because it is their Leader's first call to mankind to forsake matter when searching for God:

But hope, as the eaglet that spurneth the sod,
May soar above matter, to fasten on God,
And freely adore all His spirit hath made,
Where rapture and radiance and glory ne'er fade.

In his book, *Historical Sketches,* Clifford P. Smith tells of other significant affirmations in her years of girlhood and young womanhood. In a letter dated April 6, 1839, she referred to God as "the Source of all good"; writing in her diary in 1843, she wished only "to contemplate all in God and God in all"; and, in a letter not dated but written probably in 1848, she comforted a friend: "You must not feel sad or anxious about the future. . . . Let us remember there is One 'who careth for us'—too wise to err, too *good* to be unkind."

At twenty-one, when she was a pupil at Sanbornton Academy, Mary Baker was beginning to perceive that when truth is mixed with matter it is no longer truth. This perception caused one of her teachers, the Reverend Enoch Corser, to say, "I never before had a pupil with such depth and independence of thought." [11] Another who gave encour-

---

[10] *Retrospection and Introspection,* p. 18.
[11] Sibyl Wilbur, *The Life of Mary Baker Eddy* (Boston: The Christian Science Publishing Society, copyright, 1929).

agement was the Reverend Nathaniel Bouton, whose church in Concord was "the rallying point of the town, and the great congregation . . . came from all directions, long distances, and many on foot." [12]

Also there were the Reverend Corban Curtice and the Reverend Abraham Burnham; to them, and to others of the ministry, Mrs. Eddy made acknowledgment in her *Message to The Mother Church* for 1901:

> Full of charity and good works, busy about their Master's business, they had no time or desire to defame their fellow-men. God seemed to shield the whole world in their hearts, and they were willing to renounce all for Him. . . . Such churchmen and the Bible, especially the First Commandment of the Decalogue, and Ninety-first Psalm, the Sermon on the Mount, and St. John's Revelation, educated my thought many years, yea, all the way up to its preparation for and reception of the Science of Christianity.

Taking root in the early years of her search for God was the radical belief that He is perfect.

In the years from 1855 to 1860, she was ill almost continuously, but had lost all faith in medicine. She turned to her Bible and to prayer and, as so many have done when sick, she promised God, if restored to health, to devote her life to suffering humanity. She did not get well, but she did get better. In 1862, she visited Phineas P. Quimby, a healer in Portland, was helped briefly, but again drifted into semi-invalidism.

[12] John N. McClintock, *History of New Hampshire* (Boston: B. B. Russell, copyright, 1889).

On February 1, 1866, she slipped and fell on an icy street in Lynn, Massachusetts, and was so badly hurt that, after calling on her five times in little more than two days, the attending physician pronounced her condition critical. On the third day, while reading of the man who was sick of the palsy (St. Matthew 9:2-7), she was suddenly well. She got up from her bed, dressed herself, and was with her household when the doctor called a sixth time. This time there was nothing for him to do.

In *Miscellaneous Writings,* in *Retrospection and Introspection,* and in *Science and Health,* Mrs. Eddy marked the importance of this healing.

In *Miscellaneous Writings* (p. 24):

> As I read, the healing Truth dawned upon my sense. . . . That short experience included a glimpse of the great fact that I have since tried to make plain to others, namely Life is in and of Spirit; this Life being the sole reality of existence. I learned that mortal thought evolves a subjective state which it names matter, thereby shutting out the true sense of Spirit.

In *Retrospection and Introspection* (p. 26):

> The miracles recorded in the Bible, which had before seemed to me supernatural, grew divinely natural and apprehensible; though uninspired interpreters ignorantly pronounce Christ's healing miraculous, instead of seeing therein the operation of divine law.

In *Science and Health* (p. 107):

> In the year 1866, I discovered the Christ Science
> or divine laws of Life, Truth, and Love, and
> named my discovery Christian Science.

Although she marked the importance of the healing, Mrs. Eddy realized it had not come without invitation. She believed that study and thought and consecrated purpose had prepared her for precisely what had happened. She accepted it as a healing that was "divinely natural and apprehensible"; and she began her search to find out how it was done and how it could be done again.

Accepting divine law as the only source, she searched the Scriptures with new vision and in the perfection of God found what she believed to be the Principle of all healing and all good. Accepting Principle as God, she certified her discovery:

> That there is but one God or Life, one cause
> and one effect, is the *multum in parvo* of Christian
> Science; and to my understanding it is the heart
> of Christianity, the religion Jesus taught and demonstrated.[13]

From the day of her healing until the day of her passing, Mary Baker Eddy never relaxed her search into the perfection of God.

She did not gain understanding all at once, but she did achieve it in some degree in the first years after 1866, and in those years she was able to heal, and to heal again. The condition of her niece, Ellen C. Pilsbury, of Sanbornton Bridge, who was suffering from enteritis, was declared hope-

[13] *Miscellaneous Writings,* p. 25.

less by the family doctor. She was quickly healed by Mrs. Eddy in 1867.

In 1868, Mrs. Eddy was living in Lynn and was in her room in a boarding house when she heard a cry of fear from her landlady. Responding, Mrs. Eddy was confronted by a maniac, who threatened her with an upraised chair. Gazing deep into the man's torment, and deeper still, she reached out as he dropped the chair and touched his head as he fell to his knees.

Sobbing his penitence, he asked for the forgiveness he already had. Smiling, Mrs. Eddy told him to go in peace.[14]

There were many healings of all manner of disease by Mrs. Eddy and by her students in the first years of her journey and, having discovered what she believed was "the religion Jesus taught, and demonstrated," it was her great hope that her findings would be welcomed by all Christian denominations. She offered them, pleaded with clergymen to study them, and challenged the clergy to disprove the evidence of her work.

Through nearly ten years after her discovery she continued to attend services in a Congregational church in Lynn and continued to hope that her words would be heard, and used, by all who professed Christianity. Instead, from nearly all the pulpits, there was rejection of her teachings and ridicule for her name. The enmity must have troubled her and must have been hard for her to understand, but it was well for her and well for her teachings that rejection came.

---

[14] In 1884, when Mrs. Eddy was living in Boston, the stranger called on her, identified himself, and said he had returned to the asylum from which he had escaped. Discharged soon afterwards, he credited her with his healing, said he was living far from Massachusetts, was married, had a family, and was in Boston for the single purpose of seeing her and expressing his gratitude.

Had the clergy accepted her offer, the teaching that God is perfect almost surely would have been cast aside; the doctrine "that there is but one God or Life, one cause and one effect" almost surely would have been denied. The demonstration of healing would have been lost, as it was lost in the second century after the crucifixion, the direct result of the substitution of the opinions of the clergy for the words of Jesus.

> There followed him great multitudes of people from Galilee, and *from* Decapolis, and *from* Jerusalem, and *from* Judaea, and *from* beyond Jordan —and they heard Him speak of the poor, of those who mourn, of the meek, the merciful, the pure in heart, the peacemakers, those who are persecuted for righteousness' sake. After He had taught them many things, they heard His command: "Be ye therefore perfect, even as your Father which is in heaven is perfect."

It remained for the clergy to speak of God on lower ground—in terms of an executioner looking upon man as a loathsome insect fit only for everlasting torment in the pit of hell, as it remained for the clergy to measure life in terms of death, although Jesus never spoke of life as anything but eternal.

It would not have been possible for the clergy to have reconciled Mrs. Eddy's teachings with their own.

In Mrs. Eddy's teachings, there is full acceptance of the words of Jesus: "God *is* a Spirit; and they that worship him must worship *him* in spirit and in truth." In *Science and Health* (p. 140) there is this affirmation: "We worship spiritually, only as we cease to worship materially. Spiritual devoutness is the soul of Christianity. Worshipping through the medium of matter is paganism. Judaic and other rituals are but types and shadows of true worship."

In Mrs. Eddy's teachings, the words, "So God created man in his *own* image, in the image of God created he him," are taken to mean what they say. *Science and Health* (p. 475) contains this instruction:

> The Scriptures inform us that man is made in the image and likeness of God. Matter is not that likeness. The likeness of Spirit cannot be so unlike Spirit. Man is spiritual and perfect; and because he is spiritual and perfect, he must be so understood in Christian Science.

In Mrs. Eddy's teachings, there is no room for more than one God. In *Science and Health* (p. 340) are these words: "The First Commandment is my favorite text. It demonstrates Christian Science."

To worship spiritually, the denominational churches would have had to resolve more than one hundred differences in theology. They would have had to repudiate ritual which had accumulated over centuries. They would have been compelled to deny the existence of matter. They would have had to accept God, and not medicine, as the healer of disease. They would have had to teach that there is no such place as hell, no such person as the devil, and that death is an illusion of mortal mind. They would have had to agree that, being perfect, God knows no evil and, therefore, does not, and cannot, punish it—that "evil will in time disclose and punish itself." [15]

Mrs. Eddy came slowly to the view of having a church

[15] *Science and Health,* p. 447.

separate from all other churches. It was not until August, 1879, that she organized the Church of Christ, Scientist, and chartered it under the laws of Massachusetts. Before this, however, she formed the Christian Scientist Association.

While still searching for the cause of her healing, she recognized the exactness in "the divine laws of Life, Truth, and Love," and, after her discovery, she emphasized this exactness to her students and in her teachings. Persuaded that the clergy would not accept what she believed to be the truth, she formed the Association in 1876 for the purpose of protecting her teachings and of advancing a clear and distinguishable religion.

In the preamble to its constitution, she described the Association as "the oldest society of the School of Mind-healing, Christian Science," and in succeeding paragraphs made it clear that she now looked upon Christian Science as a religion, separate and distinct. For a time, the Association represented the Christian Science movement and through it for a number of years Mrs. Eddy conducted the affairs of the movement, including the organization of her church in 1879, the establishment of *The Christian Science Journal* in 1883, the first Committee on Publication in 1885, and the Christian Science Reading Rooms in 1888.

Meanwhile, she was building in larger dimensions. She realized, if Christian Science was to be established as a distinct religion, that there must be "a thorough preparation of the study for (its) practice." [16] Foreseeing this need, she organized the Massachusetts Metaphysical College in January, 1881, stating that the college had for "its vital purpose, the establishment of *genuine* Christian Science healing." [17]

Her use of the word "genuine" was a reference to imi-

[16] *Miscellany,* p. 245.
[17] *Retrospection and Introspection,* p. 48.

tators who were counterfeiting her teachings and calling the forgeries Christian Science. In the years of the seventies, and the eighties, there were more than twenty such imitations. They brought confusion to the public mind, made apparent the need for teachers qualified to instruct in the exactness of Christian Science, and proved Mrs. Eddy's requirement that "Truth alone must be taught." [18]

It was a requirement that heeded the instruction of the Teacher who charged the multitude, and the twelve who were His disciples, "Take heed therefore how ye hear." Mrs. Eddy's was a seeking in which the only teaching is of God and the only textbooks the Bible and *Science and Health with Key to the Scriptures.*

Except for two terms,[19] Mrs. Eddy taught all classes in the Massachusetts Metaphysical College from the time of its opening in 1881 until the early spring of 1889, when she gave up teaching.[20] After her retirement, her adopted son, Ebenezer J. Foster Eddy, taught one term and General Erastus N. Bates taught one class. On October 29, 1889, Mrs. Eddy dissolved the corporate structure under which the College was organized and closed its doors.

In the approximately nine years of its operation, hundreds of students were instructed in Christian Science and from her classrooms Christian Science went to all parts of the world. In 1884, Mrs. Eddy met the need for additional teachers. Until 1884, she was the only authorized teacher of Christian Science. In that year, she taught her first Normal

[18] From a letter to an early student, Mrs. Mary H. Philbrick, C.S.D.

[19] Two terms were under the tutelage of Mrs. Eddy's husband, Asa G. Eddy, who died in 1882.

[20] Mrs. Eddy taught her last class in November, 1898, in Concord, New Hampshire. In this class were sixty-five Christian Scientists, all of whom were invited. In addition, two Concord newspapermen were invited. There were two lessons, one on each of two successive days.

Class, of ten students. In the years until 1889, she taught other Normal Classes and sent out graduates to teach others and to heal the sick.

Mrs. Eddy closed her College in the same year, and for the same reason, that she dissolved the corporate structure of her Church. Each was at the crest of its popularity. More than one hundred and fifty applications for enrollment in her College were in her possession; overflow crowds were in attendance at church services which were held in Chickering Hall, Boston. Her reason for dissolving both corporate structures—and, in the same year, the Christian Scientist Association—was because she believed a more spiritual form of organization was needed.

In 1892, Mrs. Eddy formed The Mother Church, The First Church of Christ, Scientist, as successor in perpetuity to the Church she organized in 1879, and, in 1898, she established The Christian Science Board of Education as an auxiliary to the Massachusetts Metaphysical College.[21]

In writing of the Board of Education, Mrs. Eddy said in *Miscellany* (p. 246):

> I closed my College in the midst of unprecedented prosperity, left Boston, and sought in solitude and silence a higher understanding of the absolute scientific unity which must exist between the teaching and letter of Christianity and the spirit of Christianity, dwelling forever in the divine Mind or Principle of man's being and revealed through the human character.

---

[21] "Class teaching will not be abolished until it has accomplished that for which it was established; viz., the elucidation of the Principle and rule of Christian Science through the higher meaning of the Scriptures." (*Miscellany*, p. 241.)

While revising "Science and Health with Key to the Scriptures," the light and might of the divine concurrence of the spirit and the Word appeared, and the result is an auxiliary to the College called the Board of Education of The Mother Church of Christ, Scientist, in Boston, Mass.

Our Master said, "What I do thou knowest not now; but thou shalt know hereafter;" and the spirit of his mission, and wisdom of his words, and the immortality of his works are the same to-day as yesterday and forever. . . .

Up to, and including, 1907 (with the exception of the years 1903, 1904, and 1905, when no Normal Classes were taught, although some members of the 1903 Primary Class were permitted to use the initials C.S.B., but were not permitted to teach until receiving Normal Class instruction) there were yearly Normal Class instructions under the auspices of The Christian Science Board of Education; and these were (and are) the qualifications required of all applicants:

Loyal Christian Scientists' pupils who so desire may apply to the Board of Education for instruction; and if they have practiced Christian Science healing successfully three years and will furnish evidence of their eligibility therefor, they are eligible to enter the Normal Class. All members of this class must be thorough English scholars.
[*Church Manual,* Article XXIX, Section 1.]

In the years up to 1908, there was no limit on the number of students in each Normal Class but, after 1907, each Normal Class [22] was restricted to not more than thirty students, classes to begin on the first Wednesday in December and to be confined to one week and, instead of being held yearly, to be held once every three years.

Membership in The Mother Church is required of each applicant and "if both husband and wife are found qualified to teach Christian Science, either one, not both, should teach yearly one class" (*Church Manual*, Article XXX, SECTION 7). Each teacher in the Board of Education is elected every third year.

Also in the *Manual* (Article XXVI, SECTION 4) is a By-law which stipulates the number of students a graduate of the Normal Class may instruct each year: "The teachers of Christian Science shall teach but one class yearly, which class shall consist of not more than thirty pupils."

Mathematically, the total number of teachers is small; the number of students who can be taught each year is unimpressive. In the restriction is found once more Mrs. Eddy's refusal to be led astray by the flattery of numbers. In the parable of the *leaven, which a woman took, and hid in three measures of meal, till the whole was leavened,* she saw "an inference far above the merely ecclesiastical and formal application of the illustration." She saw that "ages

---

[22] When The Christian Science Board of Education was established in 1898, it consisted of four members. They were Edward A. Kimball, Laura Lathrop, Septimus J. Hanna and Dr. Alfred E. Baker, one of whom (Edward A. Kimball) presided, although all members were present. Shortly thereafter, Mrs. Eddy decided that Kimball, alone, should conduct the classes. He did so through 1902. Beginning with 1906, the teachers have been:

1906, Eugene H. Greene; 1907, Septimus J. Hanna; 1910, Bicknell Young; 1913, Laura E. Sargent; 1916, Clifford P. Smith; 1919, Ella W. Hoag; 1922, Frank W. Gale; 1925, Emilie B. Hulin; 1928, Irving C. Tomlinson; 1931, Duncan Sinclair; 1934, George Shaw Cook; 1937, Bicknell Young; 1940, Julia M. Johnston; 1943, Dr. John M. Tutt; 1946, Mary C. Ewing; 1949, Richard J. Davis; 1952, Emma C. Shipman; 1955, Robert Ellis Key.

pass, but this leaven of Truth is ever at work. It must destroy the entire mass of error, and so be eternally glorified in man's spiritual freedom." [23]

In *Miscellaneous Writings* (p. 166), she said, "like the leaven that a certain woman hid in three measures of meal, the Science of God and the spiritual idea, named in this century, Christian Science, is leavening the lump of human thought, until the whole shall be leavened and all materialism disappears."

As a girl of eighteen she sensed that the search for God is useless if the search is in matter; as a woman, and a teacher, she realized that progress in the Science of God does not depend upon obedience to the laws of mathematics, but upon obedience to the laws of Spirit; she knew that we need only to obey these laws, and all is open to us; she discerned these are laws none can find without preparation, laws none can harm, laws none can change.

In recognition of the changelessness of the laws she unfolded, so her words remain unchanged. [24] They will so remain. They are anchored in church law that they may fulfill Mrs. Eddy's purpose of "leavening the lump of human

[23] *Science and Health with Key to the Scriptures,* p. 118.

[24] No changes of any kind have been made in Mrs. Eddy's words since her passing in 1910. Two testimonies were deleted from *Science and Health with Key to the Scriptures.* After complete investigation by The Christian Science Board of Directors, the two testimonies were found to be unworthy of retention. One was removed; one was replaced. The change was made in 1925, and there was precedent for it. In 1907, and again in 1909, Mrs. Eddy took similar action affecting two other testimonies in *Science and Health.*

Another change was made in the *Church Manual.* In accordance with Mrs. Eddy's wish that her writings be made as accessible as possible, the Directors in 1925 included an Index in the *Manual.* In 1951, after a survey disclosed that the Index was little used, it was discontinued.

A third change was in the deletion of the list of Church Officers from the *Manual,* described in an early chapter.

Mrs. Eddy's words were not involved in any of the changes.

thought, until the whole shall be leavened and all material-ism disappears."

Mrs. Eddy was a woman of great wisdom. She knew that of first importance is the teaching and not the teacher, and for the accomplishment of her great purpose she left to the single keeping of The Christian Science Board of Directors an eternal offering: that all should hear as she heard, and all should obey as she obeyed—not in hope, but in under-standing.

CHAPTER SEVEN

Protection Was Provided

IN August, 1879, Mrs. Eddy received a charter [1] from the Commonwealth of Massachusetts in which was written this clause:

Now, THEREFORE, I, Henry B. Pierce, Secretary of the Commonwealth of Massachusetts, do hereby certify that said Mary Baker G. Eddy and others (giving names) their associates, and successors, are hereby legally organized and established as, and are hereby made, an existing corporation under the name of the Church of Christ (Scientist), with the powers, rights, and privileges, and subject to the limitations, duties, and restrictions which by law appertain thereto.

However acceptable this clause may have been to Mrs. Eddy in 1879, the more she studied it the less acceptable it became until, in 1889, it was wholly unacceptable. Under its terms, her church had "powers, rights, and privileges"— and, also, it was *subject to the limitations, duties, and restrictions which by law appertain thereto.*

This meant that having been chartered by the Commonwealth, her church was in the custody of the Commonwealth —associated with whatever laws a legislature might repeal;

[1] On April 12, 1879, at a meeting of seventeen Christian Scientists in Lynn, Massachusetts, and held for the purpose of forming a church, Mrs. Eddy suggested the church be called Church of Christ, Scientist. There was disagreement. Instead of pressing her wish, Mrs. Eddy urged that thought be given to her suggestion. A few weeks afterwards the membership approved the name unanimously. The first Sunday services were held in Salem, Massachusetts, May 4, 1879.

servant to whatever laws a legislature might enact. It was subservience not in keeping with her obedience to God.

No experience better illustrates Mrs. Eddy's growth in spiritual understanding than her experience in building The Mother Church.

In a way, the growth began in the summer of 1872. Mrs. Eddy was living in Lynn and, taking along a prospectus for a book now known as *Science and Health with Key to the Scriptures,* she went to Boston to see a publisher. In Boston, she was advised to drop the idea of writing such a book because it would have no market. Returning to Lynn, she was walking from the railroad station to her home when, suddenly, she reached out, stopped her companion, and pointing to a church building, she said:

"Someday, I shall have a church of my own."

Even then, in 1872, six years after her healing, Mrs. Eddy was becoming persuaded that her teachings were not acceptable in Christian pulpits. Nevertheless, she still hoped for a hearing. She talked with people she knew, and with clergymen she knew, but few heard in her words what was in them. In her words was not a plea for acceptance. She asked no one to believe what she said. She asked only that they listen to the testimony and examine the evidence.

She proposed nothing more, as she wrote in 1875 in the Preface to the first edition of *Science and Health,* than that they "settle the question of 'what is Truth?' on the ground of proof. Let that method of healing the sick and establishing Christianity be adopted that is found to give the most health, and make the best Christians, and you will then give science a fair field. . . ."

There were only a few who believed and, beginning June 6, 1875, sometimes as many as twenty gathered on Sunday in Good Templars Hall, in Lynn, to listen as she talked of

God and addressed herself to the purpose of building a church whose doors and windows and crossbeams would be shaped as with the hand of the Carpenter.

These Sunday services were organized by her students, eight of whom agreed to contribute $10 weekly, for one year, to pay Mrs. Eddy "as teacher and instructor, [for] the renting of a suitable hall, and other necessary incidental expenses."

On July 4, 1876, Mrs. Eddy and six of her students formed the first Christian Science organization. She called it the Christian Science Association. Its purpose was not limited to teaching and study, as became the purpose of other Christian Science associations. In addition to teaching and study, it aimed to promote a separate and unmistakable religion. In taking this action, it was apparent that Mrs. Eddy had become persuaded there would be no endorsement of her teachings from the pulpits of orthodoxy.

Nevertheless, wherever she could, and whenever she could, she delivered lectures and sermons in an effort to awaken the deeper understanding of all who were willing to listen. In one period, from November, 1878, to July, 1879, she delivered thirty-two lectures in Boston alone. There were healings. There, also, was unbelief.

Mrs. Eddy wrote of these efforts in *Retrospection and Introspection* (p. 15), saying:

> In the year 1878 I was called to preach in Boston at the Baptist Tabernacle of Rev. Daniel C. Eddy, D.D.,—by the pastor of this church. I accepted the invitation and commenced work.
>
> The congregation so increased in number the pews were not sufficient to seat the audience and benches were used in the aisles. At the close of my

engagement we parted in Christian fellowship, if
not in full unity of doctrine.

As for the Christian Scientist Association, it operated
under a constitution, had By-laws and Rules of Order, and
held meetings at regular intervals, sometimes once every
two weeks, sometimes once every four weeks. Until Mrs.
Eddy moved from Lynn to Boston in 1882, the meetings
were held in the homes of individual members, with almost
half of the meetings being held in Mrs. Eddy's home.

Orderly in everything she did, Mrs. Eddy included in
the constitution a precisely worded specification of her discovery, "to wit; that a Divine principle and given rule
applicable to every condition of man, and constituting the
Divine plan of his salvation from sin, sickness, and death
exist in the order of Eternal life, Truth, and Love, and that
Jesus demonstrated for man's example and his redemption,
this holy principle of Divine science, healing the sick, casting out devils, error, and raising the dead; clearly showing
by this Divine understanding and proof, the indivisibility
of Science and Christianity." [2]

Plainly, even after the obtaining of a charter for the
Church of Christ, Scientist, in 1879, Mrs. Eddy regarded
the Christian Scientist Association—and not the Church—as
the representative body of the Christian Science movement;
and the members thought of themselves the same way. In
numbers, they were not many. When organized, as distinct
from "formed," there were less than twenty and, in January,
1880, more than three years afterwards, there were but
twenty-nine. In 1883, there were sixty-one; in 1886, with

[2] From the constitution as reprinted in *Historical Sketches* by Clifford
P. Smith. Judge Smith called attention to the unusual capitalization and
questioned it, saying, "the capitalization and punctuation may have been
furnished by the printer."

interest in the teachings spreading from New York into the Middle West, there were 148; and, in 1889, approximately eight months before being dissolved, there were 353.

In the beginning, not all were students of Mrs. Eddy, there being a few honorary members, and some visitors. However, after 1885, membership was restricted to her own students, although not all were invited to membership. It was through the Association that Mrs. Eddy developed the Church in 1879, *The Christian Science Journal* in 1883, the Publication Committee in 1885,[3] and the Christian Science Reading Rooms in 1888.

The Association being the instrument Mrs. Eddy used to form the Church in 1879, it was natural that the attitude of the members of the Association toward the Church was one of affection rather than of obligation. Not all became members of the Church although, on May 26, 1880, when the Church asked for the money that was in the Association's treasury "to help liquidate the church debt," there was not a dissenting vote; also on June 30, 1880, the members of the Association voted to pay, in advance, four weeks' rent for the hall in which Sunday church services were held.

At the same time, not all the members agreed with Mrs. Eddy when, in 1883, she said "the association should be merged into the Church"; nor was this done. She did not press the matter.

In not pressing the matter she saw, unquestionably, that the members were not ready to hear her speak of things without corporate organizational moorings. She was willing to wait. On September 23, 1889, she perceived their readiness and wrote them of her earnest desire that "you vote To-day to dissolve this organization." They met that same

[3] This committee was the forerunner of the Committee on Publication of The Mother Church which, in turn, was formed in 1898.

day and did as she wished, "by a unanimous vote . . . at three o'clock and ten minutes, P. M."

Two months later, to the day, on November 23, 1889, she again wrote to her students, "This Mother Church must disorganize, and now is the time to do it, and form no new organization but the spiritual one." The next day the clerk of the Church informed the membership that a meeting would be held on December 2, 1889, "to consider the advisability, and to take action thereon, of dissolving the organization of the Church on the basis of material and human law."

On December 2, all articles and clauses in the regulations and by-laws of the Church were annulled except "that part of Article I which fixes its name," and in place of a Church associated with whatever laws a state legislature might determine, and servant to whatever laws a state legislature might enact, there was established "a Voluntary Association of Christians knowing no law but the law of Love, and no Master but Christ in the exercise of all the ministrations and activities heretofore performed as a Church of Christ, Scientist."

They might dissolve the material organization, and they might refer to themselves as "a Voluntary Association of Christians knowing no law but the law of Love," but they did not yet understand their Leader's teaching that to seek each other in Love is to find themselves. It was three years before Mrs. Eddy felt they understood well enough to accept her words:

> The real Christian compact is Love for one another . . . this bond is wholly spiritual and inviolate.[4]

[4] *Christian Science Journal,* March, 1892.

On September 23, 1892, three years after the dissolution of the Christian Scientist Association, eleven of Mrs. Eddy's students met at twelve o'clock noon at 133 Dartmouth Street, in Boston, Massachusetts, and formed The Mother Church. The First Church of Christ, Scientist.

It was the Church she dimly saw on that night in Lynn, twenty years before. Now in 1892, it was a Church, and not, as in 1879, an association that represented her teachings—a Church she defined as a "structure of Truth and Love"; [5] and one which, as she wrote on pages that were sealed in the cornerstone of the edifice of The Mother Church, "henceforth [would] whisper our Master's promise: 'And upon this rock I will build my Church, and the gates of hell shall not prevail against it' "—a Church that, by her instructions, requires of its members that they go into the paths of men and there speak of the Kingdom that is, and shall remain.

She found in a little-known law in the statutes of Massachusetts that her Church could be free of corporate limitations that make it "a creature of the State," and still hold property. Believing God *keeps* the things that belong to Him, Mrs. Eddy stripped her Church of dependence upon human opinions; in this way she placed it beyond the reach of all who wished to destroy it.

The *Church Manual* insures its impropriation. Mrs. Eddy provided this protection. On February 27, 1903, she wrote a letter to The Christian Science Board of Directors:

---

[5] CHURCH: The structure of Truth and Love; whatever rests upon and proceeds from divine Principle.

The Church is that institution, which affords proof of its utility and is found elevating the race, rousing the dormant understanding from material beliefs to the apprehension of spiritual ideas and the demonstration of divine Science, thereby casting out devils, or error, and healing the sick. (*Science and Health*, p. 583.)

Beloved Students: I am not a lawyer, and do not feel I sufficiently comprehend the legal trend of the copy you enclosed to me to suggest any changes therein. Upon one point, however, I feel competent to advise, namely: Never abandon the By-laws nor the denominational government of The Mother Church. If I am not personally with you, the Word of God, and my instructions in the By-laws have led you hitherto and will remain to guide you safely on, and the teachings of St. Paul are as useful today as when they were first written.

The present and future prosperity of Christian Science is largely due to the By-laws and government of "The First Church of Christ, Scientist," in Boston. None but myself can know, as I know, the importance of the combined sentiment of this Church remaining steadfast in supporting its present By-laws. Each of these many By-laws has met and mastered or forestalled some contingency, some imminent peril, and will continue to do so. Its By-laws have preserved the sweet unity of this large church, that has perhaps the most members and combined influence of any other large church in our country. Many times a single By-law has cost me long nights of prayer and struggle, but it has won the victory over some sin and saved the walls of Zion from being torn down by disloyal students. We have proven that "in unity there is strength."

With love as ever,
Mary Baker G. Eddy.

N. B. I request that you put this letter upon our Church records.—M. B. E.

Also, in 1903, in a letter to the General Association of Teachers, she urged obedience to the *Manual*, saying, "Adhere to the teachings of the Bible, Science and Health, and our Manual, and you will obey the law and gospel"; and, to Clara Shannon, a member of her household, she prophesied there would be a time when the *Manual* "will be acknowledged as law by law."

By establishing the *Church Manual* as the law of The Mother Church, by stressing faithfulness to the teachings of the Bible, *Science and Health*, and the *Church Manual*, and by making The Christian Science Board of Directors servants, in perpetuity, of the *Manual*, Mrs. Eddy placed upon the Directors, and upon the Directors only, the full responsibility of protecting "the present and future prosperity of the cause of Christian Science."

The time of testing whether the *Church Manual* would "be acknowledged as law by law" was near.

In the *Manual* were provisions that required Mrs. Eddy's written consent if certain functions were to be performed. Within, and without, the movement there was speculation on whether, with Mrs. Eddy not available in person, these functions were being performed legally.

It was not generally known that, while preparing the *Manual*, Mrs. Eddy had given thought to this same problem. Her cousin, Henry M. Baker, was a lawyer of standing in New Hampshire [6] and it was he who assured her that her way of providing for the protection of The Mother Church was completely legal. In his reminiscences,[7] William R.

[6] In 1907, Henry M. Baker, Archibald McLellan, and Josiah E. Fernald were named by Mrs. Eddy to comprise a Board of Trustees in the management of her property.

[7] *Permanency of The Mother Church and Its Manual* (Rev. ed., Boston: The Christian Science Publishing Society, copyright, 1954).

Rathvon recalled his own concern over the legality of the *Manual:*

"After I was in Chestnut Hill for a short time and studied the Manual as our Leader desired us to do, I was at first puzzled, then perplexed, and finally apprehensive, that she had apparently made no provision for those sections of the *Manual* referred to in this question to function after her signature or assent could not be had. I shared my misgivings with Judge Hanna and Mr. McLellan, both of whom felt as I did. We decided it would be best to speak to General Henry M. Baker about it as he was legal adviser to our Leader as well as her cousin, and a regular visitor to the home. He was then a member of Congress and his judgment on legal matters was greatly respected by Mrs. Eddy. One afternoon, just after he left her side, I asked him to step into Mr. Frye's [8] study as I had a matter of importance to lay before him.

" 'General Baker,' I said, 'for some time I have been quite concerned about how certain parts of our *Manual* would function if Mrs. Eddy could not supply her assent or signature as it requires. I thought best to ask you as a lawyer and one in whom Mrs. Eddy has every confidence.'

"The sun was shining on the carpet floor where he stood as his prompt and emphatic reply dispelled every cloud of doubt from my mind. 'You need not be at all uneasy,' were his reassuring words. 'It is a matter of common law in a case of this kind, where it is physically impossible to carry out specified conditions by the one named, that the next in authority assume that jurisdiction. And in this case the next in authority is the Board of Directors of The Mother Church. Any competent court in the land will uphold the

[8] Calvin A. Frye, Mrs. Eddy's secretary.

Manual just as Mrs. Eddy intends it to function whether her signature is forthcoming, or not.' "

There were others equally sure that the absence of Mrs. Eddy's signature did make a difference. Nearly ten years had elapsed since her passing, but still the argument was heard that, without her physical presence, there could be no single central authority responsible for the affairs of The Mother Church. Beginning to find support was the claim that final authority in the field of publishing belonged to the Board of Trustees of The Christian Science Publishing Society, as constituted under a Deed of Trust executed by Mrs. Eddy in Concord, New Hampshire, January 25, 1898.

The claim was made that, under the provisions of the Deed of Trust, supervision over the Trustees ended with Mrs. Eddy's passing. It was argued that it was Mrs. Eddy's intention there should be two directing bodies within The Mother Church, and that the Board of Trustees of The Christian Science Publishing Society should continue in perpetuity as a self-governing body. The dissenters did not seem to realize that, in so claiming, they were saying Mrs. Eddy believed the way to insure the continued strength of her Church was to make it a divided church.

On March 25, 1919, Christian Scientists everywhere in the world were stirred by press dispatches telling of the filing of a Bill in Equity in the Massachusetts Supreme Judicial Court. The plaintiffs were the members of the Board of Trustees of the Publishing Society. The defendants were The Christian Science Board of Directors, of The Mother Church. The Bill in Equity was not the ordinary court action seeking clarification of disputed duties. The Bill was a challenge to the validity of the *Church Manual.*

In it, the Trustees requested:

1. That the defendant Directors be restrained and enjoined from taking any further action intended directly or indirectly to impede or interfere with the plaintiff Rowlands, or either of the other plaintiffs, in the discharge of his or their respective duties as Trustees, under the trust instrument of January 25, 1898;

2. That the resolution hereinbefore recited purporting to remove the plaintiff Rowlands as trustee of The Christian Science Publishing Society and declare such trusteeship vacant, be adjudged as nugatory and of no legal effect;

3. That the defendants be restrained and enjoined from carrying out any purpose or plan by either direct or indirect means to compel the plaintiffs or any of them to resign their offices as Trustees; to impair, destroy, or in any way injure the business of The Christian Science Publishing Society as conducted by the plaintiff Trustees; or in any way to carry out any threat or purpose to injure the business of said Publishing Society either by creating and maintaining a publishing society to conduct a business in competition therewith, or otherwise;

4. That the defendants be restrained and enjoined from taking any action to defeat or tending to defeat the purposes of Mrs. Mary Baker G. Eddy, the Donor, as set forth and declared in the Trust Deed of January 25, 1898;

5. That the defendants be given such further relief as the case might require or admit of.

On the same day, and at the request of attorneys for the plaintiffs, the Massachusetts Supreme Judicial Court issued an *ad interim* injunction, restraining the Directors as follows:

Until said hearing you the said defendant Directors, your agents, attorneys and counselors, and each and every one of them are commanded to desist and refrain from taking any

further action intended directly or indirectly to impede or interfere with the plaintiff Rowlands, or either of the other plaintiffs,
in the discharge of his or their respective duties as Trustees,
under the trust instrument of January 25, 1898; and from carrying out any purpose or plan by either direct or indirect means
to compel the plaintiffs or any of them to resign their offices as
Trustees; to impair, destroy, or in any way injure the business
of The Christian Science Publishing Society as conducted by
the plaintiff Trustees; or in any way to carry out any threat or
purpose to injure the business of said Publishing Society either
by creating and maintaining a publishing society to conduct a
business in competition therewith, or otherwise; and from taking any action to defeat or tending to defeat the purposes of
Mrs. Mary Baker G. Eddy, the Donor, as set forth and declared
in the Trust Deed of January 25, 1898.

The action by the Trustees was litigation the Directors
tried to avoid. Lamont Rowlands, whose removal as a Trustee was ordered by the Directors, became a member of the
Board of Trustees of The Christian Science Publishing
Society on August 1, 1917. Because of outside interests, he
was not a regular attendant at meetings of the Trustees; in
fact, of 407 such meetings, he was absent 192 times, or
approximately 47 per cent.[9]

This absenteeism was a matter of concern to the Directors,
and for many reasons, among which was the refusal of the
other two Trustees to meet with the Directors unless Rowlands was present. Of concern, too, was a new policy proposed by Rowlands, and agreed to by his associates, which
permitted the publication of cards of practitioners who were
not recognized by the Directors as qualified practitioners;
the listing, as branch churches, of organizations not recognized by the Directors as branch churches; using the facil-

---

[9] On September 8, 1898, Edward P. Bates, one of the original Trustees,
was removed by vote of the Directors. Appointed on January 25, 1898, his
absenteeism record was 30 per cent.

ities of The Christian Science Publishing Society to publish articles—all in violation of the *Church Manual.*

Those were some of the things about which there was disagreement. There were many others; but, as was pointed out in the hearings before the justices of the Massachusetts Supreme Judicial Court, the Board of Directors held off on taking any action "in the hope that the Trustees would come back to their moorings." There still was this hope, as late as January 3, 1919, when the Directors sent a letter to the Trustees in which it was said:

> The Directors have one more proposal to make. It is that the present members of the Board of Trustees submit their resignations to The Christian Science Board of Directors to take effect when their resignations are accepted by the Board of Directors.

Upon receipt of this letter, the Trustees met with their attorneys and, in a letter dated January 27, 1919, the attorneys informed the Board of Directors that they had advised the Trustees to stand fast, because "if there be any conflict between the terms of the Deed and the language of the *Church Manual,* the legal and moral obligation of the Trustees compels them to respond to and obey the mandates of the Deed." [10]

In their communication to the Directors, the lawyers suggested another meeting, and another effort "to harmonize their different views." This meeting was held. Other meetings were held. The Directors insisted that the Trustees recede from their position that the terms of the Deed held precedence over the By-laws of the *Church Manual;* the Trustees were adamant in their refusals.

[10] The lawyers for the Trustees were Charles Evans Hughes, Silas H. Strawn, and Sherman L. Whipple.

On March 17, 1919, the Directors met, wrote and adopted the following resolution:

The following resolution is offered for adoption by The Christian Science Board of Directors, the Board of Directors of The First Church of Christ, Scientist, in Boston and the governing board of the Christian Science denomination. It is offered for adoption in the exercise of the rights and powers vested in this Church and in this Board by the law of Massachusetts, by the Deed of Trust dated January 25, 1898, through which Mary Baker Eddy, the Discoverer and Founder of Christian Science, and the Leader of the Christian Science movement, constituted the Board of Trustees of The Christian Science Publishing Society, by the By-laws of this Church, and by the usage of the Christian Science denomination.

Whereas Mr. Lamont Rowlands, who has been acting as Trustee of The Christian Science Publishing Society under which said Deed of Trust and under Article XXV of the By-laws of this Church, was put into said position for the reason, among other reasons, that he was a member of this Church who had subscribed to its By-laws and was regarded as obedient to its By-laws and government; and

Whereas Mrs. Eddy has declared that "The present and future prosperity of the cause of Christian Science is largely due to the By-laws and government of "The First Church of Christ, Scientist, in Boston" (*Christian Science Sentinel*, Volume XVI, p. 1010);

Whereas Mrs. Eddy has declared that "Law constitutes government, and disobedience to the laws of The Mother Church must ultimate in annulling its Tenets and By-laws. Without a proper system of government and form of action, nations, individuals, and religion are unprotected; hence the necessity of this By-law and the warning of Holy Writ; 'That servant, which knew his lord's will, and prepared not himself, neither did according to his will, shall be beaten with many stripes.'" (*Church Manual*, p. 28); and

Whereas the tenets referred to in the foregoing quotation are "the important points, of Christian Science" (*Science and Health*, p. 497), and the system of government and form of action referred to in the foregoing quotation is that which is shown by the By-laws of this Church; and

Whereas it has become evident that Mr. Rowlands does not understand or recognize the importance and necessity of promoting the interests of Christian Science by following the directions given by Mrs. Eddy in our *Church Manual;* and

Whereas Mr. Rowlands has shown a disposition to invent or adopt interpretations of our Church By-laws that pervert their meaning and annul their effect; and

Whereas since Mr. Rowlands began to act as Trustee of The Christian Science Publishing Society, he and other Trustees thereof have tried to change the relation which has always theretofore existed between The Christian Science Publishing Society and its Board of Trustees on the one hand and The Mother Church and its proper officers on the other hand, and he in particular has tried to convert and enlarge such trusteeship into an office or function of a new and different character; and

Whereas Mr. Rowlands and other persons acting with him, including several eminent lawyers wastefully employed have set up said Deed of Trust against the By-laws and government of The Mother Church, and have threatened this Board with litigation if this Board exercises its right and power to remove any of said Trustees; and

Whereas it has become evident that Mr. Rowlands has allowed a sense of self-interest to interfere with the interests of Christian Science; that he has become self-assertive, contentious, and disposed to make trouble without regard to consequences; and that he is, for these reasons and the foregoing reasons and other reasons, not suitable for connection with The Christian Science Publishing Society as a Trustee thereof; and

Whereas Mr. Rowlands evidently has other interests which prevent him from giving sufficient time and attention to the business of The Christian Science Publishing Society; and

Now therefore it is resolved by The Christian Science Board of Directors, the Board of Directors of the First Church of Christ, Scientist, in Boston, and the governing Board of the Christian Science movement, in the exercise of the rights and powers above mentioned, that Mr. Rowlands is no longer accepted by this Board as suitable for connection with The Christian Science Publishing Society as a Trustee thereof; that he be and hereby is removed from the Board of Trustees of said Society; and that the trusteeship in connection with said Society heretofore held or claimed by him be and hereby is declared vacant.

On the following day, a letter was sent by the Directors to the two remaining Trustees:

March 18, 1919.

Mr. Herbert W. Eustace,
Mr. David B. Ogden, Trustees,
The Christian Science Publishing Society,
Boston, Mass.

Dear Friends:—

I am instructed by The Christian Science Board of Directors to say in furtherance of the Board's interview with you on the 17th inst., at which time you were served with a notice of the dismissal of Mr. Lamont Rowlands as a Trustee of The Christian Science Publishing Society, which action was taken by The Christian Science Board of Directors under Article XXV, Sections 3 and 5, of *The Mother Church Manual*,[11] the Board calls attention to your duty under Article XXV, Section 3, of the *Manual,* requiring the remaining Trustees to fill the vacancy. It is the Board's desire that you immediately appoint some one to fill the position made vacant by their action of yesterday, and in the appointment of Mr. Rowlands' successor they expressly

---

[11] *Vacancies in Trusteeship.* Section 3. The Christian Science Board of Directors shall have the power to declare vacancies in said trusteeship, for such reasons as to the Board may seem expedient.

Whenever a vacancy shall occur, the Pastor Emeritus reserves the right to fill the same by appointment; but if she does not elect to exercise this right, the remaining trustees shall fill the vacancy, subject to her approval.

Suitable Employees. Section 5. A person who is not accepted by the Pastor Emeritus and The Christian Science Board of Directors as suitable, shall in no manner be connected with publishing her books, nor with editing or publishing *The Christian Science Journal, Christian Science Sentinel, Der Herold der Christian Science,* nor with The Christian Science Publishing Society.

request that you name a person who shall be suitable and satisfactory to the Board of Directors.

Kindly acknowledge receipt of this letter, and advise the Board of Directors when you will be able to comply with the above request.

Sincerely yours,

(Signed) Chas. E. Jarvis.

Corresponding Secretary for The

Christian Science Board of Directors.

Rowlands refused to honor the dismissal. Eustace and Ogden refused to honor the request. Together, and on the advice of the lawyers, they took the position that the Directors were wrong in their charges against Rowlands, wrong in assuming they had authority to dismiss any Trustee, and wrong in presuming to instruct the Board of Trustees to name to their membership "a person who shall be suitable and satisfactory to the Board of Directors."

They emphasized again their intention of being guided by the terms of the Deed of Trust. For the time being, that is where the matter rested—because of an unavoidable apostasy.

On the same day (March 17, 1919) that resolutions were drawn dismissing Rowlands, The Christian Science Board of Directors dismissed from its own membership John V. Dittemore.

A director since 1909, Dittemore became increasingly bitter in the months of disagreement. From the beginning, he opposed all efforts to restore pleasant relations with the Trustees; and, in the late months, he opposed all efforts by the Board to keep The Mother Church from being drawn into litigation. It was his expressed view in the first days of disagreement that all three Trustees should be dismissed and, as the days of disagreement accumulated, so did his bitterness.

He became critical, not only of the Trustees, but also of the Directors. Soon his criticism was sharply personal, and openly contemptuous. Finally, he refused to join with his fellow Directors in making decisions, and when decisions were arrived at, declined to accept them. On March 17, 1919, he was dismissed. The resolutions of dismissal follow:

Whereas Mr. John V. Dittemore, one of the members of this Board, has frequently failed and refused to obey the By-law of this Church that "the business of The Mother Church shall be transacted by its Christian Science Board of Directors (*Manual*, Article 1, SECTION 6). In particular he has violated this By-law by doing, or attempting to do, as a single member of the Board, what could be done only by the Board as such. He has violated this By-law by acting as a single member of the Board, contrary to what has been done, or deliberately left undone, by the Board. He has violated this By-law by refusing to be bound by the votes of the majority and the decisions of the Board. He has violated this By-law by disregarding the equal rights, duties, and responsibilities of the other members of the Board, and by attempting to force them to accept his opinions and submit to his will;

And whereas Mr. Dittemore has taken advantage of his position as a member of this Board to carry on a campaign for personal influence and control in the affairs of The Mother Church;

And whereas Mr. Dittemore has violated Article I, Sect. 5 of our Church By-laws [12] by reporting the discussions of this Board; and he has violated the last sentence of Article XXXIII, Sect. 2 [13] of our Church By-laws by giving directions to State

[12] *Directors.* Section 5. Members shall neither report the discussions of this Board, nor those with Mrs. Eddy.

[13] *Duties.* Section 2. The State Committees on Publication act under the direction of this Committee on Publication. ("This Committee on Publication" refers to the Committee on Publication of The Mother Church which, as stated in the *Church Manual* [Article XXXIII, SECTION I], "shall consist of one loyal Christian Scientist who lives in Boston, and he shall be manager of the Committees on Publication throughout the United States, Canada, Great Britain and Ireland.")

Committees on Publication and inducing them to act contrary to bulletins issued by their manager with the approval of this Board;

And whereas Mr. Dittemore has conducted himself in such a manner as to produce discord and trouble between the Trustees of The Christian Science Publishing Society and this Board, and to hinder the efforts of this Board to arrive at a mutual understanding with said Trustees and secure the rights of The Mother Church without litigation and without destruction or injury to any of the interests of Christian Science;

And whereas Mr. Dittemore has written numerous letters to this Board which were not calculated to help carry on its work; but which were self-assertive, controversial, and acrimonious, and which sometimes included statements about the other members and the proceedings of the Board that were unjust, distorted, and untrue;

And whereas Mr. Dittemore has frequently and continually, during meetings of this Board, acted toward the other members in a rude, offensive, and threatening manner;

And whereas Mr. Dittemore has ceased to maintain toward the other members of this Board an attitude of unity, cooperation, equality, and Christian fellowship, and has habitually adopted the opposite attitude, so that it has become extremely difficult for this Board to perform its functions;

And whereas the other members of this Board have repeatedly remonstrated with Mr. Dittemore in regard to most of the matters herein contained, but doing this has made no change for the better in his conduct;

Now therefore, it is resolved by The Christian Science Board of Directors, the Board of Directors of The First Church of Christ, Scientist, in Boston, that Mr. John V. Dittemore be, and he is by the adoption of this resolution, removed and dismissed from this Board;

Resolved further that Mr. Dittemore be and hereby is requested to return to the Clerk of The Mother Church and Corresponding Secretary of this Board all letters, documents, papers, copies thereof, and other articles which he has taken or received as a member of this Board, or an officer of this

Church, or which have been delivered to him by reason of his being a member of this Board, or an officer of this Church.

The vote was unanimous.

Yet, in spite of the provocation, the Directors continued their efforts to avoid litigation, as the Court records disclose. Their patience was not understood. The Trustees mistook it for indecision. Dittemore mistook it for weakness. Even on March 17, 1919, and after that date, the Directors hoped for an acknowledgment from the Trustees of the authority of the *Church Manual* and for recognition by Dittemore that, in his personal bitterness, he had wandered far from the teachings of Christian Science.

As for the Directors, if they erred, they did so on the side of forbearance. It may be said that forbearance did not prevent litigation. It may be that less forbearance would have prevented litigation. While she was here in person, Mrs. Eddy encountered dissension within the ranks. She, too, had forbearance; and she insisted upon it in the *Church Manual:*

> No church discipline shall ensue until the requirements according to the Scriptures, in Matthew, 18:15-17, have been strictly obeyed, unless a By-law governing the case provides for immediate action.
>
> [Article XI, Section 4.]

In Matthew 18:15-17, there are these instructions given by the Founder of Christianity to His disciples:

> Moreover if thy brother shall trespass against thee, go and tell him his fault between thee and him alone; if he shall hear thee, thou has gained

thy brother. But if he will not hear *thee,* then take with thee one or two more, that in the mouth of two or three witnesses every word may be established. And if he shall neglect to hear them, tell *it* unto the church: but if he neglect to hear the church, let him be unto thee as an heathen and a publican.

CHAPTER EIGHT

All Survived That Could Survive

Aɴʏ hope by the Directors that the Trustees would
acknowledge the *Church Manual* as the sole authority
in the affairs of The Mother Church must have vanished
on May 20, 1919. On that day, on the previous day, and on
the next day there was an exchange of communications
which made agreement unattainable. The communications
are their own evidence:

The communication of May 19, 1919:

Mr. William D. McCrackan,
The Commodore,
Forty-second street and Lexington avenue, New York City.

In view of your letter of April 22, written to Mr. McKenzie,
and your continued absence from the office, the trustees suspended you as an associate editor and omitted your editorials,
and in view of your conduct your services are discontinued as
of today.

Board of Trustees.

The communication of May 20, 1919:

The Christian Science Board of Directors,
Falmouth and St. Paul Streets,
Boston, Mass..

Dear Friends:
The continued absence of Mr. McCrackan and his neglect of
his duties in connection with his position as associate editor
made it necessary to discontinue his services and omit his further

editorials. Consequently, Mr. McCrackan's services were discontinued yesterday.

It will, of course, be necessary for the trustees to employ another associate editor, and we are now giving consideration to this subject. If you have any recommendations to make in connection with such appointment, and can furnish us the names of those you think could serve in this position acceptably, and for the promotion of Christian Science, we shall be glad to have you furnish us with the names as early as practicable.

With best wishes,
Sincerely yours,
Board of Trustees.
(Signed) Herbert W. Eustace, Secretary.

The communication of May 21, 1919:

Board of Trustees,
The Christian Science Publishing Society,
107 Falmouth Street,
Boston, Massachusetts.

Dear Friends:

The Christian Science Board of Directors instructs me to acknowledge with thanks the receipt of your favor of May 20 and to make the following reply:

Under the provisions of Article I, Section 3, and Article XXV, Sect. 4 [1] of the By-laws of The Mother Church, the directors are

---

[1] 3: *Clerk and Treasurer.* The term of office for the Clerk and the Treasurer of this Church (also for the editors and the manager of The Christian Science Publishing Society, and the manager of the general Committee on Publication in Boston) is one year each, dating from the time of election to office. Incumbents who have served one year or more, may be re-elected, or new officers elected, at the annual meeting held for this purpose, by a unanimous vote of the Christian Science Board of Directors and the consent of the Pastor Emeritus given in her own handwriting. (Article 1, SECTION 3.) *Editors and Manager.* The term of office for the editors and the manager of The Christian Science Publishing Society is one year each, dating from the time of election to the office. Incumbents who have served one year or more can be re-elected, or new officers elected, by a unanimous vote of the Christian Science Board of Directors, and the consent of the Pastor Emeritus given in her own handwriting. (Article XXV, SECTION 4.)

charged with the responsibility of electing the editors of the Christian Science periodicals.

Basing their action on the established custom inaugurated by our Leader, Mary Baker Eddy, which has never been questioned, but which has been accepted by the Christian Science movement since the establishment of the trust, the directors will be prepared to elect a successor to Mr. McCrackan on June 2, and will take pleasure in giving you due notice of such election.

The directors trust that you will appreciate the propriety of the position taken by them under the *Manual* and will be guided accordingly.

> With kind regards,
> Sincerely yours,
> (Signed) Charles E. Jarvis,
> Corresponding Secretary for The Christian
> Science Board of Directors.

Also on May 21, 1919, a fourth communication was sent to a number of newspapers from the Committee on Publication of The Mother Church. It was written by Clifford P. Smith. As appearing in the *Boston Herald,* this communication read:

To the Editor of The Boston Herald:

There is a special reason just now why editors and readers of newspapers should be cautious about accepting stories pertaining to Christian Science affairs. A very active propaganda is in operation against the government of The First Church of Christ, Scientist, in Boston.

The report that when Mrs. Annie M. Knott [2] resigned her position as one of the editors of the Christian Science periodicals to become a member of The Christian Science Board of Directors, the board "found difficulty in getting someone to take her place" is not true. Mrs. Knott resigned on the 19th of March. Her successor, Mrs. Ella W. Hoag, was elected on the 24th of March. She was the directors' first and only choice for this

[2] Mrs. Annie M. Knott, the first woman elected to The Christian Science Board of Directors, was chosen as a successor to John V. Dittemore.

position, and she accepted it immediately when it was offered to her.

Another mistaken report relates to the reasons why Mr. William D. McCrackan has declined re-election as one of the editors of the Christian Science periodicals. His actual reasons are shown by the following letters:

P.O. Box 32, Fenway Station,
Boston, Mass., May 18, 1919.
My dear Judge Smith:

I am sending you copies of two letters, one to Mr. McKenzie dated April 22, and the other to our directors, dated May 1st.

I want you to have the exact facts in regard to my position as editor. In case any false statements are printed I leave it to you as Committee on Publication to make the necessary corrections.

Faithfully,
(Signed) W. D. McCrackan.

April 22, 1919.
My dear Mr. McKenzie:

I am forwarding to you my editorial which is due on Thursday, April 24.

Since the trustees of the Publishing Society have taken to censoring the Sentinel and Journal upon advice of counsel, what is happening is that their counsel are finally determining the nature of the articles and editorials for those periodicals. It is sufficient to recall among other instances that the trustees' counsel caused to be erased from an article the second verse of the good old hymn, "Onward, Christian Soldiers," and from an editorial a statement by Mrs. Eddy concerning the Manual which she framed for her own church. This produces an intolerable situation. In justice to my service to the Christian Science field I cannot be a party to this method of making up our periodicals.

Under these circumstances I shall continue to send my editorials, but shall take no part in selecting and correcting articles.

With all good wishes,
Faithfully,
(Signed) W. D. McCrackan.

Dear Directors: May 1, 1919.

The time approaches when you will be called upon to make your annual appointments of editors of *The Christian Science Sentinel, The Christian Science Journal, Der Herold,* and *Le Héraut.* If my name should come up for reappointment, let me say that when I took office in 1916 I felt three years would constitute a full-rounded term of service for me as an editor. I have seen no reason to change my views. I served three years as Committee on Publication for the State of New York and three years as First Reader of The Mother Church. At the coming annual meeting I shall have served three years as associate editor. It is now my desire to take up other branches of Christian Science work at the close of my term.

I am sincerely appreciative of the opportunities for good which the three annual appointments by the board have meant for me.

With best wishes,
I remain, faithfully yours,
(Signed) W. D. McCrackan.

On account of the suit brought by the Board of Trustees of the Christian Science Publishing Society, The Christian Science Board of Directors is not responsible for the censoring to which Mr. McCrackan took exception.

Sincerely yours,
(Signed) Clifford P. Smith.

The letter from the Directors to the Trustees, and the publication of Judge Smith's statement in the *Boston Herald,* brought a conference between the Trustees and their attorneys, and out of the conference came legal action. Going into court, attorneys for the Trustees charged there had been a violation of the injunction issued on March 25 and demanded that the Directors, and Smith, be subpoenaed, arrested, and haled into court on charges of contempt.

In their charge, the attorneys insisted that "the action of the defendants and the notice thereof are a deliberate and purposeful interference by the defendants with the management by the plaintiffs of the affairs of the Publishing Society, the employment of editors and other officials, and . . . the result of said action is to discredit the plaintiffs and embarrass them in the performance of their duties."

Continuing, and referring directly to Judge Smith's letter, the attorneys stated:

Said letter was published and sent out by the defendants, with the purpose on their part to mislead the public and those interested in the Christian Science movement as to the circumstances under which said McCrackan's services were discontinued. The defendants knew at the time of putting out said letter that said McCrackan had been dismissed from the service of the Publishing Society by the trustees, and were fully informed as to the valid reasons which led the trustees to take such action.

The defendants and their attorney also knew, or in the exercise of reasonable diligence would have known, that the statements in said McCrackan's letter of April 22 to which they gave currency to the effect that plaintiff's counsel had caused to be erased a certain part of the hymn, "Onward, Christian Soldiers," and had caused to be erased from an editorial a statement by Mrs. Eddy concerning the *Manual*, and that such alterations in editorials were the cause, or reason, for the retirement of said McCrackan as an associate editor, and that said McCrackan resigned as associate editor and was not dismissed, were entirely false and without foundation.

Said letter was sent out for publication by the defendants, intending thereby to give a false and misleading impression and understanding as to the reason, or reasons, why said McCrackan retired from the service of the plaintiffs and as to the circumstances of his dismissal, and for the further purpose of thereby discrediting the plaintiffs as trustees in the management of the affairs of the Publishing Society, and to interfere with and embarrass them in connection with such management, and to impede the trustees in the discharge of their duties as such.

Wherefore, The plaintiffs pray that the defendants Dickey, Neal, Merritt, Rathvon, and Knott, together with their agent, attorney, and counseler, said Clifford P. Smith, be summoned to the bar of this Court, there to answer for their contempt of this Court in the violation of said injunction.

The Plaintiffs,
By their Solicitors.

Contempt proceedings against the Directors, and against Judge Smith, were heard by Justice Braley, of the Massachusetts Supreme Judicial Court through the five days of June 4, 5, 6, 7 and 10, 1919. The Directors, and their counsel, were found guilty. Each director was fined fifty dollars; Judge Smith was fined one hundred dollars.

It was February 20, 1920, and a room in the old court building in Pembrooke Place, in Boston, was filled with Christian Scientists. Five months before, or thereabouts, in this same room, the witnesses completed their testimony, and the lawyers completed their arguments; and all, the testimony and the arguments, had been submitted to Judge Frederic Dodge.

Appointed as Master by the Massachusetts Supreme Judicial Court, Dodge had presided over thirty-four days of hearings between the dates of June 3, 1919, and September 12, 1919. On this day of February, in 1920, there would be an acknowledgment of the *Church Manual* "as law by law," as Mrs. Eddy prophesied—or a decision that, in the conduct of their duties, the Trustees of the Publishing Society were above the *Manual* and were not, as were all other Christian Scientists, subject to its By-laws.

Now, Dodge was on the bench again, reading his decision, and nearing the end of its sixty-eight pages. Nearing the end, he reviewed the dismissal of Rowlands; and, pausing, gave his decision:

"... I find that Rowlands' removal was not lawfully effected by the . . . resolution adopted on March 17, 1919; and that he is still a Trustee under Mrs. Eddy's deed of January 25, 1898, notwithstanding the resolution."

The decision was a surprise to the field and to the Directors. The reaction of both was immediate. Support flooded in on the Directors; and they, in turn, instructed their attorneys to begin preparations to appeal the decision to the full bench of the Massachusetts Supreme Judicial Court.

To the great majority of Christian Scientists, it was unbelievable that such a decision could be made, and equally unbelievable that the Master could say the things he said in supporting his decision. In dismissing Rowlands, the Master said the Directors did not act in good faith. These were his words:

"So far as the assigned reasons accuse Rowlands of failure to devote time enough to the Publishing Society's business, or were made to appear as reasons requiring his removal only, and not equally the removal of his co-trustees, it may be said that they were not reasons assigned in good faith."

Within two weeks, or on March 4, the Directors sent a request to publish in the *Monitor,* the *Sentinel,* and the *Journal* a statement addressed to the field, and reading as follows:

Dear Co-Workers:
In the suit brought by the Trustees of the Christian Science Publishing Society against the Directors of The Mother Church, the Master has now filed a report of his findings and conclusions. Much of the report is unfavorable, but it is not a final decision. It is subject to review by the Supreme Judicial Court of Massachusetts, first by a single justice thereof, and later on the full court of five justices. At least some months are likely to elapse before their final decision can be obtained.
Among the Master's findings favorable to the Church are the following: He has found that all the By-laws of the 89th, or

final edition of the *Manual,* were approved by Mary Baker Eddy; that they were adopted by its Board of Directors; and that they always have been accepted as the By-laws of The Mother Church by its entire membership.

These findings recognize Mrs. Eddy's authorship of our *Church Manual;* they also affirm all that is legally essential to the stability of The Mother Church as a permanent organization. Mrs. Eddy's work as the Discoverer, Founder, and Leader of Christian Science only needs the clear understanding and active cooperation of Christian Scientists.

The discernment, steadfastness, and unity of Christian Scientists have been tested before. So once more we may be assured by these words of our beloved Leader: "Built on the rock, our church will stand the storms of ages." (*Miscellaneous Writings,* p. 140).

Faithfully yours,
Adam Dickey,
James A. Neal,
Edward A. Merritt,
William R. Rathvon.
Annie M. Knott.
The Christian Science Board of Directors.

Two days later, or on March 6, the Trustees replied:

The Christian Science Board of Directors, The
First Church of Christ, Scientist,
Falmouth and St. Paul Streets,
Boston, Massachusetts.

Dear Friends:

Your letter to the Board of Trustees requesting the publication in the *Monitor, Sentinel,* and *Journal* of a letter to the members of The Mother Church in the form which you sent us, has been given careful consideration.

When it became clear that the difference of opinion between the Directors and the Trustees as to their relative responsibilities in connection with the administration of the trust created by our Leader, would have to be submitted to the decision of the Court, the Trustees adopted the rule that the *Monitor* should report only the actual proceedings in court, without comment, and that the other publications should contain no report.

This rule was adopted because the Trustees felt strongly that the organs of the Church provided by our Leader—not as personal organs of the Board of Directors, or any of its members, or of the Board of Trustees, or any of its members, but solely for promoting and extending Christian Science throughout the world—should not be involved in controversies which might arise among the members of either board as to the scope of their respective duties.

This rule was approved by the Court very early in the proceedings, and since then has been strictly adhered to with the assent and acquiescence of all the parties.

While the communication which you request to be published is clearly not within the rule, containing, as it does, comments on the Master's Report, we have decided, in view of the nature of your request, to make it an exception, and accordingly have requested the editors to publish your letter and our reply.

In this connection, however, and to prevent any misunderstanding, may we say that the Master's findings which you quote as favorable to the Church were made not only without contention to the contrary, but with the Trustees' cordial approval.

May we also add that the Trustees, having felt constrained by the attempted removal of one of their members from his office to submit the whole question at issue to the Court, decided to wait its decision, and until such decision to make no comment or statement of their position. Accordingly, adhering to this rule, we shall offer no comment upon the Master's Report until the same has been accepted and confirmed by the Court.

Very sincerely yours,
(Signed) David B. Ogden,
Secretary.

Meanwhile, Dittemore had refused to accept his dismissal as a Director. He, too, brought suit. On April 29, 1919, or some six weeks after his dismissal, he asked the Massachusetts Supreme Judicial Court to agree that the resolution of dismissal was without legality. His plea was referred to Judge Dodge, and the Master was asked to hear the cases (Dittemore's and the Trustees') at the same time, "to find the facts, and report [them] to the court."

The Master found that Dittemore was improperly removed, and expressed the opinion that the reasons given in the resolution were not sufficient to justify the dismissal.

It was not until late in November, 1920, that the cases came before the full bench of the Massachusetts Supreme Judicial Court. The months that intervened were not calm months in the history of the Christian Science movement.

So many were the actions attributed to the Board of Directors that on April 12, 1920, the Board issued this announcement:

> By reason of certain incidents which have been reported, it appears specially necessary at present for all Christian Scientists to be cautious about accepting unauthentic statements said to have come from this Board. Any word attributed to this Board, but not satisfactorily tested, should be disregarded. In particular, vague reports "from Boston" should not be credited to us. It is to be expected that our communications will be made direct, and they will be duly authenticated. As Mrs. Eddy has aptly said, "Christian Science demands order and truth." (*Miscellaneous Writings*, p. 215).

Also, in April, 1920, William P. McKenzie and Ella W. Hoag resigned as editors of the *Journal* and *Sentinel*. The resignations were disclosed to the field in a *Special Announcement by the Board of Trustees* in the May, 1920, issue of the *Journal*. In this announcement, the Trustees explained that, in appointing successors,[3] the *Manual* "can, of course, no longer be strictly complied with. The written

---

[3] Frederick Dixon and Gustavus S. Paine were given temporary appointments by the Trustees as editors of the *Journal* and *Sentinel*. The two men also served as editors of *The Christian Science Monitor*.

consent of the Pastor Emeritus can no longer be secured, and until the question is determined as to whether Mrs. Knott or Mr. Dittemore is a director, the *'unanimous* vote' of the directors cannot be had."

Continuing, the Trustees said they had invited the Directors to name, as editors, persons agreeable to the Directors but "the Directors declined, giving as ostensible excuse the outstanding injunction." In speaking of this refusal, the Trustees said "the field should know that [while the injunction] restrains the Directors from taking any action which would impair, destroy, or in any way injure the Publishing Society's business, their cooperation with the Trustees in agreeing upon editors could, of course, not be construed as any such thing."

But, despite the disfavor with which the Trustees were held by the field, the sale of Christian Science literature (which was the Publishing Society's sole source of income) was little affected at first. There was a reason for this. In the *Church Manual* (Article VIII, Section 14) Mrs. Eddy included a By-law on the subject of *Church Periodicals*. It read:

> It shall be the privilege and duty of every member, who can afford it, to subscribe for the periodicals which are the organs of this church; and it shall be the duty of the Directors to see that these periodicals are ably edited and kept abreast of the times.

As said, until the Master's decision, there was great confidence among Christian Scientists that the Directors would be upheld. That decision brought a change. Believing that when their Leader conferred upon the Directors the authority to manage "the business of The Mother Church," she gave it undiluted, the great majority of Christian Scientists also believed that the business of the Publishing Society was the business of The Mother Church; as a result, they began to take action.

Cancellations in subscriptions to the *Monitor,* the *Journal,* the *Sentinel,* and the French and German *Heralds* began coming into the publishing offices. The one publication not affected was the *Christian Science Quarterly.* Providing for the order of church services on Sunday, and on Thanksgiving Day, the *Quarterly* was indispensable. The contents of the *Quarterly,* unlike those of the other periodicals, were confined to citations from the Bible and from *Science and Health.* In them was no opportunity for the inclusion of personal opinions.

Christian Scientists also began to act out of a growing conviction that, without the services of "the Directors to see that these periodicals are ably edited," the periodicals could not be considered as authorized Christian Science literature.

The instructions given by Mrs. Eddy in a letter written on November 13, 1909, were not forgotten. At that time Mrs. Augusta Stetson was contriving a rebellion within the membership of First Church of Christ, Scientist, in New York City. In answer to an appeal from the Trustees of the New York Church, Mrs. Eddy said to them, and to all members of the church: "I advise you with all my soul to support the Directors of The Mother Church, and unite with those in your church who are supporting The Mother Church."

In this period there was much discussion among Christian Scientists as to the reliability of the church literature. There were supporters of the Directors, and their numbers were considerable, who said that, because Mrs. Eddy founded the periodicals, they should be supported in anticipation of the time when the Directors would be sustained by the high court of Massachusetts; others, equally sincere, said obedience to the teachings of Mrs. Eddy included obedience to the *Manual*, and not the Deed of Trust, as the law of The Mother Church and opposed subscribing to, or reading the literature. Personal antagonisms began to appear.

So stirred were members of The Mother Church over the litigation that when, late in November, 1920, the Supreme Judicial Court met to hear the arguments of the lawyers representing the Directors, the Trustees, and Dittemore, the five judges found four other petitions awaiting their attention.

Through Mrs. Emilie B. Hulin, New York Christian Scientists were charging that their rights as members of The Mother Church were threatened by the Master's decision because it took away authority given by Mrs. Eddy, thus striking at the roots of church government.

Edwin A. Krauthoff and his wife, Daisy L. Krauthoff, objected to the Master's decision for reasons quite similar to those stated by Mrs. Hulin. At the time of the hearings before the Master, Krauthoff was one of the attorneys representing the Directors. After the hearings, Krauthoff resigned as counsel and, without the knowledge of the Directors, joined his wife in a separate action.

Their petition was denied by a single justice of the Supreme Court on the ground that it was filed too late. On October 20, 1920, the Krauthoffs, and again without the knowledge of the Directors, filed a second motion "in behalf of themselves and other members [of The Mother Church] as might desire to join, to be admitted as parties to the suit, and to refile the motions before filed and denied."

The sixth petition awaiting the attention of the Court

was filed by the Attorney General of Massachusetts. He acted
at the request of Christian Scientists in a number of states,
but mainly in Illinois, who were concerned over the invasion
into their rights as members of The Mother Church. After
denying the petition, a single justice of the Supreme Court
suggested to the Attorney General that if he thought the
public's rights were invaded by the Master's ruling, he
should bring in his own bill. This the Attorney General did.

As for the Dittemore case, its standing in the legal proceedings about to begin depended upon the position taken
by the Court in the dispute between the Directors and the
Trustees. Two questions were involved. One concerned the
legality of the removal of Rowlands. The other involved
the question of whether, under the Deed of Trust, or under
the *Church Manual,* The Mother Church had any authority
over its own literature. In a word, if the Court dismissed
the suit, then Dittemore's petition that he, and not Mrs.
Annie M. Knott, was a Director became a separate legal
action.

In giving the opinion that Dittemore was improperly
dismissed, the Master, although instructed by the Supreme
Court to file a complete report on the Dittemore hearings,
failed to do so, explaining that in his judgment, the delay
was necessary until there was a final decision on the complaint of the Trustees. Informed of this violation of the
Court's instructions, attorneys for the Directors filed for
the appointment of a new Master for the Dittemore case,
arguing that Judge Dodge had disqualified himself by prejudgment and prejudice. The motion was denied.

On November 29, Charles Evans Hughes began his presentation of the case of the Board of Trustees of The Christian Science Publishing Society before the five judges of the

Supreme Judicial Court of the Commonwealth of Massachusetts. As Hughes presented the case, there was no issue. Only one fact. That one fact was: When, on January 25, 1898, Mary Baker Eddy executed the Deed of Trust, she took from herself, and from her Church, all authority over Christian Science literature and placed it irrevocably, and in perpetuity, in the hands of three persons, and their successors, whom she designated as Trustees.

After declaring that The Board of Directors lacked the authority to dismiss Rowlands, and detailing the purpose of the Deed of Trust, Hughes argued that "nothing could be clearer than that [Mrs. Eddy] did not select the Directors to control that business"—meaning, of course, The Christian Science Publishing Society.

He maintained that Mrs. Eddy decided not to put the publishing business "under the control of the Directors, and that she determined, as she had a right to determine, that with respect to that publishing business there should be a separate trust, the terms of which she carefully defined.

"Now it does not require argument to point out what her intent was. Her intent was that while she remained alive . . . if a vacancy should occur in the publishing trusteeship she should reserve the right to fill the same by appointment if she so desired; that when it came, however, to declaring vacancies in said trusteeship there were to be two bodies who should act concurrently in regard to the serious consequence of declaring a vacancy in this Board of Trustees for the publishing business, which she independently created, knowing full well that she could put the power in the hands of the Directors had she seen fit to do so, and she did not see fit to do so."

At this point, Chief Justice Rugg interrupted to inquire:

"After 1909, did the First Members exercise any prerogatives of the Executive Members?" [4]

"I believe not," answered Hughes, directing his remarks to the Chief Justice, while referring to a contention of the attorneys for the Directors, "You will observe they refer in, it seems to me, a somewhat ambiguous manner, to a power coupled with an interest, and also to a power attached to an office.

"There is a sense in which the term may be used as applicable to both cases, but it needs a little analysis, as it seems to us, to indicate the fallacy in the way in which the argument is presented by the defendants. Of course, there was not interest in any proper sense in the Directors, the First Members. They were not, as First Members, or as Directors, on either side, either the legal or the beneficial owners. Certainly the Directors were not.

"They owed their positions and authority solely to the Deed of Trust. So far as the First Members were concerned, they were a portion of many hundreds of actual members of this religious society who had exercised the right to vote and who had transacted business in accordance with the constitution of the society.

"There was no power coupled with an interest, as I understand that phrase to be used in the law. The point they make, however, is that it was a power attached to an office and hence passed to the successors in office. And they illustrate by reference to the familiar cases of executors or Trustees

[4] Hughes, in summing up his case, dwelt on the early powers of the First Members. As we have seen, in 1901, at Mrs. Eddy's request, these powers were turned over to the Directors. In 1903, the First Members became known as Executive Members. From 1901 until 1908, the First, or Executive, Members had no church functions excepting to act as Readers, or as President of The Mother Church. In 1908, the titles were abolished at Mrs. Eddy's request; and also at Mrs. Eddy's request all members of The Mother Church became eligible for all duties within the Church.

who have powers which may be exercised by the remaining Trustees or the continuing Board of Directors, when a vacancy which occurs is filled, or otherwise. . . .

"We have, then, nothing but a bald attempt by the First Members to transfer this discretionary power to the Directors, and if the Directors disbanded them and if the First Members, or the Executive Members, acquiesced in that action that in no way changed the function or the constitution of the Directors. They were still not the First Members, not in any proper sense the successors of the First Members, but simply a Board of Trustees that had attempted to destroy a condonee.

"Neither that destruction nor the attempted transfer could give them the power which Mrs. Eddy had decided not to give them, but had given to both. . . .

"The church was organized on September 23, 1892, established its rules at that time, states it was organized as of that time, but, what is more, and controlling, these Directors are the Directors appointed by the Deed of September 1, 1892,[5] and the successors elected by the Trustees and their successors under that deed, themselves a self-perpetuating board that we have here to deal with, that holds no authority whatever from anyone but the donor in the Deed of Trust, and through the Deed of Trust of September 1, 1892, and their own acts, except as they have sought to arrogate to themselves a power through the invalid attempt to abdicate or transfer power on the part of the First Members.

"For these reasons we ask for the relief prayed for in the bill of complaint on the part of the publishing Trustees."

[5] Under date of September 2, 1892, Mrs. Eddy deeded to The Christian Science Board of Directors the property on which is located The First Church of Christ, Scientist, in Boston, Massachusetts.

In presenting arguments for the Directors, John L. Bates [6] took direct issue with Hughes, contending that "the donees of the power . . . were the First Members and the Board of Directors. The First Members had passed out of existence. They had become extinct. But before passing out of existence the powers which they had exercised in regard to the Church, under the *Church Manual,* had become the powers of the Board of Directors under the *Church Manual.*

"I think you are to determine who were the donees of this power, in interpreting this deed, according to the character of the donee, and not according to the name. The character of the donee was the authorized governing board of the Church, that is, the two boards together. The board of First Members, with certain executive duties to perform, and the Board of Directors, with other executive duties to perform, in 1898, constituted the entire authority of the Church.

"There were no other boards of any kind that had any vote. They, together, constituted the entire authority of the Church; and I submit that it is only reasonable to assume that Mrs. Eddy, in constituting them the power to decide as to when a vacancy should be declared, did it to protect the Church under the By-laws of the Church; and that when the duties of both boards under a By-law became united in one board, that being one of the boards she has named by virtue not of any transfer of power from one board to another, but by virtue of the Church law which consolidated

---

[6] Former Governor John L. Bates presented the arguments for the Directors, but much of the actual preparation and analysis of the case had been accomplished by his junior, Walter A. Dane; and considerable assistance had been given by Charles F. Choate, Jr., who was also serving as a Special Assistant Attorney General associated with J. W. Allen, the Attorney General, who was seeking to intervene.

the entire authority of the Church in one board, they became the donee of the power. . . .

"Immediately after that power—all the power—was vested in the Directors, a By-law was passed with Mrs. Eddy's approval which gave to the Directors alone the authority to remove a Trustee, or declare a vacancy for such reason as may be deemed expedient. Her intention there can be no question about. It will be claimed that this was two boards, one to be a check on the other. That element does not seem to exist here.

"In the first place, Mrs. Eddy, as I said, in 1901 caused this very change to be made in the By-laws. It was her intent evidently that the one board should exercise the power because she caused that By-law to be made. But, in addition to that, that board did continue to exist until 1908. If she had intended to have one board to check on the other, she would have continued the authority of that board, but she did not do so.

"It shows that her object in making that deed was to vest the donee's authority in the controlling authority of the Church, whatever it might be, and it is to be assumed that she contemplated that that might change from time to time, but whoever had the controlling authority in the Church would be the one to exercise the authority.

"Otherwise, how can you enforce it? Or, how can you protect the Church? You cannot come into court on all questions of doctrine, all questions of suitability of Trustees. How could she enforce the ninth paragraph of her Trust Deed, which provided that the Trustees must have certain qualities and do certain things, which could only be determined by an ecclesiastical tribunal?

"She vested it in the Church, to protect the Church, the financial beneficiary; and that was the great head and propelling force of the movement which she had inaugurated; it does not require any amendment; it simply requires a construction that would give force to the evident intent of the donor, to give the Church, through its governing authority, the authority to control the Board of Trustees, and to remove them for such reasons as it deemed expedient, in order that there might be protection for her purposes."

On December 1, after three days of debate, the court stenographers closed the books on their notes. The claims and counter-claims were in. All that remained was the decision of the Court.

A year afterwards, lacking seven days, the Supreme Judicial Court of Massachusetts announced its decision.[7]

After dealing with the Master's contention that, in dismissing Rowlands, the Directors had not acted "in good faith," the Court unanimously declared The Christian Science Board of Directors to be the designated protectors of the *Church Manual;* and the *Church Manual* to be the law of The Mother Church in all its affairs.

In its decision, the Supreme Court disagreed with the over-all legal opinions of the Master, as it disagreed with the specific charge of bad faith. In respect to this accusation, the Court said:

"The Directors cannot be said to have acted arbitrarily or capriciously in removing one of the Trustees. . . . This is a finding of good faith on the part of the Directors to all the reasons stated except the one for failure to devote time enough to the business.

"It is not a finding that the other reasons given were tainted or affected by the one as to the failure of Mr. Rowlands to devote time enough to the business. Those other reasons honestly assigned were such as, within the power

---

[7] For complete text, see Appendix 4.

invested in the Directors, warranted them in making a removal. It is their honest judgment upon the question of expediency in this respect which must prevail, and not that of any other body or magistrate."

In confirming the primacy of the *Church Manual,* and the Directors as the administrators of its laws, the Court declared:

"In the earliest edition of the *Manual* . . . and in all subsequent writings, there is printed an extract from the writings of Mary Baker Eddy to the effect amongst other matters that the 'Rules and By-laws in the Manual . . . were impelled by a power not one's own, were written at different dates and as the occasion required.'

"The edition of the *Manual* was in use on January 25, 1898, the date of the Trust Deed, was designated the seventh. It was different in material particulars from those which had preceded it. It is manifest that the trust deed was intended to be made subject, so far as it concerned the officers of the Church and their powers and duties touching upon the disbursement of the net income paid by the Trustees to the treasurer of the Church to such changes as the occasion might require to be made in the *Manual.* . . .

"Although the Trustees under the Trust Deed were given extensive powers concerning the publication of the so-called literature of the Church, nevertheless they were not the final arbiters concerning these matters, because they might be removed from office by other church authorities 'for such reasons' as to other church authorities 'may seem expedient.'

"The soundness of the reasons for such removal is not made subject to review or revision by any other church tribunal, body, or officer. The expediency of the reasons moving to that action are left by the deed wholly to the church authorities therein named. No discussion is needed to demonstrate that this power of removal was comprehensive, drastic, and final.

"The promotion of Christian Science as taught by Mrs. Eddy was the end and aim of the trust. To that regnant design all other provisions, not in themselves made fixed and unchangeable, must yield.

"Christian Science as thus taught was disclosed by the writings of the founder. The ecclesiastical organization established by her for the teachings and dissemination of Christian Science was 'The First Church of Christ, Scientist.' She did not reserve to herself the power of removal of the Trustees, but she reposed that authority in First Members and Directors of that Church. That Church as shown by the *Manual* at the time of the execution of the Trust Deed of January 25, 1898, was the dominant church in Christian Science.

"It was the beneficiary of all the net profits from the management of that trust. Its Board of Directors was clothed with extensive powers concerning its management. Its *Manual* appears to be a vital part of Christian Science. The presumption is inevitable that all the parties to the Trust Deed of January 25, 1898, intended that the power of removal should be vested in the responsible representatives of The First Church of Christ, Scientist, however they might be described or denominated, provided they succeeded to the powers and exercised the functions of First Members and Directors . . .

"The result is that the board of five directors [8] have the

---

[8] In designating "the board of five directors," the Court disclosed that it was not impressed by one of the basic arguments made by Charles Evans Hughes. In his summation, Hughes was critical of Archibald McLellan's status as a Director, inasmuch as he was appointed after the execution of

power, if they act in accordance with law and with the terms of the Trust Deed of January 25, 1898, to effect removal of a Trustee under that deed. . . ."

Summing up its long-awaited verdict, the Supreme Court said:

"The conclusion that the power of removal of a Trustee is now vested in the board of five Directors is contrary to that of the master, but it is in substance and effect the application of different legal principles to the facts by the master. . . .

"The result is that the exceptions of the defendants to the master's report so far as they relate to his rulings that the Directors had no power under the deed of January 25, 1898, to remove a Trustee and the removal of Mr. Rowlands was ineffectual must be sustained. On the facts found by the master, in the light of principles of law here found to be controlling, the plaintiffs cannot maintain their bill."

The Court then disposed of the other matters brought before it:

"In order to decide the fundamental issues raised on this record, it is unnecessary to consider the question whether Mr. Dittemore or Mrs. Knott is a director. That issue is directly involved in another case.

"The exceptions of Emilie B. Hulin have been waived and need not be considered.

"Suggestion of Attorney General denied.

"Both appeals of Mr. and Mrs. Krauthoff dismissed

---

a deed in which Mrs. Eddy gave to the Board certain real estate on which the publishing house had been located.

Referring to McLellan as "a By-law Director," Hughes supported the appellation by producing a letter, dated March 19, 1903, in which Mrs. Eddy said to the new Director, "I regret that your name cannot appear as a member of The Christian Science Board of Directors on their deeds. I have twice urged this question, but Mr. Elder finds it cannot be legally so."

"Bill dismissed, November 23, 1921."

In dismissing the claims of the Trustees, the Supreme Judicial Court of the Commonwealth of Massachusetts gave legal effect to Mrs. Eddy's intention that the supreme authority of the Christian Science Church should be The Christian Science Board of Directors, and the governing rules of the Church and of its activities are the *Manual*.

As with the decisions of the New York Court of Appeals in the Cole and Vogelgesang cases in 1916 and 1917, so with this decision. It was historic.

More than two years had gone since the adoption by The Board of Directors of resolutions dismissing Rowlands as a Trustee and Dittemore as a Director; since the filing, by the Trustees, of their lawsuit; since the injunction restraining the Directors from any supervision over the affairs of the Publishing Society.

As was said, it was not a calm period in the history of the Christian Science movement. In the more than eleven months of review by the Supreme Court, rumors often swept the field that the decision had been made and that it favored the Trustees. As one result of these rumors, the cancellation of subscriptions to the periodicals again gained great impetus. In addition, there was a sharp reduction in the number of churches and societies and practitioners using the periodicals for the listing of their names.

The financial loss was substantial. During the litigation, the circulation of the *Monitor* dropped from more than 80,000 to less than 18,000. Before the litigation, the *Monitor* was earning a profit; in the last three months of 1921 and the first month of 1922, the loss was $145,062.92. Subscriptions to the *Journal* dropped more than 75 per cent; subscriptions to the *Sentinel* dropped more than 50 per cent.

The number of churches and societies and practitioners who used the *Journal* as a listing place for their names fell off approximately 70 per cent. The loss in revenue from this reduction in subscriptions and listings was large.

But, in spite of the resistance to the periodicals, the movement made gains. In 1920, there was a gain of fifty-nine new societies, thirteen new branch churches, and thirty societies gained recognition as branch churches. In 1921, there was a gain of ninety-five societies; again there were thirteen new branch churches and, in 1921, thirty-four societies became branch churches. Among the recognized 2,001 branches of The Mother Church were societies in Havana, Singapore, and Copenhagen.

This was a period in which personal antagonisms loomed large and seemed to portend a lasting schism within the Christian Science movement. It but seemed that way. The antagonisms did not survive because there were no differences in opinions regarding the teachings of Mary Baker Eddy. There was acceptance of them and acceptance of her leadership. This being the case, the only things that could survive did survive.

CHAPTER NINE

A Name Is Restored

I N light of the court decision, the members of The Mother Church had only one duty—to go on being Christian Scientists in the way marked out for them by Mrs. Eddy. The test of their Leader's wisdom had been met; the challenge to the authority of the *Manual* was scattered. For the Directors, the immediate task was to unite the congregation.

It was not until January 28, 1922, that the Directors were able to act, and not until February 11, 1922, that they were able to use the *Sentinel* to publish their message to the field.

On November 26, 1921, there had appeared in *The Christian Science Monitor* the following statement:

We Lay Down Our Trust

From the beginning we have sought only to conform to Mrs. Eddy's wish, faithfully to carry out the high purpose of her Trust and to obey the laws of our land.

We differed from the Directors in our interpretation of what our Leader's wish and purpose were, and she could not speak to us in person.

We therefore sought legal interpretation of her legal instrument which declares our duty, and to that we are willing to subordinate our cherished beliefs. That interpretation now has been given. It is authoritative, and, as to us, final.

We shall cooperate with the Directors—who, as the law has

declared, are entitled to dominate the Trust—in the appointment of our successors.

(Signed)   Herbert W. Eustace.
Lamont Rowlands.
Paul Harvey.[1]

Boston, Massachusetts,
November 25, 1921.

Unwilling to acknowledge the powers of the Directors,
and seeking to deny to them the right to appoint their successors, the Trustees postponed submitting their resignations for more than two months after the court decision—and
then did so by sending them to the Supreme Judicial Court
of Massachusetts. It was an action that compelled the Court
to accept the resignations and to fill the vacancies.

Apprised of the maneuver, the Directors suggested the
names of Fred M. Lamson, Wm. P. McKenzie, and James
E. Patton as members of the Board of Trustees of The Christian Science Publishing Society. Acting for the Court, Justice John C. Crosby made the appointments on Saturday,
January 28, 1922, which was the same day on which the
resignations were received.

On February 11, 1922, in the *Sentinel,* there was the following message to the field:

A Word to the Field

By the recent decision of the Supreme Judicial Court of
Massachusetts there is placed before every member of The
Mother Church the opportunity to aid in quickly restoring our
periodicals to the rightful position as auxiliaries for publicly
presenting Christian Science, the essence of which is to be found
in its purity and entirety only in the writings of our Leader.
The claims of those who stood loyally by what they conceived
to be Mrs. Eddy's spiritual demonstration of church government

---

[1] Paul Harvey succeeded David B. Ogden (resigned), July 21, 1921.

have been vindicated. The misguided attempts to reverse what she intended to stand unchallenged and inviolate have been rebuked.

The *Manual* has emerged unbroken and unchanged. Its place in our movement is established for all time. Its intent is plain and unmistakable, for its author is its interpreter, and her interpretation is registered in the history of her church during the past thirty years.

This is not the time for exultation or recrimination. It is the hour when every intelligent plea for closer unity and cooperation among brethren should be promptly heeded and wisely observed. The past two years have been fertile in lessons pointing to the need of greater watchfulness, higher consecration, more loving consideration for each other, and greater devotion to the teachings of our Leader, in order that sickness and sin may be more quickly and effectively vanquished and universal healing and universal reformation may be brought appreciably nearer.

There have been opportunities to learn many things which should be remembered, and others which it will be well to forget in order that we may all meet without partiality and without prejudice upon the common ground of allegiance to our beloved Cause.

It is not too much to hope that all the workers in the great field of Christian Science, however widely they may have differed on the issues of the past two years, will henceforth with outstretched hands lovingly adopt as their greeting one to another the words of Abraham to Lot, "Let there be no strife, I pray thee, between me and thee, and between my herdsmen and thy herdsmen; for we are brethren." It is true that the unvarying demands of Principle can never be ignored if we are to realize the perfection which marks man's likeness to God. We should, however, first apply to ourselves the required test of obedience, and thus aid our brother in his efforts to reach the high goal, always remembering that "love is the fulfilling of the law."

The Christian Science Board of Directors.

The call "for greater watchfulness, higher consecration, more loving consideration for each other, and greater devotion to the teachings of our Leader," found its answer in the encouragement that was given to the new trustees, in the support that was given to the publications, to the editors, and to those appointed to supervise the affairs of the Publishing Society.

During the litigation, there was a great deal of confusion within the Publishing Society. In 1918, Harry I. Hunt was appointed by the Directors to succeed Allison V. Stewart [2] as publisher of Mrs. Eddy's writings. Being so appointed, Hunt believed he was directly responsible to the Board. It was an opinion that was accepted, then rejected, by the Trustees.

In dispute between Hunt and the Trustees was the authority for issuing requisitions for paper, printing, and binding. Hunt insisted the authority was his; the Trustees insisted the authority belonged to them. In March, 1920, after nearly two years of disagreement, Hunt resigned. The confusion increased, and increased so much that when the court decision was announced on November 21, 1921, reserve stocks of Mrs. Eddy's books were exhausted, and publication had been suspended on some of the titles. It was the first, and only, time in the history of the Movement that this had happened.

Anxious to restore the orderly processes of manufacturing, distribution, and management, the Directors recalled Hunt in January, 1922, but almost a year elapsed before conditions became normal. Meanwhile, the vexatious con-

---

[2] Allison V. Stewart was the last of the publishers of Mrs. Eddy's writings to deal directly with the author. He succeeded Joseph Armstrong in 1907; Armstrong was appointed by Mrs. Eddy in 1904 and continued as publisher until his death in 1907.

tract of 1917 between the Trustees under the Will of Mary Baker Eddy and the Trustees of the Publishing Society was cancelled. This was the contract under which the Trustees were authorized to publish and distribute Mrs. Eddy's writings. Following its termination on June 15, 1922, Hunt was made Publishers' Agent. As such he was Administrative Officer for the Trustees Under the Will, and directly responsible for the details of publishing the writings of Mrs. Eddy.

In their report to the members of The Mother Church at the annual meeting in June, 1922, the new Trustees indicated some of the difficulties they encountered in adjusting the affairs of the Publishing Society.

On January 28, 1922, when Lamson, McKenzie, and Patton became Trustees, paid subscriptions to the *Journal* totaled 17,685; to the *Sentinel,* 38,399; and to the *Monitor,* 17,753. On May 15, 1922, approximately four months later, paid subscriptions totaled: *Journal,* 67,624; *Sentinel,* 93,402; and *Monitor,* 41,247.

In part, the report read:

When the present Trustees took office ... the Publishing House was in need of rehabilitation, and immediate expense was involved for supplies and equipment. Also, there were claims made by the departing employees which required settlement.

It was found that subscribers to the various periodicals who had canceled a subscription during its course had not been paid back the balance due for the unexpired term of the subscription. The obligation of completing the subscription terms involved straight expense, and has still to be met in order that the Publishing Society may keep faith with its subscribers.

It was found that when advertisements of churches and societies, practitioners and nurses, were withdrawn from the *Journal,* advertisers did not at the time receive back the unearned balance; hence the new management must arrange to complete, without compensation, the terms already paid for by the advertisers.

The main problem has been the expense of the reestablishment of the *Monitor*. Four years ago, in 1918, the *Monitor* had reached the point where it was earning a profit for The Mother Church. It had then a prepaid circulation above 80,000. The loss on the *Monitor* for the four months ending January 28, 1922, as shown by the books, was $145,062.92. The deficit for the month of March was less than that for February, which was the first month under the new management.

The old subscribers must first be served and compensated for what is due them, before the Publishing Society can show any earnings from their renewals. It is obvious that new subscriptions will be desirable; but even with these in large numbers it will be necessary for some provision to be made for meeting the losses and expenses referred to so that the Trustees shall not have to encroach upon money paid in advance for subscriptions and advertisements, and still unearned.

When our Leader, Mrs. Eddy, decided in 1898 that the time had come to publish a weekly periodical, she wrote to the then Secretary of the Board of Trustees under date of August 22, 1898, saying that this periodical was to be owned by the First Church of Christ, Scientist, and copyrighted in her name. She further said, "Call on the Treasurer of this church for funds to start with."

The direction which she gave to the Board of Trustees at that time would seem to indicate that when, in its operation as an activity of The Mother Church, The Christian Science Publishing Society requires financial aid, a call may be made upon The Christian Science Board of Directors who are responsible for conducting the business of The Mother Church, for necessary aid, and they, in turn, must call upon the field.

It will be of interest to the field to know that on last Friday, the following letter was sent by the Trustees of The Christian Science Publishing Society to the Trustees under the Will of Mary Baker Eddy:

"Boston, Mass., June 2, 1922.

"Trustees under the Will of Mary Baker Eddy,

"236 Huntington avenue,

"Boston, Mass..

"Dear Friends:

"In reply to your letter of February 8 to which a tentative reply was sent on February 10, we would say that the many problems connected with the restoration of the Publishing Society to The Mother Church have been disposed of. We are ready to cancel, on any day you may set, the contract with you of October 19, 1917, for the publication of Mrs. Eddy's writings. Meanwhile, we shall cooperate in any way possible, and we shall be glad to help install whatever new arrangement you may wish to make.

"Sincerely yours

"The Christian Science Publishing Society

"Fred M. Lamson,

"Wm. P. McKenzie.

"James E. Patton."

The Trustees are thankful for the opportunity to tell the members of The Mother Church that complete harmony exists between the Directors of The Mother Church and the Trustees of the Publishing Society... the Trustees have complete freedom in the business conduct of the Publishing Society to carry on their duties as provided by the *Manual,* and the Deed of Trust.

The "harmony and cooperation" the Trustees mentioned was not pretense. It existed between the Directors and Trustees; it also existed throughout the administrative and publishing offices. The new Trustees were men who knew each other, and who were known to the field. This was true, also, of the new editors and assistant editors.

The Trustees were men of experience, two as executives in business, the third as a clergyman and as a teacher of English literature. The businessmen were Fred M. Lamson and James E. Patton. Lamson was vice-president of the Old Colony Trust Company, in Boston, a member of the Finance

Committee of The Mother Church, and long a member of the Church. Before moving to Boston and taking up the practice of Christian Science after World War I, Patton had been General Officer of the Pittsburgh Plate Glass Company, as well as being president of a number of corporations.

After studying for the ministry at Toronto University, William P. McKenzie resigned his pulpit to teach English literature and rhetoric at Rochester University. It was while there that he became interested in Christian Science. In 1894, he was elected a "First Member" of The Mother Church and, in 1896, was invited by Mrs. Eddy to come to Boston as a member of the Bible Lesson Committee. In 1898, Mrs. Eddy named him as one of the three original Trustees of The Christian Science Publishing Society. From 1898 until 1916, he was a member of the Board of Lectureship, and, from July, 1917, until March, 1920, he was editor of the *Journal* and *Sentinel*.

At the same time the Directors announced the selection of the Trustees they published the appointment of Willis J. Abbott, New York, as editor of *The Christian Science Monitor*. A writer of biography and history, Abbott was an experienced newspaperman, having worked on publications in Chicago, Washington, and New York.

Albert F. Gilmore, New York, was elected editor of the *Journal, Sentinel, Der Herold der Christian Science,* and *Le Héraut de Christian Science.* An educator, author, Christian Science practitioner, and for nearly five years Committee on Publication for the State of New York, Gilmore was a member of The Mother Church and of First Church of Christ, Scientist, Brooklyn, New York.

Mrs. Ella W. Hoag, a student of Mrs. Eddy in 1888, a member of The Mother Church in 1892 and of Second

Church of Christ, Scientist, in Toledo, Ohio, a teacher of the 1919 Normal Class of the Board of Education of The Mother Church, and a member of the Board of Lectureship, was reappointed to her post as associate editor of the periodicals.

Also chosen as associate editor of the periodicals was Duncan Sinclair, of Glasgow, Scotland, a graduate of St. Andrew's University, Scotland, as a Bachelor of Science, and a specialist in chemistry and physics. A lecturer in metallurgy and head of the science department in Glasgow University for twenty-one years, Sinclair withdrew from those activities to devote himself to the study and practice of Christian Science. He was a member of the 1916 Normal Class of the Board of Education of The Mother Church.

Elected as manager of the Publishing House was Charles E. Jarvis. A member of The Mother Church as well as of First Church of Christ, Scientist, in Los Angeles, Jarvis became Corresponding Secretary of The Christian Science Board of Directors in June, 1916, and on November 3, 1917, became Clerk of The Mother Church.

However, one other hope expressed by the Directors to the field in the message of February 11, 1922, was not realized for some time. That was the hope that "we may all meet without partiality and without prejudice upon the common ground of allegiance to our beloved Cause."

Having failed in his first effort to persuade the Supreme Judicial Court of Massachusetts to restore him as a member of The Christian Science Board of Directors, John V. Dittemore made a second appeal to the Court. While his case was pending, he conducted a very abusive campaign against the Directors of The Mother Church; failing a second time to receive the support of the Court, he widened his hostility

to include The Mother Church and sought to set up a movement to destroy the teachings of Mrs. Eddy.[3]

The years of litigation, the years immediately before, and
the years immediately after, were critical in the history of the
Christian Science movement, even more critical than the
period ending in 1888 when, in Boston, thirty-four teachers
deserted Mrs. Eddy and formed their own church, or than
the period ending in 1909, when Mrs. Augusta E. Stetson
became a public critic after her name was dropped from the
roll of membership in First Church of Christ, Scientist, in
New York City.

Then, Mrs. Eddy was here, in person, to speak for her
teachings; now, her teachings had to speak for themselves.
And, as in 1888 and in 1909, the difficulties provided opportunities for harm that were not overlooked by those who
sought to destroy what had been built.

Heard again, with increasing frequency, was the argument that, because at one time Mrs. Eddy regarded rules
and regulations in the form of church by-laws as laws of
limitation and as unnecessary in Christian Science, now was
the time to do away with the *Manual* and the denominational government of The Mother Church in order to be
in keeping with Mrs. Eddy's declaration that "organization
is requisite only in the earliest periods of Christian history."

It was a partial quotation, and it was misleading.

In writing that "organization is requisite only in the
earliest periods in Christian history," Mrs. Eddy was speak-

[3] Under the leadership of Mrs. Annie C. Bill, of England, Dittemore
sought to establish what was called the Christian Science Parent Church of
the New Generation. Dittemore died in New York City on May 10, 1937.
About two months before his death, on March 23, 1937, he wrote an
expiatory letter to The Christian Science Board of Directors. For a copy of
this letter, see Appendix 5.

ing not of The Mother Church but of the church she organized in 1879 and dissolved in 1889. Mrs. Eddy's declaration can be found on page 45 of *Retrospection and Introspection,* which was published in 1891:

> Despite the prosperity of my church, it was learned that material organization has its value and peril, and that organization is requisite only in the earliest periods in Christian history. After this material form of cohesion and fellowship has accomplished its end, continued organization retards spiritual growth, and should be laid off,—even as the corporeal organization deemed requisite in the first stages of mortal existence is finally laid off in order to gain spiritual freedom and supremacy.

The Mother Church is a different structure from the one Mrs. Eddy dissolved in 1889, and in establishing it Mrs. Eddy placed it beyond the "values and peril of material organization."

The argument that she regarded church by-laws as unnecessary had its origin in two sentences taken from a short commentary entitled *Mental Digestion,* which appeared in print following publication of the *Church Manual* in 1895. The two sentences were:

> Heaps and heaps of praise confront me, and for what? That which I said in my heart would never be needed,—namely laws of limitation for a Christian Scientist.

These were Mrs. Eddy's full words:

> Will those beloved students, whose growth is taking in the Ten Commandments, and scaling

the steep ascent of Christ's Sermon on the Mount, accept profound thanks for their swift messages of rejoicing over the twentieth century Church Manual. Heaps and heaps of praise confront me, and for what? That which I said in my heart would never be needed,—namely laws of limitation for a Christian Scientist. Thy ways are not ours. Thou knowest best what we need most,—hence my disappointed hope and grateful joy. The redeemed should be happier than the elect. Truth is strong with destiny; it takes life profoundly; it measures the infinite against the finite. Notwithstanding the sacrilegious moth of time eternity awaits our Church Manual, which will maintain its rank as in the past, amid ministries aggressive and active, and will stand when those have passed to rest.

Scientific pathology illustrates the digestion of spiritual nutriment as both sweet and bitter,—sweet in expectancy and bitter in experience or during the senses' assimilation thereof, and digested only when Soul silences the dyspepsia of sense. This church is impartial. Its rules apply not to one member only, but to one and all equally. Of this I am sure, that each Rule and By-law in this Manual will increase the spirituality of him who obeys it, invigorate his capacity to heal the sick, to comfort such as mourn, and to awaken the sinner.[4]

The argument to abandon the *Church Manual* found so many ears that Adam H. Dickey [5] went before the biennial

[4] *Miscellany,* pp. 229-30.

[5] Adam H. Dickey became Mrs. Eddy's secretary in 1908 and continued in that capacity until her passing in 1910. In 1910, he was appointed to The Christian Science Board of Directors; he continued as a Director until his death in 1925.

conference of the Committees on Publication in October, 1921, and requested these Committees to use all means within their power to call Christian Scientists back to the shelter of the constitution of The Mother Church, which is the *Church Manual.*

In part, Dickey told the Committees:

"The enemy of Christian Science is beginning to whisper: 'It is time for church organization to cease.' Error is sending out this argument that Mrs. Eddy has said that 'organization is requisite only in the earliest periods in Christian history'; therefore it says: 'Let us abandon the By-laws and the denominational government of The Mother Church,' after the manner of the wicked husbandman who said, 'This is the heir: come, let us kill him, that the inheritance may be ours.'

"As usual, error is a few years behind the time . . . the material organization to which Mrs. Eddy refers as being no longer requisite is the one she abandoned . . . for which she substituted the spiritually-organized Church of Christ, Scientist, in Boston, which, according to her statement, 'still goes on.'

". . . We have Mrs. Eddy's statement to the effect that at one time she considered laws of limitation for a Christian Scientist unnecessary (*Miscellany,* p. 229). In other words, she believed that the divine impulse operating in each individual consciousness was sufficient to guide her followers into doing exactly what was right under all circumstances; but God directed her otherwise and she found through experience that By-laws were a necessity, and under the guidance of divine Mind she began to formulate certain rules or By-laws for Christian Scientists to follow. These were written at different times and on different occasions, to cover different conditions and situations. . . .

"We know *Science and Health* was written through the direct inspiration of divine Mind, and no Christian Scientist would think for a moment of revising it. This being the case, why should we not consider the *Church Manual,* which our Leader assures us was written under similar inspiration, just as inviolable as *Science and Health?*

"No alert Christian Scientist would want to revise the *Church Manual;* nor would any well-meaning Christian Scientist conclude that our Leader had put any law therein that could be improved upon at a later date. Mrs. Eddy placed the *Manual* in the same class with *Science and Health* when she tells us on page 251 of *Miscellany,* 'Adhere to the teachings of the Bible, Science and Health, and our *Manual,* and you will obey the law and the gospel.' "

As he neared the end of his address Dickey raised a question that, even then, was a worn one; and answered it. The question was: "Is it not strange that Mrs. Eddy put the government of The Mother Church in the hands of five persons?" His answer was:

"Christian Scientists do not understand that she did this. What she did was to put the government of The Mother Church into the *By-laws.* The Church is not being governed by persons; it is governed by Principle through By-laws in the *Manual.* Our Leader tells us that man is self-governed properly only when he is governed by God. The government of the Church lies in obedience to the *Manual.* When the *Manual* is obeyed absolutely and implicitly, the Church is being governed according to the law of God. When the *Manual* is disregarded, the Church is in danger.

"The safety of the Christian Science church does not rest in the Board of Directors; it lies in the integrity of each individual member, and in the determination of the members to obey the By-laws. Without loyalty and support and obedience to the *Church Manual* this Cause could not possibly exist." [6]

Enemies struck from another direction.

As the Discoverer and Founder of Christian Science, Mrs. Eddy wrote many things, in addition to her published works. As a teacher, she wrote thousands of letters to her own students, and to others, all over the world; as an editor, she wrote many paragraphs and articles for Christian Science publications; as pastor of her church, she prepared many sermons; and, as a servant of God, she put into incomplete words many thoughts.

Now, in an effort to destroy her teachings, a growing number of letters and manuscripts, all purporting to be genuine, was being circulated. Companion to the letters and manuscripts was the rumor that Mrs. Eddy had left writings soon to be published—and that, among them, were the letters and manuscripts being circulated.

It made for a harmful situation. Among the documents were some that had been taken from the Archives of The Mother Church by a faithless student. They were incomplete notes not intended for publication but this did not keep the enemies of Mrs. Eddy from using them to injure her teachings. For the most part, however, the writings were forgeries and because they were it was hoped by sincere Christian Scientists that use of them would subside.

Instead, the forgeries gained such wide circulation that, under the heading of "Mrs. Eddy's Unpublished Writings," there appeared in the *Sentinel,* in its issue of March 3, 1923, these words of caution:

The published writings of Mrs. Eddy contain that which she desired to give to the world from her pen. Her printed words,

[6] Dickey's address was published in its entirety in *The Christian Science Journal* in June, 1922.

chosen with care and grouped with exactness, express her precise meaning and present a complete elucidation of Christian Science. She left no writings which are to be published at some future date. She left nothing unfinished in her exposition of this Science of Mind which, when applied as she directs, heals the sick and reforms the sinner.

Her personal correspondence was large, and was addressed to many individuals covering a wide range of subjects, but she expressly desired that the published writings alone should be taken as her voice to the world.

Mrs. Eddy saw that anything she had not written for publication, or that might be circulated in manuscript form, was open to adulteration, and misapplication. Respecting her wishes in this regard, hundreds of her correspondents have sent in their cherished letters to be permanently filed in the vaults of The Mother Church, where they will be protected and preserved. The field at large also can honor her wishes by refusing to accept any papers which purport to be from her pen, but which are open to doubt.

Of late, certain typewritten articles and alleged extracts from letters claiming to have been written by our Leader have been circulated which are not genuine and should, therefore, be shunned. Some of them are clever imitations of her style, and present occasional sentiments that in themselves are not objectionable, but which are mingled with others that are deleterious and foreign to her teachings. Still others of these spurious writings have been built up in part from phrases and sentences filched from genuine writings by our Leader, and which are artfully surrounded and submerged in things she never would have approved.

To counterfeit a letter is as reprehensible as to counterfeit money, and those who would heed our Leader's wishes, and at the same time protect our Cause from imposition, should reject every writing or paper claiming to be from her which does not bear such unmistakable evidences of authenticity as would be accepted as conclusive in a court of law.

To be genuine it should bear our Leader's signature, it should show the date and residence, and the name of the person to whom it was originally addressed. If any of these essentials be lacking, the article or letter should be regarded as a snare for the unwary. Passing them from hand to hand is an offense against Christian Science, as well as a direct violation of our Leader's wishes.[7]

The falsifying continued until it became necessary for the Trustees under the Will to apply to the courts for legal protection. Legal protection was given, the Supreme Judicial Court of Massachusetts saying, in a decision (Baker v. Libbie, 210 Massachusetts Reports 599, 604-607) which concerned the circulating of excerpts from letters by Mrs. Eddy:

"It is generally recognized that one has the right to the fruits of his labor. This is equally, whether the work be muscular or mental or both combined. . . . The right of an author to publish or suppress publication of his correspondence is absolute in the absence of special considerations, and is independent of any desire or intent at the time of writing. It is an interest in the intangible and impalpable thought and the particular verbal garments in which it was clothed."

In the decision, the Court also held that the proprietary rights of Mary Baker Eddy passed to her legal representatives. In so deciding, the Court used the word "publication"

---

[7] Practically all of Mrs. Eddy's letters have been acquired by The Mother Church. In addition, authorized Christian Science literature is never circulated in the form of handwritten, or typewritten, pages. It is always printed, and always under the name of the publisher.

Nevertheless, fake writings said to be the work of Mary Baker Eddy are often circulated. The trickery began while Mrs. Eddy was here in person. In the *Christian Science Sentinel,* December 11, 1937, is published a statement by the Directors reporting an occasion when a collection of fake writings was shown to Mrs. Eddy. After examining the collection, she said, "The enemy of Christian Science or a self-deceived student must have compiled it."

in the sense "of making public through printing or multiplication of copies." [8]

Ten years had gone since the setting up of the Relief Fund to shelter and to feed the unsheltered and hungry of Europe in a war of devastation; five years had gone since the denial by the Trustees of the Publishing Society of the primacy of the *Church Manual*. It was a decade marked by strife, in the world and in the movement. Nevertheless, in 1924, there were more than two thousand recognized branches of The Mother Church, 2,117 to be exact, whereas, ten years before, there were 1,616 recognized branches. This was a total increase of 501, or an average of slightly less than one new branch each week.

Compared with the immediately preceding span of ten years, the gain in branches was smaller, there having been an increase of 667 such units in the period of 1906-15. However, there were gains that were more than compensating. With each year, there was a steady increase in the membership of The Mother Church, and, in the Clerk's Report at the annual meeting on June 7, 1924, it was stated that The Mother Church "has admitted more members this year than in any previous year in its history."

At this meeting it also was reported:

"Since June 1, 1923, fifty-six churches and eighty-two Christian Science societies have been recognized as branches of The Mother Church. Twenty new organizations are lo-

[8] In the December 11, 1937, issue of the *Sentinel,* The Christian Science Board of Directors referred to this decision, and reminded all offenders: "Mary Baker Eddy always exercised her literary rights in the interest of Christian Science, and of all mankind. The present holders of her rights aim to do as she would have done. Because of these facts, before a loyal Christian Scientist accepts or circulates anything attributed to Mrs. Eddy he would do well to ask himself such questions as these: 'Is it authentic?' 'Is it in circulation with the consent of Mrs. Eddy or her Trustees?' "

cated in Europe, South Africa, Tasmania and New Zealand.
. . . Applications from 1,093 practitioners and nurses for
cards in the *Journal,* the German *Herold,* and the French
Héraut have been considered by The Christian Science
Board of Directors during the past year." The applications
numbered five times the total applications in 1915.

The 1924 annual meeting was one of unusual importance.
Ten years before, in annual meeting, the members of The
Mother Church were reminded of Mrs. Eddy's instructions
to keep before them the teaching that "God creates all
through Mind, not through matter,—that the plant grows,
not because of seed or soil, but because growth is the eternal
mandate of Mind." [9] So reminded, the members gathered
and listened to the reading of a statement "outlining the
principal lines of activity to be followed in fulfilling the
desires of our beloved Leader as expressed in her will and
in other documents indicating more specifically the channels
through which to accomplish the purposes intended." [10]

In 1924, the report for the ten-year period ending December 31, 1923, disclosed that "$1,500,000 have been paid to
over four hundred branches of this Church as aid in church
building. During the year 1923, these payments were at the
rate of one each week.

"A number of inquiries have been made . . . in regard to
the repayment of church building grants, and the following
paragraph now appears in the letter outlining plans for
giving assistance to the erection, purchase, or remodeling
of church edifices:

" 'The Trustees will not require the payment of interest
on grants made by them, nor the repayment of principal so
long as the terms of requisite declarations of trust are ful-

[9] *Science and Health,* p. 520.
[10] For complete statement, see Appendix 6.

filled. However, any organization may repay its grant whenever it desires, in which case it will secure a release of the lien on its property and give to the Trustees additional funds for carrying on its work. . . .' "

In those ten years, Christian Science lecturers traveled the world and were heard by perhaps 25,000,000 people. To illustrate, in the single year of 1923, there were 3,084 lectures in England, Ireland, Scotland, Wales, the Channel Islands, Denmark, France, Germany, Holland, Italy, Latvia, Norway, Sweden, Switzerland, South Africa, Australia, New Zealand, Tasmania, China, Japan, the Philippines, Hawaii, Mexico, Alaska, Canal Zone, Barbados, Jamaica, Bermuda, Cuba, Puerto Rico, Canada, and the United States.

In ten years, nearly $1,000,000 were spent in distributing "Mrs. Eddy's teachings by means of the literature of the Movement." Regularly, *The Christian Science Monitor* was being sent to 335 United States embassies and consulates abroad. In contrast to the losses of short years before, a check of substantial proportions was given to The Mother Church by the Trustees of The Christian Science Publishing Society. The check represented the profits of the Society for the previous year.

In the June, 1924, issue of the *Journal* were the cards of 7,335 practitioners and 161 Christian Science nurses. It was the largest number in the history of the movement, a gain of more than two thousand names in ten years.

In December, 1924, *Science and Health with Key to the Scriptures* was published in Braille.[11] The first issue was the largest single edition printed in Braille at one time. It con-

---

11 *Rudimental Divine Science* was the first of Mrs. Eddy's writings to be printed in Braille. The year was 1906. *Unity of Good* was printed in Braille in 1923; *Retrospection and Introspection* in 1930; the *Church Manual* in 1936; *Seven Poems* in 1936; and *Christian Healing* in 1943.

sisted of five hundred copies, with five books to a set, or twenty-five hundred books in all.

But, before the printing of the textbook in Braille, before the report to the membership of The Mother Church of the ten years of progress, and even while Christian Science lecturers were traveling the world bringing their Leader's message of healing, there was a decision of great significance.

In 1910, the name of Mary Baker Eddy, Pastor Emeritus, was omitted from the list of Church Officers in the *Church Manual,* after having been printed there since 1895. In the spring of 1924, in the *Sentinel,* in its issue of April 19, there was this communication from The Christian Science Board of Directors:

To every Christian Scientist falls a share of the responsibility for observing, so far as is humanly possible, our Leader's expressed plans and desires. To The Christian Science Board of Directors of The Mother Church are allotted the greatest responsibilities, as well as the greatest opportunities, in this respect. Upon them rests the duty of now replacing on page 21 of the *Church Manual* our Leader's name and title as "Pastor Emeritus," which was removed after she passed on. The Directors believe that the field will be interested in the reason for this action; and they are themselves giving a brief outline of the facts which preceded it.

In April, 1895, the then Board of Directors unanimously appointed Mrs. Eddy Pastor Emeritus "nominally; for the time and for all generations to come." On April 23, of the same year she accepted the ordination as conferred, and has since been regarded by Christian Scientists as their Pastor Emeritus.

From 1895 until after she passed on in 1910 her name, with the above title, was always printed in the forepart of the *Church Manual* under the heading "Church Officers." Soon after she passed on, the Directors who then were serving discontinued the printing of her name in this list of officers in the *Manual* because of certain conjectures and surmises then afloat in public thought, which, they believed, might cause the retention of her name there to be misconstrued and misunderstood.

As these erroneous beliefs no longer prevail, the present Directors have for some time been considering the action taken by their predecessors in 1910, and have now decided that our Leader's name as Pastor Emeritus should be replaced on page 21 of the *Manual* as it appeared for so many years prior to 1910.

The Directors believe that the list of Church Officers on page 21 should conform to Section 1 of Article 1 of the *Manual*, which distinctly and specifically names the "Pastor Emeritus" first among the church officers. There are other By-laws in the *Manual* which also refer to Mrs. Eddy as the Pastor Emeritus of her church.

Devoted Christian Scientists will ever continue lovingly to refer to Mrs. Eddy as "our Leader," a designation which is not affected by her being no longer visibly with us. With equal reason should she ever be regarded nominally as our Pastor Emeritus, for no one can possibly succeed her in either capacity.

She became our Leader for all time, not because she personally led the movement safely over the obstacles, and through the difficulties which confronted its earlier existence, but for the greater reason that her teaching and writings will always continue to lead the seeker after righteousness toward "the goal of Spirit, or life in God." (*Science and Health with Key to the Scriptures,* p. 324.)

She is our Pastor Emeritus, not merely because she once officiated as pastor and minister of the early church organization, but because as Discoverer and Founder of Christian Science, her discovery will ever minister to the needs of suffering and sinning humanity, healing the sick and comforting the sorrowing through the impersonal truth which she revealed.

Mary Baker Eddy's name was again among the Church Officers for all to see—again where it belongs, again where, so long as there is a *Church Manual,* it must stay.

CHAPTER TEN

That Which Is to Be

IT was 1925, and fifty years had passed since Mary Baker Eddy had published her book, *Science and Health,* and said in its Preface: "Truth, independent of doctrines or time-honored systems, stands at the threshold of history." [1]

Original in presentation, and revolutionary in thought, the book brought ridicule to Mrs. Eddy, and to her teachings, long before it brought recognition and inquiry. It was a book that said because sin, sickness, disease, and death are not of God, sin, sickness, disease, and death are not of man. Its teachings called upon mankind to prove their efficacy by giving to God that which belongs to Him. In a world bewitched by materialism, the teachings were heard by few ears.

Less than 1,500 copies of two printings of *Science and Health* were sold in the six years that followed publication, and Mrs. Eddy had gone deep into her purse to meet the costs of printing. On January 31, 1881, with the manuscript for a third printing in her possession, but with not nearly enough money to pay for its publication, she visited John Wilson, one of the owners of University Press in Boston.

She told Wilson she was able to pay a few hundred dollars on account, but not "one-half of the amount before commencing the work" of manufacturing, as Wilson had stipulated, nor could she pay the balance on receipt of the books,

[1] Later Mrs. Eddy changed the sentence to read: "Truth, independent of doctrines and time-honored systems, knocks at the portal of humanity."

as Wilson expected—but, having the books, she told him she was sure she could sell enough to pay him, in full.

Wilson was never quite able to explain it, but he found himself not only willing to take the risk, but also eager to take it. The books were made, and delivered, and sold—and the bill was paid. Before 1881 was over, there was a fourth printing, and before the end of 1882, a fifth printing was being distributed. By 1883, there were fifteen printings.[2]

Twenty years more, plus one, *Science and Health* was in its eight hundred and thirty-fifth printing (417 printings in cloth binding, and 418 printings in limp leather binding). It was in this year (1906) that, acting on instructions from Mrs. Eddy, University Press discontinued the practice of numbering the printings.

In 1925, *Science and Health* was second only to the Bible as the most widely read book in the English language. In 1925, the Trustees under the Will of Mary Baker Eddy observed the fiftieth anniversary by publishing a special Half Century Edition of *Science and Health*. In the same year, the Trustees under Mrs. Eddy's will brought out a new volume which became an immediate success. Entitled *Prose Works*, it is a book that now exceeds, in sales, all Christian Science titles except *Science and Health* and the *Church Manual*.

Prose Works contains all of Mrs. Eddy's writings other than her poems, *Christ and Christmas*, the *Church Manual* and *Science and Health*. Containing more than 1,350 pages, the book includes these writings: *Miscellaneous Writings, Retrospection and Introspection, Unity of Good, Pulpit and*

---

[2] The sixth printing (1883) carried the title *Science and Health with a Key to the Scriptures.* This title was continued through the fifteenth printing, after which "a" was dropped. Beginning with the sixteenth printing, *Science and Health with Key to the Scriptures* became the permanent title.

Press, Rudimental Divine Science, No and Yes, Christian Science versus Pantheism, Message to The Mother Church, 1900, Message to The Mother Church, 1901, Message to The Mother Church, 1902, Christian Healing, The People's Idea of God, The First Church of Christ, Scientist, and *Miscellany.*

Books released by the Publishing Society in 1925 included a German hymnal, a French translation of *The Life of Mary Baker Eddy* by Sibyl Wilbur, and a large-sized *Reader's Quarterly.* Circulation of the periodicals was at its highest point and, except for the war years, so was the circulation of the *Monitor.*

This same period marked the appearance of the Norwegian and Swedish translations of the *Quarterly,* as well as the monthly printing of the Bible Lessons in Braille. Sixteen pages were added to the *Journal* to provide for the expanding list of churches, societies, practitioners, and nurses. The hymnal was in the process of being translated into Dutch and Swedish. For the first time in seven years, the Board of Directors was practically free from litigation. In speaking of this comparative freedom, the Directors referred to the fact that they were "legal proceedings . . . brought against us, but never by us"; and added: "Let us be profoundly grateful that in all of them the position of the Church has been sustained, and the contentions of its adversaries have been discredited."

It was a period of seedtime and harvest in a climate quite different from that which existed when Mrs. Eddy was here in person—quite different from what it was in the first years after her passing when, not able to pursue her in person with their malice, her enemies pursued her name.

In Scotland, the Reverend James Black told the people of Edinburgh: "I admire Mrs. Eddy, the Founder of Christian

Science, in deep ways, and I frankly consider her one of the most remarkable people in religious history. . . . She has left her mark for good on countless lives; indeed, she has affected our generation more than any single man or woman."

In London, England, the Reverend Edward T. Vernon expressed the belief that "God used Mrs. Eddy for a special revelation, and there is, indeed, no reason why this should not be so. No just person can fail to admire her as a religious leader. She has founded a great church; and, let us say it frankly, brought great blessings to countless lives."

Richard C. Cabot, Professor of Clinical Medicine, Harvard University, was quoted as saying: "The good effects of Christian Science I see on all sides. I have not the slightest doubt that it does good, that it cures disease, organic as well as functional." And Charles Hunter, Professor of Clinical Medicine, University of Manitoba, was in agreement: "Christian Science has helped many persons suffering from diseases which to the medical practitioner defied diagnosis. . . . Christian Science, furthermore, has brought relief to individuals who were victims of organic disorder, proving that psychotherapy is not solely confined to functional diseases." Adding his views to those of his fellow physicians was Dr. Drummond Shields, member of the British Parliament: "Some of the most remarkable cases I know—wonderful cures—have been in connection with Christian Science, which I have seen myself, and know."

Legislative bodies in the British Isles, in Canada, and in the United States were reflecting the better understanding by refraining from enacting legislation restricting or interfering with the practice of Christian Science.

Earlier criticism of The Christian Science Board of Directors over the organizing of The Christian Science Benevolent

Association was quieted. In the dissension of a few years before, critics charged that the action of the Board was "unauthorized and unjustifiable" because, before her passing, Mrs. Eddy "had drafted a By-law of approval, had sent it to the Directors, but had withdrawn it when deciding to abandon the whole idea of a Benevolent Association."

The inspiration for the Benevolent Association developed this way. In late December, 1904, or very early in January, 1905, Mrs. Mary Beecher Longyear, of Brookline, Massachusetts, went to Concord, New Hampshire, where Mrs. Eddy was living, and requested permission to set up an institution where persons seeking relief through Christian Science treatment might obtain it.

Doubtless, in this meeting, Mrs. Eddy remembered other days in Lynn when, among her students, were those who were poor, and the time when she gave up five of the seven rooms in her house to a family in need, saying as she extended the gift: "Now you have a home offered you, and no rent to pay for it. So do not be cast down. I thank God . . . that I have a shelter . . . to go to in an hour of want, and to welcome those who need a little time to meet the hour."

Altogether, a sizable number of persons found shelter in the two-story, frame dwelling at 8 Broad Street, in Lynn, where, in a small upstairs room lighted and ventilated by a skylight, Mrs. Eddy completed *Science and Health.*

Also, she must have remembered the Easter Sunday in 1889 when she announced the founding of a "Christian Science Dispensary," which was opened at 7 Temple Street in Boston in May. Here help was given to all who came for it. There was no charge. The idea spread until there were about thirty such dispensaries in other cities, such as New York and Cleveland. The dispensaries were closed in 1894.

Thus it was that Mrs. Longyear found a ready listener to

her proposal. As they talked, Mrs. Eddy suggested that the institution be called a "sanatorium," and also suggested that, in addition to caring for the sick, provision be made to train nurses in order that all treatment be in accordance with Christian Science teachings.

Mrs. Longyear returned to Brookline and, under date of January 15, 1905, Mrs. Eddy wrote to her:

> God is moving on the face of the waters of your thoughts and His creation will appear.
>
> I propose that the institution you found be called Sanatorium . . . that it be a resort for invalids without homes or relatives available in time of need; where they can go and recruit.
>
> Our cause demands a wider circle of means for the ends of philanthropy and charity, and better qualifications for practical purposes. This latter lack in students of Christian Science is a great hindrance to our cause and it must be met and mastered. The students need to be qualified so that under the fire of mortal mind they can stand, and 'having done all, to stand.' (St. Paul).

During the ensuing year there was frequent communication between the two women until, on January 21, 1906, Mrs. Eddy wrote to Mrs. Longyear:

> Since reading your letters, pondering the subject of an institute or sanatorium, and studying our Manual, I see it is not best for you to take the initiative in the matter. It properly belongs to The Christian Science Board of Directors to do that, for thereby we shall avoid much confusion in the future. So please drop the matter.

A year went by, and almost another year before Mrs. Eddy again wrote on the subject. This time she sent a letter to Archibald McLellan.[3] In this letter, dated December 14, 1907, Mrs. Eddy said:

> My dear Trustee:—I desire to commence immediately to found a Christian Science institution for the special benefit of the poor and general good of all mankind. The founding and endowment of this institution will cost at least one million of dollars.
>
> Please come to me at your earliest opportunity, and I will give you further details.
>
> Most truly yours,
> Mary Baker Eddy.

The letter was published in the *Sentinel* in its issue of December 21, 1907, and, in the December 28 issue of the periodical, McLellan referred to the favorable editorial comment the announcement had received, using, as one illustration, a paragraph from the December 24, 1907, issue of the *Boston Herald:*

"The intimation from Mrs. Eddy that she intends to set apart one million dollars for a permanent fund with which to relieve poverty and extend aid to the needy, is a departure significant as a precedent, as well as commendable in itself. The Christian Science sect has been severely criticized for its omission to carry on relief and charitable work under institutional auspices. Mrs. Eddy, with her unchallenged

---

[3] McLellan was one of three Trustees under the Deed of Trust executed on March 6, 1907. The others were Henry M. Baker and Josiah E. Fernald. In this Deed, Mrs. Eddy assigned to the three Trustees, "their heirs, successors and assigns, all my interest in and to any real estate wherever situated; also, all my interests of every kind and description in and to any estate, personal or mixed, which I now own, or possess."

power, can alter this, and by implication would seem to be willing to do so."

Commenting on this editorial, McLellan wrote:

"Alluding to this article in the *Herald,* Mrs. Eddy says that about 1878 she opened a Christian Science 'Home' in Lynn, Mass., in which indigent students were given their board and instruction in Christian Science gratuitously, but the misconduct of some of these students caused her to close this 'Home.' "

Continuing, McLellan said that Mrs. Eddy had given her consent to the use of her name in the founding of the institution, which would be known as "Mary Baker G. Eddy's Charitable Fund," and disclosed:

"The sum of one million dollars will be devoted to this sole purpose. Mrs. Eddy's benevolence will be open to all those individuals who are genuinely interested in Christian Science for its truth's sake, and who shall present to the Board of Directors of the Fund satisfactory certificates as to their indigence, their religious views, and their moral character. These certificates must bear the signature of some well-known Christian Scientist who can vouch for the facts stated therein. The students of Christian Science will be maintained by this Fund until such time as the Board of Directors shall have pronounced them good healers of the sick, and delivered to them certificates to this effect. The beneficiaries of this Fund, and the families of those who have families, are to be supported from the income of the Fund, and the number of students and their families to be supported will depend upon the amount of this income. Among those to be taught and supported will be some persons who are trained and qualified nurses and genuinely interested in Christian Science."

More months passed—nearly nineteen of them—before

there was a next step. In these months Mrs. Eddy moved from Concord to Boston, founded *The Christian Science Monitor,* watched over her Church, and, as was her practice, gave long, careful, and prayerful thought to the work yet to be sent forth.

On July 27, 1909, an envelope containing a new By-law for the *Church Manual* and a signed letter was sent to The Christian Science Board of Directors.

The letter:

> The Christian Science Board of Directors,
> Beloved Brethren:—
> Please vote on the adoption of the following by-law, and if adopted publish it in our periodical and in the Church Manual.
> Mary Baker Eddy.

The By-law: *The Mother Church shall establish and maintain a Christian Science resort for the so-called sick.*

The Directors adopted the By-law and, after so doing, talked among themselves of how best to carry out their Leader's wishes. There was correspondence with Mrs. Eddy in which the Board expressed its concern over the readiness of The Mother Church to assume the additional responsibility.

Instead of using the "unchallenged power" attributed to her by the *Boston Herald,* Mrs. Eddy communicated with the Directors on August 11, 1909, to this effect: "If The Mother Church is not ready to establish and maintain a Christian Science resort for the sick, she [Mrs. Eddy] is willing to let this matter rest for the present and suggests that you vote on the repeal of the by-law providing for the same."

The By-law was repealed and Mrs. Eddy's secretary, who had given her message to the Board, was apprised of the action.

To the day of her passing, the "resort for the so-called sick," as she called it, was often in Mrs. Eddy's conversation. At the same time, she was content to leave the decision of when to build in the care of the Directors. She knew the work would be done; she knew, as she wrote to Mrs. Longyear, that God's "creations will appear."

Six years, less one day, after her passing The Christian Science Board of Directors used the *Sentinel*, December 2, 1916, for this message to the field:

... This period of six years [since the passing of Mrs. Eddy] has been for Christian Scientists largely a period of adjustment. It has been a testing time, a period wherein opportunity has been given to demonstrate the great fact that the Church of Christ, Scientist, is an emanation of divine Mind, and therefore that divine Mind, not human personality, directs its destiny.

Today we may all rejoice in the fact that no demands have been made upon it which have been beyond its strength, and no problems have been presented for which the by-laws have not already provided the solution. These six years have afforded an opportunity to Christian Scientists throughout the world to adjust local problems, to build many church edifices, and to lay in their own consciousness the foundations for broader developments in all of the departments of this great movement.

The Mother Church is extending the channels of its usefulness. It is taking a forward look, to make provisions for that day, now near at hand, which will compel a broader, more comprehensive, and more universal activity. In this hour when human thought is turning instinctively from mortal strife and suffering to the substantial things of Spirit, Christian Scientists find themselves, as watchmen on the watchtowers of Zion, confronted with the necessity of providing for the care of those who from the depths of suffering and despair have caught the message of hope which Christian Science brings, and who are turning to it for relief from their sorrows and afflictions.

In pursuance of the special wish of the Leader, repeatedly enjoined upon us, a new channel of usefulness for the Mother Church has been established in the institution of The Christian Science Benevolent Association. Among the humanitarian purposes of this Association for which there is at present a definite need, is that of caring for some of the early students of Mrs. Eddy, and for others who helped lay the foundation of this movement and who are now in need of proper provision for their peace and comfort.

During these six years it has been the policy of the Directors of The Mother Church to avoid making calls on the field for financial assistance; but an era of more intimate cooperation is now dawning, and in furtherance of this idea the following data are given, which will prove of much interest to the field:—

Numerous valuable parcels of real estate, adjacent to the property already owned by The Mother Church [4] and necessary for extensions and betterments, have been acquired and are now

---

[4] In a statement to the field (*Sentinel,* October 7, 1916) telling of preliminary steps that "have just been taken toward the formation of a new and important department...to be known as The Christian Science Benevolent Association," the Directors, after reviewing some of the earlier history of the Benevolent Association, and giving the details of Mrs. Eddy's proposed By-law establishing "a Christian Science resort for the so-called sick," closed their announcement with these paragraphs:

"Although temporarily delayed, this Board has not lost sight of its obligation to found this work for which the demand has so definitely and rapidly increased, but has only awaited the time which seemed right for carrying out the project.

"A short time ago Mrs. [Mary Beecher] Longyear offered to make a gift of a valuable tract of over twenty acres of land, beautifully situated in the suburb of Brookline, as a site for the first Christian Science home or sanatorium to be established and conducted by The Mother Church. Our appreciation of this generous offer was immediately expressed, and Mrs. Longyear was notified that the gift would be accepted.

"The project will be developed as rapidly as possible. Plans for buildings will be started at once, and it is hoped that the actual work of construction will commence not later than the early spring. Such announcements as are necessary will be made from time to time through our periodicals."

in friendly hands. It will be necessary to provide the sum of $526,500 before title can be taken to these properties.

Deeply impressed by the need for adequate preparation on the part of us all to assist in the fulfilment of the glorious mission of Christian Science, we call upon the field for renewed consecration to the work of healing the sick, saving the sinner, and comforting the afflicted. The time has come when every Christian Scientist must be ready and willing to prove his faith by his works, and to make the healing instantaneous and permanent. No Christian Scientist is exempt from this demand. We must all be healers of the sick, fulfilling the responsibility which each one assumed when he claimed the name of Christian Scientist. Now as always The Mother Church looks to the whole field of Christian Scientists for cooperation in working out its divine mission.

True giving is the realization of the inexhaustible nature of divine supply, and can only be manifested as our understanding of that supply unfolds. Then we begin to demonstrate the scientific fact that "giving does not impoverish us ... neither does withholding enrich us" (*Science and Health,* p. 79), and we break the pretended law which would pauperize mankind by arguing a sense of personal possession.

We therefore briefly summarize the channels which are now open to the field and to which it is heartily invited to contribute, both individually and through the church and society organizations:

1st: For real estate as hereinbefore stated . . . . . $526,500.

2nd: To erect and equip the buildings and provide a maintenance fund for the first institution of the Christian Science Benevolent Association, not less than . . . . $600,000.

Chartered in 1916, the Sanatorium was opened in 1919. Then, as now, those seeking admittance were not accepted, or refused, by reason of their ability to pay, or not to pay, the established rates. Being a work that was of benefit to mankind, it was not a work where there could be a distinction between rich and poor. This work was healing that came not from waiting upon each other, but from waiting upon God. The choice, therefore, was not between rich and poor because God was, and is, no more and no less available to one than to the other. The choice was in the testimony of the petitioner, in his worthiness, in his humbleness, in his consecration to the purposes of God.

There was reason for the requirement. This was an undertaking to demonstrate Christian Science healing in an institutional way. Being institutional, and being healing, charity was in its framework. Consequently, a minimum of 25 per cent of the cost of operation was for the care of the poor.

Charity is a word often found in Mrs. Eddy's writings. To her earliest pupils, she said, "Great charity and humility is necessary in this work of healing," and warned her pupils, "Cast not your pearls before swine," and gave them this assurance, "If you cannot bring peace to all, you can to many, if faithful followers in His vineyard." [5]

These were words remembered by all Christian Scientists. As congregations, they were assuming the responsibility for the care of the sick, and for the healing of the sick. Theirs was a covenant that could not be divided between Christian Scientists, as distinguished by the terms church members and church directors. In Mrs. Eddy's teachings, the welfare of the movement is an individual responsibility, and obedience to her teachings is no less the duty of the individual church member than it is the duty of the individual Director of The Mother Church. All are Christian Scientists, and all are her followers.

Following Mrs. Eddy's wishes, a training course for nurses became a part of the work of The Christian Science Benevo-

[5] *Miscellaneous Writings,* p. 7.

lent Association. Of three years' duration, the training course was under the direct supervision of instructors who were experienced graduate nurses before becoming Christian Scientists. Graduate nurses were selected because of the desire to have student nurses instructed in the ordinary services so essential to the proper care of the sick.

In the instructions there was no recognition, by the graduate nurses, of medical theories, and no acknowledgment of the reality of disease. Instead, there was only awareness of the supremacy of God's law, and only acceptance of the eternal changelessness of law in which there is no sickness, of any kind. This was instruction that called for spiritual understanding of a high order. It was instruction that was in full observance of Mrs. Eddy's teachings.

This must not be interpreted as meaning that Christian Science nurses are not qualified in the practical aspects of caring for the sick. They are so qualified and are so trained. Applicants for the Nurses Training Course are carefully chosen. Before being permitted to identify themselves as graduates of the Sanatorium training course in *The Christian Science Journal,* they are required (1) to prove their competency by demonstration, (2) to complete the training course, and (3) to have received class instruction from an authorized teacher of Christian Science.

Writing in the *Sentinel,* April 8, 1922, Elisha B. Seeley called attention to the "importance [Mrs. Eddy] attached to right mental environment. On page 424, of 'Science and Health with Key to the Scriptures,' she writes:

" 'It is equally important in metaphysical practice that the *minds* which surround your patient should not act against your influence by continually expressing such opinions as may alarm or discourage,—either by giving antagonistic advice or through unspoken thoughts resting on your patient.' It can be truthfully said that no such false mental influence exists among the workers at the Sanatorium, but that the spirit of hope and expectancy prevails and is based upon an enlightened understanding of the presence, power, and substance of Spirit or Mind; and this proves that 'the law of the Spirit of life in Christ Jesus' makes free 'from the law of sin and death.' " [6]

On December 31, 1919, the financial statement disclosed expenditures of $586,253.37 for the calendar year just past. This sum included the spending of $441,908.01 for construction of buildings and improvements in grounds. On hand was the sum of $197,360.32, approximately one-quarter of which was in cash and the remainder in Liberty Bonds.

In the three months of operation, the patients numbered ninety-nine, and the cost of caring for non-paying patients was much in excess of the total income.

Eight years afterwards, or at the close of the 1927 calendar year, there had been 10,140 patients, and the prophecy made by the Directors on August 20, 1919, was verified. In a letter under this date, read in all Christian Science churches and societies, the Directors made an appeal for funds for the Benevolent Association, and in the letter were these words of prophecy: "... The unfolding and development of its philanthropic and charitable purposes will continuously present new needs and opportunities."

Opened on October 1, 1919, the Sanatorium stands at the summit of a hill where, in the days of the Massachusetts Bay Colony, a single tree stood out against the sky—a bearing for sailors and a sign for travelers on the long voyage from Europe that Boston Harbor was near.

Here on an elevation called Single Tree Hill were driven the marking stakes for the buildings that are now the Sana-

[6] Romans, 8:2.

torium. It is wooded on the summit, and in a setting of trees, and paths, and flowers the buildings are scattered. Below the summit is the Chestnut Hill reservoir, and winding around the clear waters is a road over which Mrs. Eddy often traveled in her daily drives from her home in Chestnut Hill.

It is a place, and a setting, she would have chosen. She would have liked the memory of the single tree meeting the storms of the sea and standing as a marker for the harbor ahead. She would have found it appropriate that in the same place now stands an institution which bears the stamp of her teachings—a seal that the victory, even over the last intruder, is never in doubt.

With the Sanatorium in operation, the activities of the Benevolent Association were widened to include help to "deserving Christian Scientists who have years of creditable endeavors and achievement behind them . . . who are living amid surroundings that are obstructive to comfort, activity, or clear thinking."

Quietly, several years before, the Directors had begun inquiring into the conditions under which a number of older Christian Scientists were living, and it was learned that some were in want, some were housed in depressed neighborhoods in large cities, some were in public institutions and dependent upon the charity of others.

In December, 1925, in the *Journal,* the Directors told the field "the time is at hand when the world is to be shown that our church does care for its own, and that our religion is not without profit in the sense that the apostle uses the word when he says, 'If a brother or sister be naked, and destitute of daily food, and one of you say unto them, Depart in peace, be ye warmed and filled; notwithstanding ye give them not those things which are needful to the body; what doth it profit?' "

There was no special call for funds beyond a brief announcement in the *Monitor*, but in their communication in the *Journal* the Directors said, "Many churches, societies, associations, and individuals have contributed until now an adequate amount is in hand with which to begin work. This it is estimated will be about one-fourth of the amount needed to complete the buildings, furnish them, and to take care of the first operating expenses."

The surroundings chosen as a place for a home for those in need were those Mrs. Eddy had selected in 1891 when seeking to free her own thoughts from the demands of a movement that was reaching out and over the world. This was a farm near Concord. She called it Pleasant View.

Here the hills and white birches must have beckoned her toward the farmhouse where she was born not far away, in Bow, New Hampshire; here, when she took possession, were poor acres, a few pine trees, and a house that was less a house than a hut. Instead of these, she saw flowers and hedges, sloping lawns, fruit trees, shade trees, shrubs, a home with wide verandas.

These things all came while she lived here, and coming with them was a pond, the gift of her people. This was beauty of which she could write, "I love your promise; and shall know, some time, the spiritual reality and substance of form, light, and color, of what I now through you discern dimly; and knowing this, I shall be satisfied." [7]

It was from Pleasant View that Mrs. Eddy directed the building of The Mother Church; it was while here that she established the Bible and *Science and Health with Key to the Scriptures* as the only preachers in her church, thus

[7] *Miscellaneous Writings*, p. 87.

preventing any dilution of her teachings; here she listened, and wrote, and revised, and refined the By-laws that are the *Church Manual;* gave the instructions that became *The Christian Science Sentinel;* founded The Christian Science Board of Lectureship, The Christian Science Board of Education, and The Christian Science Publishing Society, as now constituted; completed the work of making the *Quarterly* the source of the Lesson-Sermons in use in all Christian Science churches and societies; here she listened, and revised, and refined successive editions of *Science and Health.*

These were some—but only some—of Mrs. Eddy's achievements at Pleasant View. It was here she made the deep soundings in the eternal verities, and heard, with growing clearness, the voice of the Gardener saying to all mankind, "Lo, I am with you alway, *even* unto the end of the world."

With the exception of the house with the wide verandas, the setting was the same in 1927 as it was thirty years before when Mrs. Eddy walked along the flowered paths or sat on a bench beside the quiet pond. Old when restored by Mrs. Eddy, and now no longer usable, the frame house was torn down. Where it stood was erected the main building of the Pleasant View Home which, in July, was ready to receive its first guests.

In the *Sentinel*, July 2, 1927, was published a general notice to all Christian Scientists:

The time is at hand when a large amount should be in the hands of our Treasurer to make final payments upon our new Pleasant View Home at Concord, New Hampshire. The building is completed, furnishing and equipment are being installed, and future residents will soon be notified to arrive about July 15.

There should be no outstanding obligations when our home is opened for the fulfillment of the high ideals it expresses. Its roof is broad and its walls are sturdy, but they are not built to carry a debt.

When opened, the building carried no debt.

While the building of the Pleasant View Home was under way, the Directors announced the formation of the Charitable Institutions Fund to "which large or small gifts may be made, and from which appropriations will be made as they may be needed for The Christian Science Benevolent Association, The Christian Science Pleasant View Home, or any similar institution that may be established by The Mother Church in accordance with Section 8, of Article 1 of the *Church Manual*." [8]

Continuing, the Directors said:

"The respective needs of these institutions vary from time to time, and other institutions of like character may be established elsewhere and where as the need and the supply may become manifest. The Treasurer of The Mother Church will continue to have a Benevolent Association Fund and a Pleasant View Home Fund, so that contributions or gifts can be made to either of them, but it is expected that many givers for such purposes will mark their gifts for the Charitable Institutions Fund, so that the larger purpose of this Fund may have adequate support. . . .

"The support of the Christian Science field for both the Benevolent Association and the Pleasant View Home has been generous and timely. The development and the results of the Benevolent Association are most gratifying, and we have every reason for expecting that the Pleasant View

---

[8] *Trusteeships and Syndicates*. Sect. 8. Boards of Trustees and Syndicates may be formed by The Mother Church, subject to the approval of the Pastor Emeritus. (Article 1, SECTION 8.)

Home, in a different way, will help to fulfill the demand and need stated by our Leader, Mary Baker Eddy . . . as follows:

" 'Our cause demands a wider circle of means for the ends of philanthropy and charity, and better qualifications for practical purposes.' "

At the same time that they made this announcement, the Directors informed the field of changes in the direct management of the affairs of the Benevolent Association and the Pleasant View Home. "Until now," said the Directors, "each of these auxiliary institutions has had a Board of Trustees consisting of the same individuals who are Directors of The Mother Church.

"Now the by-laws of these institutions have been amended so that each of them has its own Board of three Trustees whose duties are similar to those of the Trustees of The Christian Science Publishing Society. Accordingly, the members of this Board have retired from these trusteeships, and have been succeeded by three newly appointed trustees."

The reason for their retirement was to give to the Directors "more time for duties that cannot be delegated to others."

In the same year, 1927, in February, the Directors told the field that time had come for the building of a Sanatorium on the Pacific Coast, and named these conditions:

1. It should be located at a point at least three days' distant by train from Boston.

2. It should be under the direct supervision and control of The Mother Church.

3. Its funds should be handled through the Treasurer of The Mother Church.

The field was advised that the Sanatorium probably would "be located at or near San Francisco."

In October, 1927, a Building Committee was placed in charge of all operations, and the committee continued in this capacity until January, 1930, when articles of incorporation were filed. These articles provided, among other things, that: (1) the members of the Corporation should be the five members of The Christian Science Board of Directors, "whosoever they might be"; and (2) the Directors should "hold title to the sixteen acres of land upon which the sanatorium is built."

Among the first acts of the Directors was the appointment of a Board of Trustees consisting of three Christian Scientists whose job it was to complete the work of building. On May 23, 1930, the sanatorium was opened. As in Chestnut Hill, instruction was in full observance with Mrs. Eddy's teachings—in the awareness that now, or ten thousand years from now, truth does not yield to please the hour. As at Chestnut Hill, each patient was free to employ his own practitioner.

The land on which the sanatorium was built was rolling and heavily wooded with eucalyptus trees; known as Arden Wood, it was located between Twin Peaks and the ocean. These, too, were surroundings in friendship with the purpose.

About four months after the opening of the San Francisco sanatorium in 1930, the Directors announced the widening of the circle "for the ends of philanthropy and charity." In London, England, a committee known as the Committee on Christian Science Houses was appointed to assist needy Christian Scientists to enter Christian Science nursing homes, then being established in England and Wales.

This extension of the work of The Mother Church followed the revision of an Act passed by the British Parliament in 1927. In this Act, which was passed over many protests, all nursing homes in England and Wales were placed under medical supervision.

Instead of lessening, opposition to the legislation increased. It was reflected in Parliament where Neville Chamberlain, Minister of Health, told the House of Commons: "Christian Science is not carried on as medical treatment; it is not a species of quackery which pretends to be something it is not."

Finally persuaded, members of Parliament inserted a clause in the legislation which authorized the Minister of Health to exempt any nursing home which operates "in accordance with the practice and principles of the body known as The First Church of Christ, Scientist." The exempting clause required that such places be identified as "Christian Science Houses."

With the way cleared for the opening of the homes, the Committee was authorized by the Directors "to receive applications for exemption, make recommendations to the Minister of Health, and to insure that such Houses as receive exemption continue to be carried on in accordance with the provisions laid down in the Act of Parliament."

This development has grown into a supervisory group for all nursing homes. Known as The Committee on Christian Science Nursing Homes of The Mother Church, The First Church of Christ, Scientist, in Boston, Massachusetts, this supervisory group is appointed by the Directors. Now, wherever such nursing homes may be, they are under this committee. It is a work of help and charity unique in the world.

Increasingly, the competency of Christian Science practitioners, nurses, sanatoriums, and nursing homes is being recognized by insurance companies in the United States, Canada, and other countries.

Occasionally, since the organization of The Christian Science Benevolent Association, the question has been raised as to the appropriateness of the words "Benevolent Association," as applied to sanatoriums in which are guests who pay for accommodations and care. The word "Benevolent" is used correctly. Benevolent is a word of many synonyms, all well within the use to which it is put. So, too, with the word "charitable." Under the laws of Massachusetts and of California, the Chestnut Hill Sanatorium and the Pacific Coast Sanatorium are classified as charitable institutions.

In Mrs. Eddy's writings there is a paragraph which says: "A certain apothegm of a Talmudical philosopher suits my sense of doing good. It reads thus: 'The noblest charity is to prevent a man from accepting charity; and the best alms are to show and to enable a man to dispense with alms.'" [9]

This is a reference to the ancient teaching that in the ladder of charity are eight steps, the highest of which is to help another to help himself, the second highest of which is to help those whose work it is to help others to help themselves.

To temper poverty is not the primary purpose of the Benevolent Association. Mrs. Eddy knew, and her teachings disclose, that to supply food and shelter is the easiest task of all giving. To do this, and only this, is to give merely the means of physical existence, and leave nothing of spirit.

The mission of the Benevolent Association is to provide not only conditions under which men and women are kept aware of their human imposts, but also conditions under which men and women are permitted to grow in the understanding of that which was, and is, and is to be—the love of God.

[9] *Miscellaneous Writings,* Preface.

CHAPTER ELEVEN

All Churches Closed

UNLESS there is freedom of religion it is useless to speak of any other form of freedom. This fact seemed hard for people to understand even though freedom of religion had been professed for three hundred years and was written into the nation's Constitution.

Forty-seven years had gone since 1880 when the Massachusetts legislature denied the attempts of Mrs. Eddy's enemies to put a stop to her work of healing—yet, in 1927, there remained five states in which it was a crime to treat the sick through prayer. These five were Alabama, Maryland, Ohio, Texas, and West Virginia, and twenty-three more years passed before Ohio—last of the five—revised its medical laws to provide freedom of religion within its borders. The year of revision was 1950.

Meanwhile, in 1927, legislatures in the Union of South Africa and the Province of Quebec rejected proposals which confused the practice of Christian Science with the practice of medicine. Also, in 1927, the states of Indiana, Minnesota, Missouri, and Rhode Island enacted legislation protecting Mrs. Eddy's teachings.

There was further illumination when, in 1929, a bill was passed by the Congress of the United States to regulate the practice of healing in the District of Columbia. As enacted, the bill provided for examining and licensing persons engaged in the practice of "drugless healing ... but this Act shall not be construed to apply to . . . persons treating human ailments by prayer or spiritual means [provided] the laws and regulations relating to communicable diseases and sanitation are not violated."

The bill, including its important provision, was introduced by a medical doctor. He was United States Senator Royal S. Copeland, of New York.

At the annual meeting of the members of The Mother Church in 1929, the Committee on Publication reported:

"During the past year nearly every legislative body where Christian Science is represented has held either an annual or a biennial session. Consequently, the Committees on Publication have had to examine many bills for the purpose of maintaining freedom in relation to health and religion.

"In most instances, however, the provisions calling for amendment or opposition were not intended to restrict the rights of Christian Scientists and were amended in an agreeable way. For instance, in Arkansas, 'Christian Scientists, practicing within the limits of their calling,' were exempted from a general requirement that persons practicing 'the healing art' should pass an examination in anatomy, physiology, chemistry, bacteriology, and pathology.

"Thus Arkansas has become one of the more than forty states which has made provision for the practice of Christian Science, either explicitly, or in general terms, when enacting requirements for the practice of material methods.

"For the purpose of making Christian Science better known to the public, The Christian Science Board of Directors has authorized the Committee on Publication to furnish newspapers notices of our Sunday services containing excerpts from the Lesson-Sermon. Each notice or report includes a quotation of moderate length from the Bible and a brief quotation from our textbook chosen correlatively from the Lesson-Sermon for that week. These notices are now accepted by many newspapers in countries where English is spoken and the demand is increasing rapidly."

In 1930, eighty-two churches and societies were added to the list of branches of The Mother Church. Fifty of the branches were in the United States, four were in Canada, twenty-one were in Europe, two were in Africa, and five were in Australasia. Altogether, there were 2,451 branches, along with thirty-nine college organizations, five of which were admitted in 1930.

In the late nineteen-twenties and nineteen-thirties, a new church or society was being formed every four or five days. In 1931, among the 2,519 branch churches and societies, and forty college and university organizations, was the first branch church in Poland. In 1932, the first branches of The Mother Church were formed in Greece, in Belgium, and in Czechoslovakia; and, in 1933, in Nairobi, in the British crown colony of Kenya in East Africa, a new branch was founded 2,000 miles away from the nearest Church of Christ, Scientist.

In Cairo was another church, the first in Egypt; there were two branches in Brazil, and five additional branches in Australasia. In 1933, there were 2,639 branch churches and societies, forty-seven college and university organizations and, devoting full time to the healing work of Christian Science, were 10,747 practitioners and 505 nurses.

This was growth that recalled to the Directors a letter signed by one of Mrs. Eddy's secretaries, which was sent to the congregation of the Second Church of Christ, Scientist, in Manchester, England. The letter was published in the *Sentinel,* February 10, 1910, and it read:

Your letter of recent date addressed to Mrs. Eddy has been received and read with interest. On behalf of our Leader, permit me to express to you her loving appreciation for your assurances of loyalty and gratitude, and further to inform you of her pleasure in learning that you have established a new branch in the vineyard whereon is to grow the fruits of healing and regeneration. Second Church of Christ, Scientist, of Manchester, thus starting as the second outgrowth of multiplication and not division, is moving forward in accord with the "eternal mandate of Mind." [1]

The first college organization was formed at Harvard University in March, 1904, although there had been informal meetings among the students since 1898.

Mrs. Eddy's interest in youth was deep and abiding. One of her last writings for public print was an article entitled *Youth and Young Manhood*. It appeared in the *Cosmopolitan Magazine* in November, 1907. In it she said:

> King David, the Hebrew bard sang, "I have been young and now I am old; yet I have not seen the righteous forsaken, nor his seed begging food."
> I for one accept his wise deduction, his ultimate or spiritual sense of thinking, feeling and acting, and its reward. This sense of rightness acquired by experience and wisdom, should be early presented to youth and to manhood in order to forewarn and forearm humanity. [2]

Almost two years before, on December 28, 1905, in writing of *Christmas for the Children,* she said, "Too much cannot be done towards guiding well the germinating and inclining thought of childhood," [3] and she provided for the protection of college organizations in the *Church Manual:*

[1] *Science and Health*, p. 520.
[2] *Miscellany*, p. 273.
[3] *Miscellany*, p. 261.

Privilege of Members. Sect. 8. Members in good standing with The Mother Church, who are members of the faculty, instructors, or students in any university or college, can form and conduct a Christian Science organization at such university or college, provided its rules so permit. All members in good standing with The Mother Church, who are graduates of said university or college, may become members of the organization by application to, and by the unanimous vote of, the active members present, if the rules of the university or college so permit. When called for, a member of the Board of Lectureship may lecture for such university or college organization.

[Article XXIII, Section 8.]

This By-law, which first appeared in the *Manual* in 1904, brought questions:

"Could college organizations have, as members, Christian Scientists who are not members of The Mother Church?" The answer was given by The Board of Directors. Substantially, it stated that while organizers, and officers, must be members of The Mother Church in good standing with The Mother Church, each organization could have in its membership others who are Christian Scientists, but not members of The Mother Church.

"Could graduates who continued their active support and encouragement of college organizations be considered 'active members'?" The answer was "no"; and it was explained that "active members" are students, members of the faculty, or instructors of the university or college.

A third question came from individuals who became Christian Scientists, and members of The Mother Church, after graduation. They inquired if they could be admitted to membership in the organizations of their alma mater. The answer was "yes," but first they had to be elected "by the unanimous vote of the active members present, if the rules of the university or college permit."

As organizations, these groups belong to The Mother Church and may look to the Directors for counsel and information, but they have a different status from branch churches and societies. Their services are open to the college public only but, on occasions, invited guests may attend meetings. They also differ from branch churches and societies in that their members are not required to withdraw from their respective branch churches, or societies, in order to be members of the college organizations.

In 1931, at a world conference of Workers for the Blind called by President Hoover and attended by delegates from thirty-seven nations, it was disclosed that the Christian Science church led all churches in the publication of religious literature printed in Braille. In this same year in England, and with only three dissenting votes in more than two hundred, the Lower House of the Convocation of Canterbury of the Church of England adopted a resolution designed to advance spiritual healing.

With the Bible, *Science and Health* was listed in the catalogue of one of the large mail-order establishments; *Retrospection and Introspection* was published in the French, Swedish, and Norwegian languages; the Lord's Prayer with its spiritual interpretation was published in Danish, Dutch, Norwegian, and Swedish; also published was a revised *Hymnal,* the total printing being 565,000 copies; the average circulation of the periodicals for the six months ending March 28, 1933, was: *Monitor,* 129,260; *Sentinel,* 170,784;

Journal, 113,342; German *Herold,* 29,176; French *Héraut,* 14,577; Braille *Herald,* 526; Scandinavian *Herald,* 5,347; Dutch *Herald,* 3,130.

The *Monitor* was being mailed to subscribers in nearly every country in the world, even to islands in the Pacific where, excepting for three boats a year, there was no outside communication . . . in 1934, workers in Christian Science began regular visits to CCC (Civilian Conservation Corps) camps; in the *Sentinel,* August 11, it was reported that young men who were interested in Christian Science "were strengthened, and others heard some new [to them] and usable truths" . . . in 1935, The First Church of Christ, Scientist, in Shanghai, was dedicated, and in its overflowing Sunday School were classes made up of American, British, Chinese, German, and Russian children.

At the annual meeting in June, 1937, the Committee on Publication reported: "Our legislative work has afforded us the outstanding experience of the year. We are glad to report that public thought, which is reflected in legislative bodies, has become sufficiently free from prejudice so that Committees have been able to prevent the passage of many measures which would have restricted the rights of Christian Scientists."

In Germany, the growth of the movement was receiving the watchful attention of Hitler. The growing circulation of the German *Herold* was watched; so was the growing number of churches; so were the crowded services. The experience of the two Churches of Christ, Scientist, in Dresden, was not uncommon. So many were the people who were turned away from Sunday and Wednesday services that it was necessary to form a third church.

Yet, in spite of the crowded churches, an ancient evil was returning to Europe. Ruled by greed and sustained by hate, a system of force was openly speaking of mastery of the peoples of the world. Religious persecution was being revived. Alert to the deception that identifies war only with guns, the Directors, at the annual meeting of The Mother Church in June, 1938, reminded the dictators of the world "that no state can long endure without the spiritual influence of the Christian Churches."

And said further:

"As students of Christian Science we have a definite responsibility in respect to the upholding of such fundamental issues of life as the cultivation of goodwill and the preservation of a system of government which protects the civil rights of its people, and ensures to them freedom of speech, of the press, and of religious worship.

"This special responsibility is imposed upon us primarily because we know that the divine qualities of thought which constitute realities in life, righteousness in government, and unity among men, are not something to be denied or bestowed by the will of man, but belong alike to all. They emanate from infinite Principle, and are as universal in their operation, and as permanent in their character as Principle itself.

"We also know, and are daily demonstrating, that the obstructive forces which would deprive man of a free and full enjoyment of these blessings are unreal in their nature and powerless in their effect. They are, as Isaiah tells us, nothing, and 'a thing of nought.' In reality, they belong to nobody and operate nowhere.

"Understanding this, it manifestly becomes our duty to apply what we know to the betterment of world conditions, prayerfully and with love for God and man, and do it with the same diligence and consistency which we commonly employ in working out a solution of personal problems.

Individuals, like nations, however, are prone to become so engrossed in purely personal or local affairs that they take little or no account of conditions which they believe do not concern their immediate welfare.

"While we should not magnify error, or become unduly alarmed by the present-day suggestions of war and disaster aggressively presented through many channels, we must be keenly alert not to allow a false sense of security to lull us to sleep and make us indifferent to situations of national and international character which, unless corrected, are destined to affect our interests as directly as if the scene of their action were within the bounds of our own community.

"The rousing words of our Leader on page 177 of *Miscellaneous Writings* are particularly fitting at this time. She says: 'Never was there a more solemn and imperious call than God makes to us all, right here, for fervent devotion and an absolute consecration to the greatest and holiest of all causes.' And she adds: 'Will you give yourselves wholly and irrevocably to the great work of establishing the truth, the gospel, and the Science which are necessary to the salvation of the world from error, sin, disease, and death? Answer at once and practically, and answer aright!' "

Before 1939 was over, the world was being told that a few tons of steel was the prophet of a new order. Again, jungle ideas were roaming the world, this time adding the savagery and the corruption of communism to the brutality of war.

Fuming up from the caldron of atheism, communism began spewing over Europe before the end of World War I. Wholly materialistic in their purposes, the ringleaders of communism set forth to take God from the thoughts of men.

Dimly, they must have realized that churches are important only as they speak of God, and mankind is important only as it reflects Him. Early, these ringleaders testified to their fear of God by killing priests and burning churches, and, as the first step leading to the loss of spiritual values in other lands, they began sending saboteurs into other lands to turn pulpits into political forums and men into mechanisms.

In Italy, on March 23, 1919, Benito Mussolini began marching his recruits, and on October 28, 1932, he took over control of Italy. Caught between the materialistic forces of communism and fascism, Italy embraced fascism.

Adolf Hitler and Erich Ludendorff joined in a beer putsch in Munich on March 9, 1923. The putsch was not immediately successful, but was the birth of nazism. Ludendorff was arrested and paroled. Hitler was arrested, and sentenced to prison for five years. Through political influence, the sentence was shortened, but, while he was in prison, in Landsberg, he wrote *Mein Kampf,* the guidebook of the Nazis. Hitler came into power in Germany on January 30, 1933. Shortly thereafter, he abolished freedom of speech, and made equality before the law the exclusive possession of Aryans, or Germans of "pure" Nordic strain.

Already, Hitler had rejected the perfection of God for the distinctions of ethnology.

Because of the high rate of currency exchange, as well as the growing poverty in the countries of Central Europe, The Christian Science Board of Directors assumed in large part, and for several years after World War I, the cost of supplying Christian Science literature to Christian Scientists in Germany, Austria, Latvia, Esthonia, Finland, Poland, Russia, and other countries. Wishing to pay something for the literature, followers of Mrs. Eddy in these countries began reimbursing the War Relief Fund until, in the *Sentinel,* May 19, 1923, it was announced:

The Mother Church now has a credit to the War Relief Fund in the Deutsche Bank, in Berlin, of a considerable number of German marks representing these payments from the churches and societies in Germany, a sum which, while not of much value in the money of certain other countries, yet expresses much sacrifice on the part of the depositors.

Continuing, the Directors told of how

The Trustees under the Will of Mary Baker Eddy sent, without charge to the branches of The Mother Church in Germany, one thousand copies of the English-German Christian Science textbook; and The Christian Science Publishing Society has been able through the generosity of subscribers to *Der Herold* and *Le Héraut* [the German and French *Heralds*], also of contributions to the free fund, so called, to send free subscriptions for Christian Science literature to those in Europe who might not otherwise be able to have these aids to their study of Christian Science.

The War Relief Fund has supplied, largely and at specified rates, approximately ten thousand copies of the textbook and three thousand copies of other writings of Mrs. Eddy, also about four thousand subscriptions to the periodicals and more than fifteen thousand other pieces of literature, exclusive of *Quarterlies*. The larger part of this has gone to Germany. Literature has also gone to Austria, Hungary, Jugo-Slavia, Latvia, Czechoslovakia, Finland, Esthonia, Russia, Roumania and the Ukraine.

It has now become necessary to withdraw the offer to supply literature to Germany at the rate of one thousand marks to the dollar, because the balance in the War Relief Fund reserved for this purpose is nearly exhausted. The demand for literature, especially in Germany, is very great, many of the Reading Rooms having had lists of individuals awaiting their turn to be supplied with the textbook.

Some Reading Rooms advise that no sooner is a shipment of books received than their shelves are nearly depleted, so eager are the seekers for Truth to own the textbook of Christian Science. In consequence, they have discontinued keeping such lists because of the lack of books to meet the demand.

Having become aware of this demand for our literature and the difficulty in obtaining it, some individual Christian Scientists and some churches have requested the Directors to be allowed to help in continuing to supply the need. The Directors have accordingly authorized the Treasurer of The Mother Church to receive special gifts for the purpose. Such funds as may be received by the Treasurer, designated to be used to supply literature to the Central European countries, will be expended by the Board at such stated rates in the currency of the recipients as from time to time may seem reasonable and right, also to supply the literature free of charge in such cases as circumstances may warrant.

It is probable that by far the greater amount contributed will be applied to the needs of Germany where the Scientists are most numerous and the need is greatest. Any balance of funds remaining on hand after the necessity for which this fund is established has passed will be placed by the Directors in such other church as seems at the time best to meet a particular need.

Growth continued, although economic conditions were difficult in Germany. There were but five churches, three societies, and thirty practitioners in Germany when World War I began; there were thirty branch churches, thirty societies, one hundred and five practitioners, and one Christian Science nurse in Germany when Hitler came into power in January, 1933.

It was not long before Hitler put a stop to the sending of literature to Christian Scientists in Germany. This stop-order was issued in 1936, but in the summer of 1935 sums owed the Publishing Society were frozen in German banks, and members of The Mother Church living in Germany were prohibited from paying the small per capita tax, as stipulated in the *Church Manual*.[4]

[4] Every member of The Mother Church shall pay annually a per capita tax of not less than one dollar, which shall be forwarded each year to the Church Treasurer. (Article VIII, Sect. 13. *Church Manual*.)

Hoping to obtain a relaxation of the order, Clifford P. Smith went to Germany in September, 1935. He was partly successful. After much negotiation, the details of a new arrangement were announced by The Christian Science Board of Directors in the *Sentinel* on September 12, 1936:

The only arrangement now approved by the German Government for sending Christian Science literature to Germany is one by which The Mother Church, The Trustees under the Will of Mary Baker Eddy, and The Christian Science Publishing Society can send literature to branch churches and societies which are recognized as such. Therefore, branch churches, branch societies, and individual Scientists in all other countries are advised not to send any Christian Science literature to Germany, either to branches of The Mother Church, to groups of students, or to individual Christian Scientists.

The literature sent to the branches of The Mother Church in Germany is donated to them, but they can sell it to their members, or to other Christian Scientists, and put equivalent amounts in their respective literature funds, which must be expended in Germany for purposes connected with Christian Science.

Christian Science congregations continued to grow. On December 18, 1937, the Directors opened "A Literature for Germany Fund," and invited contributions in money as well as in English-German literature. At the same time, the Directors were not unaware of the hostility that was crowding closer to the movement—and, at the annual meeting of The Mother Church in 1938, they made it the subject of an encompassing statement.

Speaking of the healing ministry of Christian Science, the Directors emphasized "that life . . . is not a physical thing, to be destroyed by sin, disease and death, but is a condition of thought to be corrected and transformed"—and stressed that this healing ministry "indicates the day is approaching when responsible heads of governments will see that undue reliance upon material means and methods to accomplish their ends inevitably results in failure and defeat."

They urged the responsible heads of all governments to "realize that no nation is stronger than the moral fibre of its people, and that a nation can become truly great and permanently secure only to the extent that spiritual qualities are cultivated in the thoughts of its citizens and permitted freely to operate in the government of their lives."

To these were added other words intended for the eyes and thought of all who seek through programs of human degradation to be masters of mankind: "The history of the past teaches that nations whose governments have been conceived largely in self ambition and brought forth by human force are literally 'of few days, and full of trouble.' As expressions of economic and political systems they were essentially as fleeting and unsound as the mentalities which gave them birth. Nothing remains of them but the briefest possible records of material achievements, and their apparent greatness is little more than a passing shadow on the dial of time.

"In spite of the material tendencies of the past, there were always a few who courageously stood for the development in national life of individual initiative, integrity, and high moral standards. In much the same way there are thoughtful men and women today who are concerned when the state undertakes to subordinate religious interests to social and economic expedience. . . .

"Such men and women are the hope of the race, the bulwark and inspiration of every nation. Without them civilization would perish and freedom of thought and action would disappear from human experience. These courageous individuals, strengthened by the truth that frees, stifle aggression, preserve peace and freedom, and promote the brotherhood of man. They represent the type of thought which in some degree has been touched by an understanding of spiritual truth, and among them will be found Christian Scientists."

Events came swiftly after the signing of a non-aggression pact by Hitler and Stalin in August, 1939. Before September was over, Poland was crushed, and divided between the two dictators. Europe was deep in war. In Warsaw, a Christian Science society was denied permission to identify itself in the *Christian Science Journal;* in 1940, a society in Lódź was suppressed, and its meeting place turned into a mess hall for Nazi police.

Then came Monday, June 9, 1941.

In Germany and in Austria, every Christian Science church, every Christian Science society, every Christian Science reading room, and every Christian Science practitioner's office was closed; all records and all files in all offices, all churches, all societies, and all reading rooms were seized; all funds and all literature were confiscated; every known Christian Scientist was arrested.

Every known Christian Scientist was questioned in minute detail. There were queries concerning personal matters, queries as to how long the individual had been a Christian Scientist, whether he became one of his own choosing, or whether he had been coerced; and, if coerced, by whom. There were many questions regarding Christian Science treatment, and practitioners were ordered to give the names and addresses of all persons treated, and of all persons healed. There were questions as to the individual's sympathies toward Hitler, toward nazism; whether the individual was, or had been, a member of the Nazi party.

On July 14, 1941, Hitler published an edict making permanent the action of the previous month. This edict was served on all church officials of all Christian Science churches in Germany, as it was served on Friedrich Stender, in Hamburg:

> Secret Government Police
> Government Police Headquarters
> of Hamburg
> Stadthausbrücke 8

File No. II B I — 3703/41
Herr Friedrich Stender as President of
First Church of Christ, Scientist,
Hamburg
Alsterdorferstrasse 100, Hamburg

Der Herr Reichsminister des Innern [Minister of the Interior] has, through the edict of July 14, 1941, by reason of Section I of the regulation of the Reichspräsident [Chancellor] for the protection of the people and state dated February 28, 1933, dissolved and banned the sect "Christliche Wissenschaft" [Christian Science], becoming effective at once for the entire Reich. Its property is confiscated.

Referring to the penalties of Section 4 of the above-mentioned regulation, all activity is forbidden which attempts to continue this organization or to establish it anew with the same or similar aims.

Also the Minister of the Interior, according to the law of July 14, 1933, regarding the confiscation of property inimical to people and state, has found the endeavors of the above-named organization in Germany to be hostile to the people and state.

> by (signed) Göttsche.

(Official Seal)
Secret Government Police,
Government Police Headquarters
   of Hamburg.

In Germany, a program of dishonor was under way. Christian Scientists joined the Jews and political prisoners in the concentration camps. Other Christian Scientists were jailed. Others, after receiving warnings, were permitted to return to their homes.

Needing to grow quiet again in the companionship of the truth, members of the eighty-five churches and societies in Germany, nine of which were in Berlin, found within themselves resources that were there right along.

Meeting places were locked and guarded by the police, but there were services wherever two or three might meet, for they were mindful of Jesus' words, "Where two or three are gathered together in my name, there am I in the midst of them." Practitioners' offices, 113 altogether, were locked, and healing was prohibited, but there was healing because there were ways to speak to the sick and distressed that materialism could not understand.

For weeks a family in Berlin risked its freedom trying, by short wave, to hear the services of The Mother Church. One night the voice of the First Reader announcing Silent Prayer came to the family—faintly, but clearly; in silence, the family joined its prayers with the prayers of the vast congregation listening in lands far beyond Boston, and with the prayers of the thousands who were within The Mother Church itself; joined their voices in repeating The Lord's Prayer; listened to the reading of the Lesson-Sermon; heard the singing of the closing hymn; listened to the benediction —and shut off their muffled radio trusting no hostile ears had heard the forbidden message.

Taunted and threatened, Christian Scientists were ordered to deny their religion; refusing, they were jailed. Bibles were buried, and buried with them were copies of *Science and Health,* the *Church Manual,* the *Quarterly,* the *Hymnal,* all to be taken from their hiding places in back-yard gardens or open fields and studied again, after nightfall, with a concentration camp the penalty, if caught; and some were caught. It was the determination of the police to wipe Mrs. Eddy's teachings off the face of Germany; and they said so, in these words: "It is the spirit of your movement we want to destroy."

In Denmark, Norway, Holland, Belgium, France, Italy, and the other European countries that were overrun, the discipline was not so strict—at first; nor were the penalties so severe—at first. Not all churches were closed, not all practitioners' offices were locked,[5] although, on occasions, there were arrests and jail sentences; on other occasions, Christian Scientists were seized and drafted into German labor battalions.

But the edict of July 14, 1941, did not keep the literature out of Germany or out of the occupied countries. Friendly hands carried the *Quarterlies* into Germany and into the occupied countries. To illustrate, in Munich, two practitioners received *Quarterlies* at regular intervals. They made typewritten copies and distributed these to more than a hundred and fifty Christian Scientists in Germany. In turn, more than a hundred and fifty Christian Scientists made a second distribution. Many hands in many countries copied and distributed current *Quarterlies*.

The *Quarterlies* were sent to the Munich practitioners by two German soldiers stationed in Paris. The soldiers were Christian Scientists. They received the *Quarterlies* from sources in Switzerland.

[5] Denmark: churches 1, practitioners 9; Norway: churches 1, societies 1, practitioners 4; Holland: churches 2, societies 7, practitioners 27; Belgium: societies 2, practitioners 6; France: churches 5, societies 2, practitioners 38; Italy: churches 1, practitioners 2; Finland: practitioners 1; Esthonia: societies 1; Greece: societies 1; Latvia: churches 1; Roumania: societies 3, practitioners 3.

Before 1943 was over, churches, societies, and practitioners' offices in the occupied countries were closed, and all Christian Science literature was ordered seized. In The Hague, the home of a Christian Science teacher was invaded, and the teacher was threatened with imprisonment if she persisted in practicing her religion.

"You can't put me in prison," she said.

"You will learn that I can," returned the stranger, who was the chief of the German secret police in the Netherlands. "I have confiscated all your books, and I am warning you against practicing Christian Science."

"You can't stop me praying."

"Pray all you want to, but don't do anything else."

Nodding her assent, the teacher smiled, "That is all we ever do."

Encouraged by Hitler's agents, the Japanese government struck at Christianity in Japan on October 17, 1940, ordering a general acknowledgment of the Japanese emperor as God. Advised beforehand of the decree, Christian Science societies in Japan (there were two: one in Tokyo, one in Yokohama) dissolved as organizations but continued to meet and hold services in private homes.

Soon after the attack on Pearl Harbor on December 7, 1941, the edifice of First Church of Christ, Scientist, in Shanghai, was seized, and its Sunday School room used as an ammunition dump. In Hongkong, Tientsin, the Dutch East Indies, Malaya, and other far eastern countries, Christian Scientists were dispossessed of their meeting places and their church buildings.

At Singapore, church dedication services were in progress as Japanese troops began the attack on the city; in the Philippines, literature was hidden, and hidden with it were chairs, and desks, and benches, and organs—sometimes just in time to escape capture.

In time, the war was ended; but before it was ended, the impossible ideal a few thought fragile was sheltering a multitude. Among the sheltered were truants who now knew that to doubt God is to have faith in evil.

CHAPTER TWELVE

Expansion and Extension

O N December 14, 1939, the Directors appointed the Christian Science Wartime Committees of The Mother Church in the United Kingdom, Canada, and France.[1] Because the United States was not a belligerent, it was necessary to work within the terms of neutrality in the shipment of relief supplies to some of the warring nations.

To do this, The Mother Church, on April 13, 1940, became a registered voluntary relief agency, through which its branch churches and societies in the United States could channel the export of clothing, food, and supplies made in their workrooms or collected by their committees. On June 3, 1940, *The Christian Science Monitor* announced the opening of the War Relief Fund, saying, "The Christian Science Board of Directors expects to extend this relief to other countries when and as the way opens."

Once again events were to prove Mrs. Eddy's teaching that kindness survives all its enemies.

On May 10, 1941, the *Sentinel* reported the setting up of Christian Science War Relief Shipping Depots in Portland, Oregon, and New York City. Two weeks later a third depot

---

[1] The Committee consisted of three members: Lieutenant Colonel Robert Ellis Key, District Manager of Committees on Publication for Great Britain and Ireland; John Sidney Braithwaite, and Miss Dora Cooper. In 1945, following the resignation of Colonel Key, all British activities were merged and placed under the direction of Major General Spencer E. Holland.

was opened in Los Angeles, California, and the work of the three installations was synchronized with the work of the branch churches in their areas and with the original shipping depot in Boston. Each depot was equipped to make shipments directly overseas but in the early months, for the most part, shipments to the United Kingdom were channeled through branches of the British War Relief Society.

But, before this, it had begun to be clear that the United States would be an active participant. Factories were crowded with war work; industrial facilities were being greatly expanded; millions of young Americans were in military training.

To meet the needs of the increasing numbers of Christian Scientists in uniform,[2] the Directors, on March 27, 1941, appointed William L. Hodges as the first Wartime Minister.[3] He was sent to Camp Edwards, Massachusetts. Here he found no welcome. In Army tables of organization there were provisions for Protestant, Roman Catholic, and Jewish chaplains, but there was no provision for a Christian Science Wartime Minister who was a civilian.

Hodges appealed to the commanding officer at Camp Edwards for permission to assume the duties of a camp Wartime Minister but, pending authority from Washington, the commanding officer could do nothing.

As he was preparing to leave for Boston to make a report to the Directors, Hodges called on the chaplains and asked a few questions:

"Am I correct in my understanding that this camp furnishes a Roman Catholic priest who is commissioned by the

[2] Christian Scientists numbering 101,167 were in uniform in the armed forces of the United States in World War II.

[3] Wartime Ministers kept their civilian status. Only chaplains were part of the Armed Services.

Army to serve the spiritual needs of the Roman Catholic boys in the camp?"

The answer was in the affirmative.

"And is there a Jewish rabbi who is a commissioned officer, a chaplain, who will minister to the spiritual needs of the Jewish boys?"

The answer was, "Yes."

"And is there a chaplain of the Protestant faith to minister to the needs of the Protestant boys?"

He was informed that this was correct.

"Then," asked the Wartime Minister, "which one of these is equipped to give a Christian Science treatment to a Christian Science boy, should such a request be made?" [4]

Soon after the entrance of the United States into the war, there were chaplains' schools and in them were Christian Scientists. Before the surrender of Japan on August 14, 1945, there were 214 Christian Science ministers serving Christian Scientists in the armed forces of the United States, and twenty-six Christian Science chaplains. Serving Christian Scientists in the armed forces of the British Empire were thirty Christian Science Officiating Ministers and eight Authorized Workers. Under British law, Christian Scientists could not serve as chaplains because they were not ordained clergymen, hence the title "Christian Science Officiating Minister." Also, because Church of England law denied to women the appellation of "minister," it was necessary to confer on women workers the title "Authorized Workers." Throughout the war, the cost of the British Christian Science ministry was met by The Mother Church.

With the United States at war, the Army Chaplains' School was opened in August, 1942, at Harvard University.

[4] *The Story of Christian Science Wartime Activities, 1939-46.* (Boston: The Christian Science Publishing Society, copyright, 1947.)

After a year the school was transferred to Fort Devens, Massachusetts, and thence to Fort Oglethorpe, Georgia. The Navy Chaplains' School was located at Williamsburg, Virginia.

Candidates for chaplains' commissions included Protestant clergymen, Jewish rabbis, Roman Catholic priests, Mormons, Christian Scientists, and representatives of the Salvation Army. The first Wartime Minister assigned to serve the Army Chaplains' School was Charles C. Paul. He was succeeded by Mrs. Emily Hart Walker. The first Wartime Minister assigned to serve the Navy Chaplains' School was W. Marlborough Addison.

Required of all candidates, when the war began, was that they be graduates of an accredited college or university, and possess the degree of bachelor of theology. Informed of the absence of ordained ministers in the Christian Science Church the Army Chief of Chaplains waived the requirement of a degree in theology, but held to all other requirements. Requirements in the Navy were similar.

As always with chaplains, experiences were many:

Ammunition boxes piled together and swathed with white mattress cloth made an altar, and wrapped in white gauze supplied by medical men was a wooden cross; and all, the altar, the cross, and the improvised lectern covered, too, with white mattress cloth, were emphasized against a background of palm leaves gathered that night; inside the rough-hewn chapel, candles shed their gentle light on the faces of soldiers listening—it was Christmas Eve, in North Africa. . . .

Locating soldiers for whom there were special messages; and there were more than six thousand of these . . . the healing of the badly wounded face of a lieutenant, and the request of an Army nurse, who witnessed the healing, for help, for herself, her own healing of rheumatic fever, and the request of the attending Army doctor for help, for himself. . . .

The response of a British captain in the China-Burma-India theater to a letter from The Mother Church regarding his application for membership:

"Your query concerning the length of time [I have] been a regular attendant at the 'local church,' if you will forgive me caused a smile—one week our 'local church' might be a jeep in a jungle clearing, next week a bamboo basha [small hut]. Another Sunday under a tree in a native village, on top of a mountain range, in a clearing of elephant grass, or in a bombed-out Methodist chapel in a little Burmese town. . . ."

Forty-six of ninety-six German prisoners-of-war in a Kansas hospital asked the Volunteer Worker to leave three Bibles, three German translations of *Science and Health,* and three *Quarterlies.* They said they had heard about Christian Science in the places where they lived in Germany, and now wanted to take up its study. Not long afterwards they were discharged from the hospital. They continued their studies in a prisoner-of-war camp. . . .

"It was at the close of a hot day at the top of a high hill," wrote a soldier from New Guinea, "where a cool breeze was beginning to blow. The service was in the Officers' mess of the 5th Fighter Command. It was a brush hut, simply furnished with a few mess tables and forms. At the appointed time we quietly entered, sat down, and upon looking around, saw Americans and Australians, various ranks and uniforms, all different, yet all one. . . ."

Various ranks and uniforms, all different, yet all one—in New Guinea, and in hundreds of places all over the world because, above the guns, men and women

Hear at times a sentinel
Who moves about from place to place,
And whispers to the worlds of space,
In the deep night, that all is well.

In the years of war, daily from Boston went copies of *The Christian Science Monitor* for distribution in Army camps and Navy installations within the United States and overseas. During the peak months, the distribution totaled 22,275 daily copies. At its height, the weekly distribution of the *Sentinel* was 6,827 copies; of the *Journal,* 3,906 each month; of the *Herold* (German) 659 each month; and of the *Héraut* (French) 174 each month.

More than seven thousand library editions of the Bible and *Science and Health* were distributed; more than three hundred thousand pamphlets; more than seventeen thousand copies of Mrs. Eddy's writings, other than *Science and Health;* more than eighty thousand leaflets, and about fifty thousand vest-pocket editions of the Bible and *Science and Health.*

Thousands upon thousands of cases of clothing and hundreds of thousands of packages of food were shipped. Packets of used literature, each packet containing a copy of the *Sentinel,* the *Monitor,* and the weekly magazine section of the *Monitor* were sent biweekly to any person in the armed forces who made the request. The list of recipients grew from fifty to seventeen hundred.

There were many little things, and there were many big things. A woman in England wrote to The Mother Church asking that someone write to her son, a British soldier who was a German prisoner. It was the beginning of a correspondence with 155 prisoners-of-war in the same camp, the beginning of the sending of parcels to 217 British prisoners,

59 of whom were not Christian Scientists; the beginning of the 17,300 parcels that were sent to prison camps—and, thoughtfully, of another gift:

In the *Sentinel,* on September 30, 1944, it was announced that all World War I and World War II veterans who were in hospitals anywhere in the world could ask, and would receive, Christian Science treatment, at no charge.

In the east and in the west, the guns were silent. And in the stillness, men and women were beginning to see that a stronger force had moved in to occupy the place that once knew only violence, beginning to perceive that it is only when peoples and governments are solicited and seduced by materialism that they go to war against each other; in the stillness, beginning to understand that as in spirit all men are of one Father, so in geography are all nations knit together in a manner that makes impossible any doctrine of isolation.

In Germany, Christian Scientists were returning to their families from labor battalions, from concentration camps, from prisons. Prisoners-of-war were again in their home-lands. In Europe and in Asia, churches that had been closed were open, as the meeting place of the Christian Science society in Brussels was closed, then opened.

Under severe handling by the Gestapo, the president of the Brussels society had given information regarding the congregation, the finances, the literature, and the purposes of the society. With this information in its possession, the Gestapo held the president personally responsible for the continued inaction of the society. To protect the congregation, the president disassociated himself from the organization. The congregation continued to meet in secret and put together a building fund of 88,000 francs. When the

Gestapo was no longer in power, the Brussels society resumed services in the quarters that had been closed.

In China, Japan, the Philippines, the Netherlands, France, Italy, Poland, Czechoslovakia, and elsewhere, Committees on Publication were returning to their work; in each of the four military zones in Germany there was an assistant committee and in the eastern zone provisions were made for the restoration of forty-one branches of The Mother Church, along with a hundred and eleven informal study groups. In lands where, in the years of strife, there had been no call of church bells, congregations again were qualifying for recognition as churches and societies and individuals as practitioners that they might have their cards reinstated in *The Christian Science Journal.*[5]

With the war's close, a gift of seventeen tons of books and periodicals was made to the German churches. This shipment was followed by another gift of 10,000 German *Herolds* monthly, and 19,000 *Quarterlies*. Between September, 1947, and June, 1948, branch churches, societies, and individuals contributed $439,945 for the purchase by The Mother Church of 44,542 CARE food packages that were sent to branch churches and societies in Great Britain, France, Germany, Italy, the Netherlands, Greece, Belgium, Bulgaria, Czechoslovakia, Denmark, Finland, Austria, Norway, and Poland.

Rehabilitation work for returning servicemen was proceeding under the direction of the Manager of Camp Welfare Activities in cooperation with branch churches and societies. Recognized, in 1948, were sixty-six new branches

[5] In 1948, the cards of 80 churches and societies and of 104 practitioners from belligerent or conquered countries were published in the *Journal* that were not published in 1945. The cards of churches, societies, and practitioners in the Russian zone of Germany and in the Russian sector of Berlin are still omitted from the *Journal*.

of The Mother Church, twenty-five of which are in Europe, and thirteen new organizations in universities and colleges. In 1951, approximately two hundred and fifty Christian Scientists classified as displaced persons were arriving in, or were on their way to, the United States under the sponsorship of individual Christian Scientists in the United States.

In Los Angeles, thirty-nine branch churches and two societies participated in a joint lecture in the Hollywood Bowl, and 15,500 persons were in attendance. At the annual meeting in 1952, the Treasurer of The Mother Church reported the release of the per capita tax funds which were frozen in Great Britain, and stated in his report: "Far more important than the receipt of the money itself is the fact that this action was based upon an examination of Article VIII, Section 13, of our *Church Manual* by the Bank of England, and is a recognition on the part of the British Government of the right of members of The Mother Church residing in England to give financial support to The Mother Church in accordance with our *Manual.*"

During 1952, the Publishing Society distributed approximately a million Bibles, biographies, pamphlets, leaflets, phonograph records, and similar items in addition to its regular distribution of periodicals. A summerhouse near the pond at Pleasant View was completed and opened. In 1954, the facilities of the sanatoriums were used by 7,019 guests.

At the close of April 30, 1955, the yearly operating expenses of the two sanatoriums was $1,319,160. Of this amount, $574,780 was paid by guests. The balance of $744,380 was provided by bequests and gifts from church members and by The Mother Church.

Only a few years, less than five, had elapsed since August 6, 1945, when, in Hiroshima, a city of 343,969 persons, there were 78,150 dead, 37,425 injured, and 13,083 missing. The evil that had visited death and destruction upon a city in Japan, and that men called war, was reappearing. Once again, in its preoccupation with the make-up of the atom, humanity was forgetting that the force that plays the major part in world order is religion. In the summer of 1950, Korea was invaded by communist forces.

As in World War I and in World War II, there was an immediate need for more chaplains. The regulation of three years' seminary training before an applicant could qualify for a chaplain's commission, which was relaxed in World War II to permit the admission of Christian Scientists, was again in effect. Again the parochialism of the regulation was protested. Again the regulation was modified.

Under the modified ruling, which was made final, "A Christian Scientist who has served as a Reader for three years, or who has had his name listed as a practitioner in *The Christian Science Journal* for three years is eligible to apply, provided he is within the age limit, and has a college degree."

Before long, eighteen Christian Science chaplains were serving in Korea and Japan, responding as Christian Science practitioners, holding Christian Science services, and serving as Protestant chaplains. When the armistice was signed, nearly five hundred Christian Science workers were serving military personnel and hospitalized veterans, at home and overseas.

Mindful that there is a rock of eternal purpose, and knowing that hate can never move in the direction of the larger victory, these men and women served above the struggle.

The first Committee on Publication (then known as the Publication Committee) was formed by Mrs. Eddy through the Christian Scientist Association on February 4, 1885, and was disbanded on June 12, 1888, about one year before the Association was dissolved. This committee was the forerunner of the one established by Mrs. Eddy's By-law of December, 1898, which provided for a committee consisting of three members. They were Irving C. Tomlinson, Alfred Farlow, and Judge Septimus J. Hanna. In January, 1900, Mrs. Eddy changed the provision from three members to one member, Alfred Farlow.

This is the assignment that was given to the committee, as it is now constituted:

> It shall be the duty of the Committee on Publi-
> cation to correct in a Christian manner impositions
> on the public in regard to Christian Science, in-
> justices done Mrs. Eddy or members of this church
> by the daily press, by periodicals or circulated lit-
> erature of any sort.
> [*Church Manual,* Article XXXIII, Section 2.]

Having established the committee and its assignment through By-laws, both were put under the protection of the *Church Manual.* In forming the Committee on Publication Mrs. Eddy had no purpose other than the one stated. Knowing that her teachings were often misunderstood and, consequently, misrepresented, Mrs. Eddy, it seems clear, in establishing the Committee on Publication and making its central purpose one of dealing with misrepresentation, was making doubly sure that Christian Science should be known to the world for what it is—not for what it is not.

Certain that only the truth is permanent, she could not

have established the committee with any intention "to stifle and to mislead," as some critics contended. What the committee does is to provide facts and authentic information where needed and where acceptable. It never attempts to censor, and never attempts to prevent the circulation of material hostile to Christian Science.

There have been occasions—some, not many—when individual Christian Scientists have displayed more zeal than wisdom in their attempts to smother untruthful statements. However, this is not official policy and never has been. The official policy of the committee toward censorship and hostility was stated by the Board of Directors in the *Sentinel*, December 12, 1929, as follows: "An author and a publisher may have shown a lack of feeling, or even positive injustice, but as Christian Scientists we must observe the ethics of our religion in all relations, and in every situation."

Nor is there any record to show that Mrs. Eddy ever even tried "to stifle and to mislead" anyone. There is no reason why she should. There is nothing secret in her teachings. In them are no hidden meanings and no mysteries. They say only one thing, and they teach only one thing:

God is All-in-all.

For herself, and for her teachings, Mrs. Eddy asked of all people but one thing:

Think on God only in the deepest reason; act only in the sense of right.

More, probably, than any other religion, Christian Science depends upon the written word. In fact, it depends upon the written word to an extraordinary degree.

Mrs. Eddy used the written word to teach her first students, giving them handwritten manuscripts for study and return that she might question them. In her classes in the Massachusetts Metaphysical College, the only textbooks were the Bible and *Science and Health with Key to the Scriptures*. In Christian Science churches, the only preachers are the Bible and *Science and Health*. In Christian Science lectures, the words must be put into manuscript form, must correctly express Christian Science, and must be spoken as written. In giving Christian Science treatment, the practitioner searches the written word to gain the understanding of God that brings healing.

In an editorial in the June, 1932, issue of the *Journal*, Clifford P. Smith referred to this uncommon use of the written word, and pointed out that, because it is both a science and a religion, Christian Science requires the "careful and correct expression . . . most likely to be obtained in print," that, as a religion, it "depends on the written word for expansion in the thoughts of its adherents, and for extension to other peoples," that, as a science, the requirement of "careful and correct expression is imperative, not only for expansion and extension, but for protection and stability."

Mrs. Eddy knew about careful and correct expression, knew about it better than any of her followers. In *Retrospection and Introspection* (p. 61) she declared:

> Posterity will have the right to demand that Christian Science be stated and demonstrated in its godliness and grandeur,—that however little be taught or learned, that little be right.

Her insistence that rising generations "have the right to demand that Christian Science be stated and demonstrated" is consistent with her instructions to the Committee on Publication "to correct in a Christian manner impositions on the public in regard to Christian Science."

It has been nearly one hundred years since Mrs. Eddy

heard the first maledictions, and saw the first drawing aside, of those who were her neighbors.

Meanwhile, the nation has grown from thirty-six to forty-eight states, and from approximately thirty-five million persons to more than one hundred and sixty million. Frightened by guns, the world has become divided until about 40 per cent of its total population are under the immediate control of atheistic masters. From its discovery in an upper room in a home in Swampscott, Massachusetts, Christian Science has become more than three thousand branch churches and societies in all the continents of the world.

The antagonisms have subsided, but they have not disappeared. With an increasing population, an increasing number of branch churches and societies, and the steady expansion of the movement, the activities of the Committee on Publication have increased greatly, and in this increase again is seen the unchanging capacity of the *Church Manual* to do the work of The Mother Church.

To say the same thing in different words, the duties or functions, in the sense of the purpose or mission of the Committee on Publication, are completely set forth in the *Manual*. At no time has anything been added to this purpose or mission. All that has happened is the introduction of new means, new methods, and new mechanics for carrying out the central purposes that have existed from the beginning.

In the early nineteen-twenties, radio broadcasting was very new, and, although very new, its possibilities were under study in the office of the Committee on Publication. It was clear that the use of radio for the protection and furtherance of Christian Science was within the church By-laws, which were written a score of years before radio broadcasting was even speculated upon by physical scientists.

Alert to every advance in communication, Mrs. Eddy

would have made use of radio as she made use of written and spoken words in all their helpful forms in seeking wider, and better, understanding of her teachings. In the Deed of Trust executed by her on March 6, 1907, she provided "for the advancement of the cause of Christian Science as taught by me"; and in the *Church Manual* (Article I, Section 6), there is this By-law: "The business of The Mother Church shall be transacted by its Christian Science Board of Directors."

After much discussion, and with the approval of the Directors, the services of The Mother Church were broadcast. Following the broadcast, thought was given to the preparation of Christian Science programs, and, after a while, they were offered, mostly in the form of explanatory outlines.

In 1953, and in a step which followed closely Mrs. Eddy's provision for testimonies in Wednesday evening meetings, as well as in Christian Science periodicals, the Committee introduced a radio program which presented over the air first-person accounts of Christian Science healing. All testimonies were given voluntarily, and without remuneration to the testifier; but, of course, not until there was complete verification.

These programs are now heard over eight hundred radio stations in Canada, South Africa, New Zealand, the Philippines, Australia, British West Indies, Iceland, and the United States—in the main, wherever there is an English-speaking audience. The programs are prepared in the office of the Committee on Publication under the close supervision of the Board of Directors and are recorded on tape in the Committee studios on the ninth floor of the Publishing House in Boston.

Intentionally, the programs are patterned for listening by

non-Scientists; and, as stated by the Committee, they are programs that "are missionary, in that sense. We want to help mankind in our own way. At the same time, we hope to present to the public an accurate picture of what Christian Science is, and what it is not. In that sense, it is a public relations undertaking."

The step from radio into television was natural, but it was not taken quickly. There were many who said television was not a suitable vehicle for a Christian Science program, and, within the television industry, there were some who claimed that the rich tapestry of the Scriptures was too time-worn for today's use, that Holy Writ itself must needs be subject to constant change to attract a modern audience.

The pessimism was not accepted. After study and preparation, the Committee on Publication had a program idea which carried further the use of first-hand testifiers by enabling the audience to see the people who were healed. The main distinction between the radio and television format is that the television format presents two or more testifiers whose experiences are somewhat similar. That is, they complement each other. In both radio and television programs, the experiences themselves are accompanied by brief, simple explanations of Christian Science teachings.

To televise the programs, a sum of money was appropriated by the Directors, and it was planned to start with fifteen stations and to add enough stations so that by the end of the first year the total number would be forty-five.

Instead, before the year was four months old, the program was appearing on more than one hundred stations. So great was the public interest that nearly all the stations were using the program on a sustaining basis. In the rich tapestry of the Scriptures were the golden threads of life, of healing, of peace, and of plenty—and the pessimists were wrong, even as they were wrong when Mrs. Eddy began her teachings.

The Committee on Publication for The Mother Church is elected annually by The Christian Science Board of Directors, and the vote must be unanimous. Three other committees are elected by the Directors. One is the Committee for London, England, and the counties in which London is located; one is the Committee for Massachusetts; the third is the Committee for the District of Columbia. These three committees, as well as all other Committees on Publication, and their assistants, are under the supervision of the Committee on Publication for The Mother Church.

In countries where no branch churches have been established, the Committee on Publication for The Mother Church has the authority to appoint assistant committees; but where there are branches of The Mother Church, "the Readers of the three largest branch churches in each State of the United States and in Canada shall annually and alternately appoint a Committee on Publication to serve in their localities." (*Church Manual,* Article XXXIII, Section 3.)

There is an exception to this rule. As also stated in Article XXXIII, Section 2, of the *Church Manual,* "For the purposes of this By-law, the State of California shall be considered as though it were two States, the dividing line being the 36th parallel of latitude." In the counties of Great Britain, and Ireland (excepting the counties in which London is located) the local committees are appointed annually by the Readers of the three largest branch churches in the county, as in the states of the United States and the provinces of Canada. These committees are under the immediate supervision of the Committee on Publication in London.

In each branch of The Mother Church is an assistant committee nominated by the executive boards of branch churches and societies, with the appointment being made by the state committee. These assistants function as assistants to the state committee and do not function as officials in the branch churches themselves. Altogether, there are more than six thousand committees and their assistants.

Always thorough in the protection of her teachings and the manner of their presentation, Mrs. Eddy made it the duty of The Christian Science Board of Directors not only to appoint the Committee on Publication for The Mother Church and the committees in London, in Massachusetts, and in the District of Columbia, but placed upon them the responsibility of approval of all other committees.

Although Mrs. Eddy specifically charged the Committee on Publication with the duty of correcting "impositions on the public in regard to Christian Science," it was not her desire that the Committee should wait for the appearance of such impositions before acting. The work assigned to the Committee goes deeper than correcting false statements. It works to prevent them through education, such as the radio and television programs, through supplying speakers for non-Scientist groups, such as luncheon clubs, denominational churches, business organizations—provided a request is made.

The Committee on Publication has many activities, devoted to carrying out its basic mission, that were not in existence ten years ago, or twenty years ago, or forty years ago—all proving that Mrs. Eddy did not put her Church in a straitjacket when she established the *Manual* as the law of the Church.

The Committee prepares the Lesson-Sermon news items that are released to thousands of newspapers each week; it makes available for other publications reproductions of religious articles from the *Monitor;* it assists libraries in securing authorized and approved literature on Christian Science; when requested, it studies various problems for the Directors and reports its findings to them.

Of high importance is its work with legislatures in every land where there are branch churches and societies. Whether in Europe, or Asia, Australasia, Africa, or the countries of the Western Hemisphere, the committees keep in active touch with public officials in matters of legislation that affect both the Christian Scientist and the non-Scientist.

Securing recognition of the right to rely on God for healing is a signal contribution to the concept of human liberty as practiced in the United States. In securing this right, the Committee does not seek a special right for Christian Scientists, or the right of an individual to depend upon Christian Science for such healing.

In constitutional terms, what the Committee is asking is the fuller recognition of the right of an individual to turn to God for help, no matter what the difficulty. Often it is assumed that the right of freedom of religion means the right to attend the church of one's choosing, or the right to think as one pleases. This is not the position of the Christian Scientist. In Mrs. Eddy's teachings, the full right of an individual to turn to God for help includes the right to rely on God for healing, as taught in the Bible. In Mrs. Eddy's teachings, there is literal acceptance of the words of the Apostle James: "Be ye doers of the word, and not hearers only."

There is no favor-seeking in this effort to establish recognition of worship and individual conscience. It is an effort to deepen and strengthen the recognition of the God-given rights of freedom which belong to every individual, whatever his religion may be and wherever he may be.

These, then, are some of the present activities of the Committee on Publication. To a marked degree it, too, is work that finds expression in the written word, and, as with the radio and television programs, it is an effort with the single purpose of helping "mankind in our own way." This, too, is in the way of Mrs. Eddy's great wish.

CHAPTER THIRTEEN

Without Malice, without Guile

IN *The Christian Science Journal* of February, 1932, is told the story of a man who found his faith restored by visits to a church not his own.

It happened not long after Mrs. Eddy's passing in 1910. A woman was waiting on Huntington Avenue in Boston, and her eyes were drawn to the thoughtful expression on the face of a man who was standing and gazing at The Mother Church. Finally, the woman said: "That is a beautiful building."

For a full minute there was no acknowledgment of her words. Then, although the stranger did not turn his head, she heard him say, "I wonder if you know how beautiful it is."

"I think so," she replied, and added, "It is my church."

He turned, looked at her, and looked again at the church. "It isn't my church," he reflected, "but I knew Mrs. Eddy before the church was built. I knew her when she first came to Boston. She had nothing but her faith in prayer; but she had that, and she prayed. Her prayers were answered. They brought her the interest of people; and she taught them to pray."

Conscious of the pauses between his words, the woman could almost see him picking at his thoughts, choosing from among them: "After a while they needed a church. They had little money, but they had their prayers, and they built a church out of prayer. Pretty soon there were more Christian Scientists in Boston, and they needed a bigger church. Still they did not have much money, but they knew how to pray and the value of prayer, and soon these prayers built a larger church. That church, too, is built of prayer."

There came a longer pause; then he was saying: "I am not a Christian Scientist, but I believe in God, and always have. Sometimes my faith grows a little weak, and when my faith weakens, I come up here and look at these buildings prayer has built; and I go away, heartened."

The Mother Church, the smaller church, was built in 1894; the extension, the larger church, was built in 1906. The first of three sections of the quarters of The Christian Science Publishing Society was built in 1908; the second section was built in 1910. For the most part, these were the buildings the stranger saw on that day of remembering. There have been many changes since that day.

The third section of the quarters for the Publishing Society was built in 1914. Of the Publishing Society, it may be said it had its beginnings with the publication of *The Science of Man, by Which the Sick Are Healed*.[1] Written by hand, copyrighted in 1870, and containing such declarations as "Not death, but the understanding of Life, makes man immortal" (*Science and Health*, p. 485), it is the foreword and outline of all Christian Science literature.

In the thirty-eight years that separated the copyrighting of *The Science of Man, by Which the Sick Are Healed,* and the building of the first of three units for the Publishing Society, much was done. *Science and Health* was published

[1] In slightly different wording, *The Science of Man* was issued in pamphlet form in 1876, 1879, and 1883, after which the pamphlet was discontinued. In 1881, Mrs. Eddy incorporated the salient paragraphs of *The Science of Man*—in their original wording—into *Science and Health*. They are contained in the chapter titled "Recapitulation."

in 1875. In 1908, demand for the book was so great that Mrs. Eddy had discontinued numbering the editions, as we have seen. The last numbered editions were 417, in cloth binding, and 418, in leather binding.

On April 14, 1883, *The Christian Science Journal* made its appearance. From 1883 until 1908, the *Journal* had more than ten different publishing addresses, but instead of being an eight-page paper, published every other month and having a circulation of a few hundred, it contained, by the end of that period, more than one hundred pages, was published every month, and had a circulation of 38,000. In the years between 1887 and 1893, Mrs. Eddy wrote and published five books: *Unity of Good, Rudimental Divine Science, No and Yes, Retrospection and Introspection,* and *Christ and Christmas.*

In 1890, she introduced the *Christian Science Bible Lessons* (now the *Quarterly*). She published, in 1895, the *Church Manual,* and, also, in 1895, brought out *Pulpit and Press.* By itself, this was a large amount of writing. In addition, she was constantly revising *Science and Health,* watching over the *Journal,* building her church, and guiding a movement that was beginning to reach across the oceans.

In all this work she had little help. In writing, she had no outside help; in publishing, she had the fine help of John Wilson and William Dana Orcutt, of the University Press; but in the mailing of her books, there were frequent occasions when shipments were wrapped and addressed and mailed by her students and by herself from her home in Lynn, and later from the Massachusetts Metaphysical College.

Hoping to rid herself of the details of publishing, she appointed William G. Nixon as her book publisher in August, 1890. He gave small service. In January, 1893, Ebenezer J. Foster Eddy became publisher. He was no improvement over Nixon. In July, 1896, Mrs. Eddy replaced Foster Eddy with Joseph Armstrong. In this banker from Kansas, she found a publisher.[2]

In 1898, so extensive was the circulation of Christian Science literature, that Mrs. Eddy formed The Christian Science Publishing Society through a Deed of Trust, and, in the same year, founded the *Christian Science Sentinel*,[3] a weekly, which, in 1908, had a circulation of 66,000. In 1903, she established *Der Herold der Christian Science*, the first of her periodicals to be published in a language other than English. On November 25, 1908, which was the day before Thanksgiving, the first issue of *The Christian Science Monitor* was mailed to its subscribers.

In 1908, the Publishing Society had seventy-eight employees. The *Monitor* added appreciably to that number.

The thought of publishing a daily newspaper was not new with Mrs. Eddy. Before 1902, when she appointed Archibald McLellan to the editorship of the *Journal* and *Sentinel*, she wrote a letter in which she said: "Until I start a widespread press, we should have in Boston a born editor." She considered McLellan "a born editor" but, before giving him the responsibility of acting in that capacity on a daily news-

[2] Since 1890, there have been six Publishers and four Publishers' Agents of Mrs. Eddy's writings. In 1907, Allison V. Stewart succeeded Armstrong. In November, 1917, Stewart resigned to give all his time to his work as a member of The Christian Science Board of Directors. In 1918, The Christian Science Publishing Society became the Publisher. Since 1922, Mrs. Eddy's books have been published by the Trustees under the Will. The Publishers' Agents have been: Harry I. Hunt, Hudson C. Burr, Alfred Pittman, and Horace J. Carver.

[3] From September 1, 1898, the day of its appearance, until January 19, 1899, the *Sentinel* was known as the *Christian Science Weekly*. Believing the word "Weekly" did not identify the periodical as "a watcher for the Field," Mrs. Eddy changed it to *Sentinel*.

paper, she provided him with the opportunity of obtaining practical experience.

In 1908, when it became generally known that a newspaper was being planned with McLellan as its editor, many persons sought to dissuade Mrs. Eddy from taking on such an obligation at her age, then, of eighty-seven years. Failing, they tried to convince her that to use the words "Christian Science" in the name was to make success impossible for the newspaper. In his book, *Twelve Years with Mary Baker Eddy,* Irving C. Tomlinson told of the last minutes of attempted persuasion:

"The members of the household were on tiptoes, waiting outside the door of Mrs. Eddy's room, while the final decision was being made. The conference was brief. A moment or so, and the editor emerged. Said he, 'Mrs. Eddy is firm, and her answer is, "God gave me this name and it remains." ' "

What those who resisted did not understand was that, in the work of The Mother Church, the presence of a daily newspaper is quite as appropriate as the presence of the *Journal,* the *Sentinel,* or any other periodical. Although Discoverer and Founder of Christian Science, Mrs. Eddy was never under the handicap of familiarity with its friendship. She saw Christian Science as always new and sought, in its unfoldment, the further advances she believed to be always waiting.

In its first issue, Mrs. Eddy gave her reason for publishing the *Monitor,* and included her reason for publishing all her periodicals:

SOMETHING IN A NAME

I have given the name to all Christian Science periodicals. The first was *The Christian Science*

Journal, designed to put on record the divine Science of Truth; the second I entitled *Sentinel,* intended to hold guard over Truth, Life, and Love; the third, *Der Herold der Christian Science,* to proclaim the universal activity and availability of Truth; the next I named *Monitor,* to spread undivided the Science that operates unspent. The object of the *Monitor* is to injure no man, but to bless all mankind.[4]

"To spread undivided the Science that operates unspent" —"to injure no man, but to bless all mankind."

These are words of great significance. "To spread undivided the Science that operates unspent" is a call to mankind to recognize the fullness, the allness, and the availability of God's abundance; "to injure no man but to bless all mankind" is instruction to all who serve the *Monitor* to use its presses only as weapons of truth and equity.

In the years since, obedience to the instructions has brought the *Monitor* into high position among the great newspapers of the world. As a gatherer of news, and as a provider of news, its interests are in what is on the up side rather than in what is on the down side in the affairs of mankind.

This does not mean that it censors all news of crime or disaster. If the crime or disaster has social significance, it is reported, briefly, factually, and without luridness. World news is so well covered and so well presented that offers have been received from many newspapers urging its sale as a news service. Similar requests, although less numerous, have been made for the syndication of national and regional news services.

[4] *Miscellany,* p. 353.

The same respect for the reader that exists in the news columns is disclosed in the advertising columns. Here there is an absence of advertising of liquor, tobacco, patent medicines, hair restorers, undertakers, cemeteries, and loan sharks, as well as other commonly and vulgarly advertised goods and services.

More than thirty thousand advertisers, of whom twenty-five hundred are national, use the *Monitor*'s pages to sell their products. Six editions are printed daily. The Atlantic (four editions) serves Boston, New England, the eastern United States, Canada, and overseas countries; the Central serves the central states; and the Pacific edition serves the western states. In addition to basic regional news and advertising, the Boston and New England editions have special local news sections.

Circulationwise, the *Monitor* is far down the list among American newspapers. Sixty or seventy newspapers surpass it in circulation, but none surpass it in prestige. There are many illustrations of this prestige; and here is one that happened in World War II.

Among the tragedies of the war was the decision by the President of the United States to evacuate all persons of Japanese ancestry from the three states of California, Oregon, and Washington. In all, more than one hundred and ten thousand men, women, and children, most of them native-born Americans, were ordered from their homes and placed under guard in Army detention centers before being transferred to what were called Relocation Centers. The Relocation Centers were built in states other than those bordering on the Pacific and were under the supervision of a civilian agency of the federal government.

In the first weeks of the evacuation, there was much public interest in the undertaking. Hundreds of requests were made by newspapers, and by magazines, for permission to send correspondents into the Army centers to report on conditions, and to interview the victims of the unconstitutional executive order. It was not feasible to grant the many requests, nor was it proper to deny information to the public.

Aware of this, the commanding general [5] of the Western Defense Command and Fourth Army selected *The Christian Science Monitor* as the newspaper through which to release the first series of articles on conditions within the Army centers, and directed an officer to get in touch with the San Francisco office of the *Monitor*.

The conversation between the correspondent and the officer went something like this:

"I understand you would like to visit some of the centers and write your findings for your newspaper."

"Yes, sir."

"When do you want to start and where do you want to go?"

The newspaperman was suspicious. "Is this a personally conducted tour?"

"No. Go by yourself."

"To any center?"

"Yes, but there are two conditions."

"What are they?"

"The first condition is that you cannot enter an evacuee's quarters unless you are invited. Nor can you ask to be invited, no matter how well you may know the occupant. The reason for this is that their homes, so to speak, are mostly of two rooms. That means they are pretty crowded for space, especially where there are children. And there are lots of children. It is not a comfortable situation, but the evacuees

[5] Lieutenant General John L. Dewitt.

are making the best of it. Consequently, no one, no soldier, and no officer, is permitted to go into these homes unless invited and, of course, unless there is trouble."

"What's the other condition?"

"I want to see what you write before you send it in for publication."

"You mean you are going to censor what I write?"

"No. My instructions are to check your copy for facts. Nothing else."

"Suppose I am critical?"

"That is your privilege, so long as you are factual."

"Who goes with me?"

"You go alone. Tell me when you want to go and where you want to go. A civilian employee of the Army will meet you at each center, will take you inside, and will turn you loose—unless you want him to go with you to answer questions."

With the exception of one or two minor changes to agree with the facts, the series of articles was published in the *Monitor*. They served well. They quieted many rumors and were widely commented upon. Later, reporters for other newspapers, as well as magazines, were given access to the centers. The *Monitor* articles were the first to be authorized as a series.

The mail circulation of *The Christian Science Monitor* is the largest of any newspaper published in the United States. Recipient of more than seventy awards for excellence in newspaper publishing, and for its many contributions [6] toward creating better understanding among people, the *Monitor* has subscribers in one hundred and twenty countries, including all the free countries of the world, includ-

[6] For story of one contribution, see Appendix 7.

ing, too, Russia, Bulgaria, Poland, China, Roumania, and Czechoslovakia.

Harry I. Hunt, who became the first publishers' agent in 1922, was experienced in the printing and distribution of Mrs. Eddy's books. In World War I, as an assistant to Allison V. Stewart, he had the foresight to order the large quantities of Oxford India paper from England [7] that kept the printing of *Science and Health,* and other titles, from being seriously affected by wartime conditions.

As the war neared its close, Hunt had another problem. Years before, when Mrs. Eddy first offered *Science and Health* in a binding of limp leather, she employed Dudley and Hodge, bookbinders in Boston, to do the work. Goatskins were used. They came from India and were supplied by the Publishers. In 1900, two people, a man and a woman, were able to fill all orders.

By 1922, many skilled workers were needed, and the demand for books bound in limp leather was steadily increasing. Meanwhile, as the war neared its close, and with but six months' stock on hand, all shipments of goatskins were stopped. Hunt was told that because of the need for silver rupees to pay Indian troops serving in the armed forces of the Empire, there was a great shortage of such coins in India. Herders refused to accept paper money, and it was not until the war was over, and silver was again in circulation in

[7] Except for the Bible, *Science and Health* was the first book published in the United States that was printed on Oxford India paper. The paper was supplied by the Oxford University Press in 1895 and the arrangement continued until 1939, when the plant was taken over by the British government for war work. Until 1895, the paper had been used exclusively in the printing of Bibles. Permission was given Mrs. Eddy to use the paper because the sale of *Science and Health* stimulated interest in the Bible. The Spanish translation of *Science and Health* (*Ciencia y Salud*), printed in 1947, was the first translation to appear on domestic Bible paper.

India, that shipments were resumed. One boatload of goat-skins from China alleviated the emergency.

The Dudley and Hodge bindery was leased in 1920 and operated until 1938, when it was sold to outside interests. In 1930, the European Bureau of *The Christian Science Monitor* in London became the European Bureau of The Christian Science Publishing Society. In 1931, authorized Christian Science literature was being published in sixteen languages; at different times, in the *Monitor,* religious articles were appearing in twelve languages. In the same year the Publishing Society had approximately one thousand regular employees, and more than three thousand others were active at various times.

A new publishing house was needed and in the *Sentinel,* October 17, 1931, plans were announced for the building of one. In part, the findings of a special committee were:

1. That at an early date, additional space would be required for the Publishing Society, the executive offices of the Church, The Mother Church Sunday School, and the publishing of the writings of our Leader, Mary Baker Eddy.

2. That within a comparatively brief period extensive and costly replacements in the mechanical department would have to be made.

3. That by building at once an appreciable contribution could be made to the world-wide effort to relieve the unemployment situation, and at the same time savings could be made in the cost of the building.[8]

4. That the orderly arrangement of departments in the

[8] The approximate cost of the building was $4,500,000. The architect was Chester L. Churchill. On the basis of 1956 prices, the architect estimated the cost of replacing the building would be in excess of $12,000,000. To illustrate: at the time of construction, bronze was used for many purposes. In 1956, the cost of bronze would make its use almost prohibitive, whereas, in 1933, bronze was bought at practically the same price as steel.

new publishing house would make it possible to avoid great loss of time and motion on the part of workers who, under existing conditions, were inconvenienced and, in some instances, were remotely separated from the departments dependent upon them for prompt and effective service.

Completed in 1935, the Publishing House is unique. Money for its building came from Christian Scientists, and their friends, in many countries; materials used in its building came from many countries; when it was finished, there was no debt. In the lobby is a tablet of Portanelle marble from Portugal on which is fixed an inscription in bronze letters:

CHRISTIAN SCIENTISTS

AND

THEIR FRIENDS

THROUGHOUT THE WORLD

PROVIDED

THIS BUILDING

TO SPREAD MORE WIDELY

THE TEACHINGS

OF THE

DISCOVERER AND FOUNDER OF

CHRISTIAN SCIENCE

MARY BAKER EDDY

LET HER OWN WORKS PRAISE HER

IN THE GATES.

PROVERBS

XXXI — 31.

Opposite The Mother Church, the building runs a full block along Norway Street. In its garden court, flowers and junipers, magnolias, lilacs, evergreens, rhododendrons, and azaleas speak of friendship whatever the month, whatever the week, while between Falmouth Street and Huntington Avenue is the Church park. Here, in all seasons, the visitor may stretch out his steps on art brick walks, or linger beside flowers and foliage, evergreens, magnolias, and pink geraniums.

While the Publishing House was being built, the *Christian Science Hymnal* was being revised and greatly enlarged. It was published in 1932; also, in the same year, the Directors established what is now the Archives of The Mother Church. In 1941, the *Christian Science Sentinel* was published in a new size. This was the fourteenth change in the *Sentinel* since its introduction in 1898, many of the changes having been made by Mrs. Eddy.

In the same year the Trustees under the Will called in William Dana Orcutt and told him of their decision to reset all of Mrs. Eddy's books so as to give them a more modern appearance. It was a sensitive decision. There had been no typographical changes in Mrs. Eddy's books since she had made them in 1902; at that time, Orcutt had carried out her wishes.

In that year, in response to Mrs. Eddy's request, Orcutt took to her home in Concord proof sheets of a new edition of *Science and Health* which contained a new chapter entitled "Fruitage." In the proof sheets were typographical changes in the running heads, the front matter, and in the placement of other material. As for the type pages, they were left undisturbed.

After studying the changes and returning the proof sheets to Orcutt, Mrs. Eddy said, "That is exactly right." Hearing those words, Orcutt remembered others, from an earlier conversation in the same room at Pleasant View: "A book is like a friend. We become familiar with a friend's face, and keep the well-known features in our mind. I think readers of *Science and Health* would be a little shocked to see the pages with which they are so familiar now in a different form." [9]

As he listened to the Trustees in 1941, Orcutt thought of the words he had heard so long before; and he wrote of his thoughts, and of his work, in his book about Mrs. Eddy and her books:

"Ever mindful of Mrs. Eddy's personal injunction... that 'the page of a familiar book was like the face of an old friend,' I made as few changes as possible in bringing the typography up to modern requirements. The most notable variation is to be found in the treatment of the chapter heads and the running heads, mostly minor matters, and yet important in themselves." He recalled: "In view of the dangers of war, it was decided at this time to take three sets of molder plates, and to store these in different parts of the country to reduce the risk of destruction by bombing or by fire."

The year was noteworthy for another event of rare moment to Orcutt and, in its way, an event of rare moment to the entire field of publishing.

One day not long after graduating from Harvard in 1891, Orcutt was talking with Mrs. Eddy in her study at Pleasant View. The subject was Orcutt's lack of interest in continuing as an assistant to John Wilson at University Press. Having been attracted by the art of the early master printers, Orcutt found only disappointment in the printing standards of the nineties. To him, they were standards of dullness, and

[9] William Dana Orcutt, *Mary Baker Eddy and Her Books* (Boston: The Christian Science Publishing Society, copyright, 1950).

he said so at length, closing his peroration with this outburst: "I want to devote myself to something in which there is beauty."

He saw her smile, then heard her quiet voice: "Have you never realized that if a man has beauty in himself, he can put beauty into anything? Of course you are right in your conception of the ideal book, but it seems to me that what Mr. Wilson has in mind for you would give you the most wonderful opportunity in the world to put your ideas into action."

Orcutt went back to the master printers and, in November, 1900, wrote to Joseph Armstrong suggesting a special edition of *Science and Health* that would "represent the highest expression of the printer's and binder's art." Armstrong was sympathetic, but invited Orcutt's attention to the fact that changes were still being made in the textbook; therefore, he could give little encouragement.

Three years later, when Orcutt was in Pleasant View on another publishing matter, Mrs. Eddy said to him, "I was sorry to disappoint you on that beautiful edition of *Science and Health* you wanted to make. I am pleased that you wish to do this for me; but Mr. Armstrong was right, the time has not come."

It was his first inkling that Armstrong had submitted his letter and sample pages to Mrs. Eddy.

On August 15, 1939, the time came. On that day Orcutt was told to proceed with the work for which he had prepared himself. In doing so, he had crossed the Atlantic twenty times, had visited the libraries of Europe, and had communed with the books in the Riccardi and Laurentian libraries and the da Vinci Archives in Florence, with the books in the Ambrosian Library in Milan. In 1941, the

Subscription Edition of *Science and Health with Key to the Scriptures* was published.[10]

Orcutt devoted an entire section in *Mary Baker Eddy and Her Books* to the Subscription Edition and its new type, which was named Laurentian. In opening the story, he wrote:

"The production of the Subscription Edition of *Science and Health* is an epic in the history of American bookmaking, and becomes an integral part of this story because whatever later use may be made of the Laurentian type, this design will always be associated with that volume."

In closing, he told his readers:

"Never was a volume started during a period more fraught with threatened complications, never was a volume that moved more smoothly from start to finish. Difficulties raised their heads only to eliminate themselves before thwarting the progress of the work. Each participant called in to play his part proved to be the exact person best fitted to perform it; each component part when combined with the others demonstrated the 'rightness' of the selection.

"All this could not have been mere coincidence. . . .

"All this is beyond the reward for careful workmanship.

"Could it not be that there was another unseen but beneficent influence that guided the book throughout the various processes with a certainty more powerful than we know, and

[10] The Subscription Edition of *Science and Health* was issued in June, 1941, in a limited edition of one thousand copies. In format, it is a super royal quarto, 10 by 14 inches, 725 pages, set in Laurentian type, especially revised and cut for this volume. It is printed in red and black on pure linen-rag, handmade paper, bulking three inches. The binding is in full imported morocco, blind stamped. Each copy is enclosed in a cloth-covered, fleece-lined wooden box. The edition was oversubscribed before publication. (William Dana Orcutt, *op. cit.*)

that the serenity of the atmosphere through which it passed was an assurance of the 'rightness' of the undertaking?

"I like to think so, and I shall always think so."

It was thirty-two years after her discovery of Christian Science, twenty-three years after writing *Science and Health*, and six years after forming The Mother Church that Mrs. Eddy established The Christian Science Board of Lectureship; in establishing it, she provided, in perpetuity, for the commissioning of selected men and women to carry her message of healing to people everywhere.

This was in 1898, and on all those selected to speak in her name, and so long as her Church shall be, she placed an obligation:

> If there be an individual who goes to hear and deride truth, he should go away contemplating truth; and he who goes to seek truth should have the opportunity to depart in quiet *thought* on that subject.[11]

This was instruction that carried one meaning. In speaking in her name, they were to speak in truth and not in controversy.

During her sojourn, Mrs. Eddy sought no converts by disputation—and, there being no strife in the design of her ministry, she denied to all who spoke in her name the use of controversy. Mrs. Eddy did not believe truth to be an instrument of strife. Believing strife to be transient, and accepting truth as the only influence that is permanent, she was sure that everything that is opposed to truth is destined to oblivion. Being sure, she did not believe it possible for

[11] *Church Manual*, Article XXXI, SECTION 4.

her enemies to destroy her—but did believe it possible to destroy their enmity.

In the work Mrs. Eddy called upon lecturers to do, they were certain to encounter hostility, as did she—for she was first to enter the darkness of bigotry and walk through it. In early years she lectured in Lynn, in Boston, in New York, and in Chicago; and, in *Retrospection and Introspection* (p. 40), she told of having notices of a lecture torn down, and of being denied the use of a church, or a public hall, in Westerly, Rhode Island, because on a previous visit to the community she had healed a woman said by doctors to be dying.

In a way, the immediate predecessor to the Board of Lectureship was a Board of Missionaries, the members of which were subject to call for work in "sections that have no local healers or teachers in Christian Science." (Article IX, first edition, *Church Manual.*) From 1897 until 1906, when the function was discontinued, missionaries were under the direction of the Directors and, according to the *Manual* (Article XXXVI, fifty-third edition), were "to do whatever is needed and required of them,—be it to fill a vacancy, or to spread the gospel of Christian Science, or to correctly propagate this Science in whatever locality it is most needed."

Appointed as lecturers in 1898 were Edward A. Kimball, Carol Norton, and three former clergymen, the Reverend George Tomkins, the Reverend William P. McKenzie, and the Reverend Irving C. Tomlinson.[12] At the time, the minimum fee for each lecture was fifty dollars, in addition to traveling expenses. This cost was met by the local church, which also provided the hall in which the lecture was given.

The first lecture by a member of the Board of Lectureship

[12] For list of lecturers, and their years of lectureship, see Appendix 8.

was given by Irving C. Tomlinson in Lynn, Massachusetts, on September 28, 1898. Since that day, 154 (men, 123; women, 31) Christian Science lecturers have appeared in nearly every civilized country in the world. They have given tens of thousands of lectures, and have been heard by millions, and millions, and more millions of people.

Of the one hundred and fifty-hour, nine [13] have spent twenty, or more, years taking to the world the teachings of a woman whose vision was of a world in which good has overcome evil and left no roots.

Appointed each year by The Christian Science Board of Directors, lecturers begin each lecture year on July 1. In the *Manual* (Article XXXII, Section 4) it is stated that "The Mother Church and the branch churches shall call on the Board of Lectureship annually for one or more lectures." Also, in Article XXXII, Section 1, it is specified: "When the need is apparent, the Christian Science Board of Directors of The Mother Church may call on any member of this Board of Lectureship to lecture at such places and at such times as the cause of Christian Science demands." For several years, there have been twenty-eight names on each list of lecturers.

As a religious leader, Mrs. Eddy was not a critic of other religions, nor was she a Herod for her own. She believed, and deeply so, that she had found the way of healing that was practiced by Jesus, but there is nothing on record to show she ever asked another to accept what she said without proof of its truth. Her expectation was that all who spoke in her name would do so without malice and without guile.

In his book, *Twelve Years with Mary Baker Eddy*, Irving

[13] Professor Hermann S. Hering, Paul Stark Seeley, Bicknell Young, Frank Bell, William D. Kilpatrick, Dr. John M. Tutt, Robert Stanley Ross, John Randall Dunn, and Bliss Knapp.

C. Tomlinson recalled Mrs. Eddy's specifications for the growth of Christian Science: "The way to establish the Cause is through writing and preaching, teaching and lecturing. This is temporal. But the way to establish the Cause through revelation is by healing and this is permanent."

CHAPTER FOURTEEN

The Home on the Hill

WHILE she was here in person, Mary Baker Eddy was referred to in the newspapers as "the most discussed woman in the world." The reason for all the discussion was plain; and still is plain.

Mrs. Eddy was a woman who said there is no life in matter. She said there is no death. She said God is the healer of all sickness, the destroyer of all evil—and she taught that to be alone and at one with God is to know these things to be true.

These are teachings of great simplicity, and, because they are, they are looked upon with suspicion. How can a world that, through centuries, has been taught to believe the reality of sickness, sin, punishment, and death accept teachings which said that man, created by God in His *own* image, is subject to none of these things?

Acknowledging the words, "Let no man say when he is tempted, I am tempted of God: for God cannot be tempted with evil, neither tempteth he any man," Mrs. Eddy believed religion to be *both* the study of, and participation in, spiritual values.

She taught that all who hear God and obey Him, find Him; and, finding Him, find no sickness, no fear, no hate, no malice, no envy, nor any of the evils that troop together to infest the human mind. She was sure that to get rid of these weeds all we need to do is to claim the qualities already ours, in the realization that when God created man, He bestowed His blessings upon man—not one at a time, but all at once.

In her teachings, there is a requirement that her followers claim their heritage, that they accept the availability of God, accept His dominion over all things, and understand the words, "Verily, verily, I say unto you, whatsoever ye shall ask of the Father in my name he will give *it* you"—and a demand that all who call themselves Christian Scientists prove their relationship to God by their deeds.

The practitioner's home was on a hill. She looked out one morning to see a man laboring up the hill, stopping every few minutes to rest. She immediately began to know that her home was God's sanctuary and that error had no power to enter where Truth and Love resided.

She turned to the definition of "Church" in *Science and Health* (p. 583) and repeated it thoughtfully, refusing the lie entrance to her consciousness. Presently there was a tapping at the door. The man looked rather bewildered as she greeted him, saying, "When I started up that hill to come here I thought I'd never make it, and now I'm perfectly all right." She invited him in and shared with him her clear realization of Truth which had denied the material evidence presented to her as she saw him coming toward her home.

He then told her of an argument he had had with a former employer that morning who owed him quite a sum of money, for which he had done hard, manual labor. They had almost come to blows over it. As he left the man, a sharp pain struck him in the region of his heart and continued to grow steadily worse. Being a student of Christian Science, he decided to ask for help.

The hill looked mountainous to him as he started to climb it. The pain continued to jab harder every step he took, until he felt he would never get to the house, but the moment he rapped on the door it left, and with it his resentment toward his debtor. He declared he had hated the man every step up the hill.

The practitioner reminded him that there was only one kind of man, and that was the man in God's image and likeness, who is honest and always pays his debts. A portion of the Lord's Prayer was considered, "and forgive us our debts, as we forgive our debtors," together with the spiritual interpretation by Mrs. Eddy (*Science and Health,* p. 117) "and Love is reflected in love."

The man silently pondered this for a few moments, after which he decided to see the man again, but this time as the perfect, loving son of God. On leaving he remarked, "Well, I've gained another hill in Christian Science, and am indeed grateful for the lesson learned this morning."

Later in the day he called to report his collection of the money, plus interest, and the complete restoration of harmony between himself and the other man.

—*The Christian Science Journal,* April, 1943.

It has long been my desire to send a testimony to our periodicals in order to put into words something of the gratitude I feel for Christian Science and all it stands for. Hearing of it many years ago,

I laughed with others at what I thought it was. Then, about 1920, I read the textbook, *Science and Health,* by Mrs. Eddy, and that reading healed me of prejudice and intolerance toward Christian Science, but I did not pursue its study further.

Some years later, through a brother, I came to realize something of what a vast and important subject it is. I was also assured that it could be demonstrated as one studied, and so I started to read once again. This time I was ready, and realized with some surprise that some of my thinking since 1920 had its source in the textbook.

An early healing, from which I have subsequently learned much, was the overcoming of susceptibility to an irritating rash caused by the leaves of a plant which I had been growing for winter house decoration. Shortly after I took up Christian Science it became necessary to repot a number of these plants, and I declared emphatically that it was ridiculous that a plant which we loved, and which gave us such pleasure and joy throughout the winter, could harm us.

Neither my wife, nor I, has been affected by the leaves since, and we can handle the plants with impunity. How often that healing puzzled me in its very simplicity when later other things, seemingly much more important, appeared harder to demonstrate? Then realization came that our attitude toward the plant had been entirely in accordance with Principle, Love.

We had loved it, cared for it, watered it, protected it, and, above all, in spite of its seemingly unpleasant characteristic, we had felt no resentment toward it, so the simple, emphatic declaration healed. . . .

—*Sentinel,* October 16, 1937.

I am very grateful to Mary Baker Eddy for her wonderful revelation of the Science of healing. I was reared in an orthodox church, and in one of its colleges I studied for the ministry. After graduation I occupied a pulpit for about a year, at the end of which time my health broke down, tuberculosis developed, and a doctor advised me to go to Colorado.

While convalescing, I had a great deal of leisure on my hands. I had heard much of Christian Science and its growth, so I decided to buy a copy of its textbook, *Science and Health,* by Mrs. Eddy, and familiarize myself with her teachings, in order that when I returned to my pulpit, I should be in a position to expose its fallacies and refute its claims.

As I read the first chapter on *Prayer,* I was impressed with it as being the most profound and the most consistent treatise on the subject that I had seen, and I had not read very far into succeeding chapters before I realized I could not answer the author's arguments. Her inspired statements appealed to me as self-evident truth. I could not resist them.

This was the beginning of my conversion to Christian Science. And what a contrast with my former belief! I had always been taught that God was omnipresent, omniscient, and omnipotent, but these great verities were treated merely as theory.

I had not been taught that they could be used practically in dealing with life's problems. But in Christian Science I found these great truths are the very basis of demonstration, the working Principle of healing and of all good.

In the old belief it was thought that the crucifixion of Jesus was necessary to appease the wrath of God toward sinful man, and to provide a ready pardon for those who sought it, condemning to eternal punishment those who failed to avail themselves of such pardon. How unreasonable and unjust! On the other hand, how beautiful the atonement appears in Christian Science!

As Mrs. Eddy says in *Science and Health* (p. 497), "We acknowledge Jesus' atonement as the evidence of divine, efficacious Love, unfolding man's unity with God through Christ Jesus the Way-shower; and we acknowledge that man is saved through Christ, through Truth, Life and Love as demonstrated by the Galilean Prophet in the healing of the sick and overcoming of sin and death."

Again, in the old thought it was believed that sickness, sorrow and poverty are in accordance with God's will, to which it was man's duty to submit. But in Christian Science I learned that God does not afflict His children. To do so would be contrary to His nature. Divine Love knows only health and joy and abundance—and He bestows these blessings impartially upon His children.

I rejoice that Christian Science with its benign message is ever more spreading throughout the world, and I pray that the day may be hastened when all people of all nations shall see its light, and shall come to know its glorious redemption. I am deeply grateful that I have found the truth which is Christian Science.

—*Sentinel,* May 5, 1938.

I came into Christian Science through a quick and easy healing of a burst varicose vein, although I understood very little of how this healing came about. I realize now that it was demonstrated through my desire for good, and the consequent opening of the channels for Truth to flow in. However, I did not, in spite of this healing, study Christian Science seriously, with the result that revengeful, hateful, jealous thoughts found me easy prey, and the poison of this wrong thinking produced a belief in a terrible illness.

Not having kept my lamp filled and trimmed, as it were, I had no light in the darkness. Materia medica was resorted to, with the result of a surgical operation to discover what was wrong with my internal organs.

The night before this operation I asked to see a Christian Science practitioner. She came to me, and said: "My child, remember that God is everywhere. His love surrounds you, and only good can come to you. All here are reflecting Him, in their goodness and kindness. Had you realized some of the truth before, you need not have been in the hospital but now, doubtless, your extremity is God's opportunity. When tomorrow you go on the operating table, know that only good exists, that there is no fear, as God governs, and know that, as you go off to sleep in Love so shall you awake."

When I had recovered consciousness sufficiently to begin to think, I asked to see the surgeon who had operated. I asked him if all was well, and he shook his head. I asked if it was cancer, and he said, "Yes, in the big intestine, inoperable and incurable." I asked if it meant I was to die, and he said, "Yes."

The efficacy of the practitioner's statement made on the previous day was demonstrated, in that I had no reaction of fear whatsoever, and was able to declare that I was not going to die, and that I had no fear. I then asked if I might have a Christian Science practitioner to see me, and I heard the discussion outside the door, on my request. The surgeon said, "Let her have what she likes, so she may die in peace."

The practitioner came to see me, and quoted these words from *Unity of Good,* by Mary Baker Eddy (p. 41): "The sweet and sacred sense of the permanence of man's unity with his Maker can illumine our present being with a continual presence and power of good."

Later when I could read for myself, I continued with that sentence, which the practitioner, at the time, realized it was wiser not to read, but which later helped me more than I can say. It continues: "Opening wide the portal from death into Life." That practitioner came to me unfailingly all the time I was in the hospital, and thus was my recovery rapid. On my return home I was helped by my Christian Science nurse to realize that Truth eliminates every vestige of fear. My practitioner never let me forget that the casting out and banishment of evil is what cures.

I asked not to be told how long the doctors had given me to live. I had an idea it was a year, and I dreaded the meantime, with the frightened thoughts of those around me who were not Christian Scientists. The time arrived when I realized how wonderful I felt. A great load seemed lifted off me, and I understood this when my husband told me that now all was well.

It transpired that the doctors had told him I must die in eight months, and this was the ninth month; therefore he, and all those around me, felt that the danger was past. This made me realize how one must protect oneself against the thoughts of others, whom the very fact of living seems to fill with fear.

A year from the date of the hospital episode I met at a social function one of the doctors who had attended the operation. He could not believe it was I. He asked a confirmation of the fact by a mutual friend, and showed him a notebook with an entry against the date of my supposed demise.

That Christian Science rescued me from the grave is more than evident. I am everlastingly grateful my husband, who though not understanding the truth of Christian Science, having never seen the proof by demonstration, consented, after an interview with a Christian Scientist of much experience, to my wishes to see no more doctors, and this in the face of opposition from relatives. This was a brave stand to take.

To Mind, Who guided my practitioner, I am

unspeakably grateful. She is a wonderful woman, realizing as she did the firm handling that I required, leaving no opportunity whatsoever for doubting the certainty of the healing, and no room for any self-pity. Her constructive understanding conveyed to me Truth and Love.

This healing took place long enough ago for mortal mind to have no chance now of saying, "Wait and see." It is with deep gratitude that I send out this message to all who may have the claim of some latent fear, or active fear of such illness, to tell them, one and all, that such a fear is without foundation whatsoever, and is absolutely and entirely unnecessary.

—*Sentinel,* December 5, 1936.

It is difficult to tell of the experience, but the student of Christian Science will readily see in it that acceptance of the truth made the overcoming of fear possible, even as in the case of disease; and the divine Principle is to be relied upon at all times.

While the *Titanic* was sinking, and during the whole time I was working at the boats, I held to the truth, thereby eliminating all fear. I do not pretend that any man can go down on a ship at midnight, in mid-Atlantic, and succeed in eliminating fear, without hard work. It was hard work, and yet the very conditions which existed on the port side were in themselves a demonstration of the workings of Truth, for not the slightest hitch occurred, and all the boats were got away, the last one, which was a flat-bottomed collapsible, floating off the deck. Now it is proverbial that the last thing a sailor will think about is his belt; certainly no thought had entered my head of my own life belt; and I was far too busy at the boats to leave them, even if I had thought of it. And this is how I came to obtain my belt.

Murdoch had been appointed Chief, I was First, and Blair was Second Officer; in that rank we joined the *Titanic* in Belfast. Shortly before we sailed from Southampton, Wilde, who was formerly Chief of the *Olympic,* and was to have been given command of another of the White Star steamers, which, owing to the coal strike and other reasons was laid up, was sent for the time being to the *Titanic* as Chief, Murdoch ranking back to First, myself to Second, and Blair standing out for the voyage. Now it will be seen why it was Wilde, on wanting some articles which were received by the First Officer in Belfast, came to me.

I took him to the First Officer's room and showed him where they were, and was on my way back on deck again when I heard Wilde say, "I am going to put on my life belt." At the precise moment I was passing my own room door, facing which is a wardrobe, and on the top of this was my life belt. On hearing Wilde's remark, I instinctively looked into the room, reached for the belt, and put it on.

I now resumed my work at the boats, finally calling for men to follow me up on top of the officers' quarters to cut adrift the last boat, which was stored there. This boat we had not even time to open up, so just hove her down to the deck from which we had launched the others.

As I saw her slide over the edge of the quarters I turned and ran across the deck to the other side of the ship to see if anything further could be done. Looking down I could see that all material work was finished, so from where I was on top of the quarters and above the bridge, I faced forward and walked into the water. The sudden immersion in this penetratingly cold water for a few seconds overcame all thought, and I struck out blindly for the crow's nest which is on the foremast and was at that time just a little above the water.

In a couple of seconds I realized that the crow's nest and all other material help was of the same value, and almost immediately I found myself drawn with great force against the grating covering the mouth of the forward blower, a huge ventilator leading down to the forward stokehold. In this position I went below the surface with the ship.

I want to emphasize strongly this point, that as soon as I collected my thoughts after taking to the water, I remember saying to myself, "Now I'll see how much I have learned from Christian Science." A doubt never entered my mind as to the possibility of my surviving; in other words, of the ability of the divine power to save me.

I think I can conscientiously say that with this thought all fear left me, and I commenced again to realize the truth of being. It was at this moment that I was drawn into the water, still realizing the truth, and while I was below the surface, these words from the 91st Psalm came to me so distinctly that I seemed to realize their full import: "He shall give his angels charge over thee."

Immediately, I think, I was thrown away from the blower and came up to find a piece of wood in my hand which seemed to be attached to the top of the funnel by a wire. I remained still, while the water rushed past me, carrying the people with it away from me. A second time I went down, still holding fast to the truth, and again came to the surface. My piece of wood was gone, but alongside me was the flat-bottomed collapsible boat which I had thrown down on the other side of the ship. This I laid hold of, but made no attempt to board it.

I want it to be clearly understood that during this time in the water the fact came calmly and clearly that there was a divine power which could be utilized in a practical manner, and also it seemed perfectly natural to rely on this power with the spiritual understanding which is so often spoken of in the Bible, and which is explained in *Science and Health with Key to the Scriptures,* by Mrs. Eddy.

Now, with the sinking of the *Titanic,* there also was the fear of suction to be overcome, and at this time the forward funnel fell, throwing the boat, myself, and other survivors about twenty feet clear of the ship, so that of suction we felt nothing.

About thirty of us floated the remainder of the night on the upturned boat, and I could not overcome the intense cold experienced. Yet, when a man handed me a bottle of something that smelt somewhat like the essence of peppermint, the

thought of material means was nothing short of re-
pulsive, and needless to say, it was not taken. At
daybreak, we found two life-boats floating nearby,
into which we were taken.

I was the last member of the *Titanic* to board
the *Carpathia,* and after interviewing the captain,
discarded my wet clothes in favor of a bunk in
which I remained for about half an hour, and was
not in the bunk, or bed, again. Reaction or effects
from the immersion—which I was confidently assured would take place—there were none; and
though surprise has been expressed by very many,
it only goes to prove that "with God, all things are
possible."

—*Sentinel,* Vol. 20, August, 1918.

Four years ago I first heard of Christian Science.
In the very first conversation with a Scientist I was
conscious that this Science was something quite
other than I had known before, something to set
store by. I became much interested, and during the
years I have studied it and attended the Sunday
services and Wednesday meetings, I have been
gaining better understanding of the Bible. Many
passages which previously seemed incomprehensible have become clear.

I am deeply grateful for the sense of security
which Christian Science gives us, by teaching us
how we can, in our own thinking, demonstrate love
to our neighbor and in that way help him. I come
in daily contact with many people, and in dealing
with them I have plenty of opportunity to apply
Christian Science. If we hold steadfastly to the

thought that our neighbor, in his true being, is an idea of God, and therefore a reflection of divine Love, the error which would thrust itself upon our thought must give way, and we can shut out inharmony.

In physical difficulties Christian Science has been my physician. Colds, influenza, and fear have yielded to the truth. Once I was taken ill with a severe stomach trouble, and could not retain my food. After trying for a week to overcome the effort myself, I asked a practitioner for help. In a few days I was completely restored. . . .

I am very grateful to the practitioner for all that she has taught me, and for her constant willingness to help in times of trouble. The disquiet and fear which previously overwhelmed me and life's many adversities, have disappeared with God's help. Regarding the future, I am calm and hopeful, for I know God is with me.

—*Sentinel,* December 4, 1937.

While I was at work, I had from a human standpoint a serious accident. I came in contact with a high voltage current, and fell from a height of six meters to the street. In a most helpless condition (with a fractured skull and injuries to my back) I was taken to a hospital. My wife immediately informed a Christian Science practitioner.

For days I lay in a delirious fever, and on top of this, inflammation of the lungs set in. My relatives were told to prepare for the expected end. Instead of the expected end, however, there came in the hour of crisis a turn for the better, which rapidly increased, to the amazement of the doctors. Four weeks later I was so far recovered that I could get up, and in another three weeks I was released. During my seven weeks' stay in the hospital there was no surgical operation. Nor were any drugs used. During the whole period of my difficulty I had only the help of the practitioner; the doctors merely observed the stages of my recovery.

—*Sentinel,* October 16, 1937.

In our home we have experienced many healings. I was healed of a poisoned finger without losing one hour from work. The children have been relieved of so-called contagious diseases, mostly with the aid of a practitioner. One healing stands out especially.

Our boy, when seven years old, broke his leg just above the ankle in the school playgrounds. The doctor rendered first aid, and put on splints. He wanted to remove him to a hospital, but at our request he was taken home. A Christian Science practitioner was called. The next day the boy himself removed the splints.

After ten days the doctor and school nurse came and examined the leg, and through the Children's Aid Society started prosecution for criminal neglect. They said the boy would be lame, and his leg crooked. The magistrate, during the hearing, told a story of a friend of his who was healed of total blindness through Christian Science, so the court case was turned into a testimony meeting.

The case was adjourned for one week. During the week, at the request of the Christian Science

Committee on Publication, an X-ray photograph was taken. This was sent to the medical officer, and the same afternoon the case was dropped as the leg was shown to be normal. I may add that a letter of apology was sent to me by the prosecutor. . . .

In two weeks the boy was out of bed, and about. We did not allow him to go back to school until the fifth week, after a slight limp had disappeared.

—*Sentinel,* November 11, 1933.

From early childhood I suffered a great deal from nervousness and timidity due to a deformity. As I grew into manhood, this caused me increased embarrassment and a dislike to associate with my fellow men. It had a tendency to make me moody and despondent, destroyed my ability to think clearly, and left me in a state of mind without hope of God in the world, tempting me at times to end it all by self-destruction.

I can sincerely say that this uplifting study has given me an inner victory over myself which words cannot express.

—*Sentinel,* November 6, 1937.

As a child, I saw my brother healed of bowlegs by Christian Science. The legs were so badly bowed that he could not stand on them. Orthopedic methods were given a full trial without effect. Then absent treatment in Christian Science was asked for, and my mother started to read *Science and Health with Key to the Scriptures* by

Mary Baker Eddy. Within three weeks the legs were straight and strong.

I have experienced quick healings in Christian Science, but I have also learned that, even if a healing does not come at once, it will still certainly come if the truth is persistently and correctly applied. About twenty years ago I began to lose the use of my legs. I sought help in Christian Science but the condition grew worse until I was no longer able to attend to my profession.

At the time I held an established post in the British Home Civil Service, and when my regulation sick leave was exhausted I was required to have a full medical examination, but explained that I was relying on Christian Science for healing and did not desire any material treatment. An ambulance took me to a service hospital, where I spent a week under thorough medical examination. The surgeon in charge then told me that I was suffering from some form of paralysis for which there was little likelihood of cure. He also told my wife that I could not be cared for at home, as among other things bed sores would soon develop. I did not see his written report to my department, but the outcome was my being invalided from service.

I returned home and was effectively cared for there without any special nursing attention. When bed sores began to develop, they were quickly healed by Christian Science. However, for almost ten years I was unable to stand or walk; I could only sit up for a short time each day, not always that. The difficulty in moving spread, and other complications developed. Several times it appeared that I was about to pass on. I could eat little and slept poorly. Our home, an upper flat in central London, was for four or five years under air attack. Financial supply had to be found, too.

But all the time spiritual growth was going on through Christian Science. Sometimes I studied alone. Sometimes I had treatment from a steadfast practitioner, who brought me great inspiration. Always I had the unfailing support of my wife. When too weak to turn the pages of *Science and Health* I started to learn it by heart so as to grasp every detail. I learned more than half the book by heart. Its teachings were food and rest to me.

As I studied and received treatment, great spiritual joy filled me—joy that God governed and nothing could interfere with His purpose of present perfection and satisfaction for all. And with the joy came an ever keener sense of spiritual innocence, a perception that man, being the individual expression of divine Mind, could never have entertained at any moment any incorrect thinking which could have caused or could justify suffering. The recognition of good's allness and evil's nothingness followed and irresistibly took charge of the physical condition. In the tenth year improvement began. I started to walk again, and sleep and appetite returned to normal. There were no setbacks, and certain readjustments were not easy, but step by step the healing finally was established.

Along with the physical healing, successive new opportunities for interesting work opened up.

Sometimes these made demands which seemed beyond my strength at the moment; but as I went forward in God's strength, the demands were met. At last I found myself leading a fully active life again, occupied more satisfactorily than ever before. All the good of those years has remained with me; all the loss and evil are as though they had never been.

I am grateful to Mrs. Eddy for discovering the spiritually scientific law by which Christ Jesus healed and for giving it to mankind in *Science and Health*. I am also grateful to her for the spiritual education I received through various activities of the Christian Science movement—the Sunday School, a Christian Science Organization at college, membership in The Mother Church and a branch church, class instruction, and the help of practitioners. This spiritual education prepared me to meet the experience here related and enabled me to reap its full blessings. I am grateful for the love and support of fellow Christian Scientists during this time. Most of all I am grateful to God, the divine Principle, who is also divine Love.

—Journal, April, 1955.

About three years ago, when I left to return to Holland, forever as I then thought, I was broken up bodily and mentally after a long period of hard work. For many years I had been trying to find help from a great number of doctors, magnetizers and, in the end, even native soothsayers and idol worshippers in the villages.

For fifteen years I had been suffering from insomnia, a serious form of heartburn, and a·complete nervous breakdown. Also, all my life I had an impediment in my speech, which was very inconvenient and troublesome, especially for a businessman.

I had asked for Christian Science treatment. . . . During the first six months there was no improvement because I lacked confidence in God, good. Then the lady who was helping me in my struggle asked if perhaps I was secretly criticizing, which was quite to the point. From that time there was rapid improvement . . . all the sickness and the speech impediment, as a discordant dream, now belong to the past.

—*Sentinel,* January 25, 1936.

About ten years ago I learned to know and love Christian Science, and as I read the many wonderful testimonies in *The Herald of Christian Science* (German edition) and became absorbed in the study of the Christian Science textbook, *Science and Health with Key to the Scriptures,* by Mary Eddy Baker, the thought came to me that I, too, should put into practice what I had learned.

I received an injury to my ankle bone, which resulted in blood poisoning. The foot was very much discolored, and in a short time the leg became swollen up to the thigh. The pain was very severe.

After I had spent a few days in this condition, it became clear to me that only Truth could free me from my false thinking. It was a hard battle, but Truth won a complete victory. With my small understanding of Christian Science, I declared the truth, which, as Jesus said, frees us from every error. The results of divine Love exceeded all my expectations; for almost visibly the swelling disappeared, the pain ceased immediately, and I was healed.

Spurred on by this proof of divine omnipotence, I studied our textbook more earnestly. For several years I have been able, partly through the help of a Christian Science worker, to make many beautiful demonstrations for my family, as well as for myself.

—*Sentinel,* September 21, 1935.

I am grateful for the healing in Christian Science of an injury to one of my eyes. I was accidentally jabbed in the eye with a sharp arrowlike stick. I was helped to the home of friends, where I telephoned a practitioner. I then withdrew and remained alone for a time, declaring that there are no accidents in divine Mind. . . .

The next morning I called a Christian Science nurse to dress the eye. Although well-meaning friends had urged me to let them examine the eye, I refused to allow anyone to look at it except the nurse, and I refrained from looking at it myself. I did not want to see something, the seeming reality of which I was denying.

When the nurse examined the eye, she began singing our Leader's beautiful hymn (Hymnal, pp. 207-12) beginning "O gentle presence," as she removed a sizable splinter, the presence of which I had endured with little pain, through the help of Christian Science. My healing followed quickly, and was permanent. Many times since I have sung this hymn in my heart, learning its healing power.

In connection with this, it was suggested to me that I sue for damages. I refused on the ground that I could not consistently deny the reality of the injury when I wanted healing, and then claim that I had been injured in order to get damages. That would be "joining in a conspiracy against" myself, as Mrs. Eddy points out on page 339, of *Science and Health*.

—*Sentinel,* December 10, 1938.

The year of 1926 found me in a world of darkness and doubt. My mother had just passed on, and I was left alone and discouraged, for at the time I was an albino and was suffering from congenital nearsightedness, the pupils of the eyes moving back and forth.

This developed into blindness and severe headaches, the latter lasting from a week to a month. I had worn glasses for about thirty years, but was unable to get any strong enough. I was always told to expect the worst, until a friend said that God could heal me as He healed in Jesus' time.

It was several months later that I was led to attend the Christian Science Sunday services. My little cousin, reading the announcement in the daily paper, made me curious to know what Christian Science services were. I did not know that this

Science was what my friend had referred to. The services were so peaceful and uplifting that I could not stay away.

I learned through hearing the Lesson-Sermon from the *Christian Science Quarterly* that Christian Science heals. On inquiring how one could get help I was told that there were practitioners. Again truth was guiding me, for a friend offered to take me to see a practitioner seventy-two miles away.

I shall never forget that hour spent with her. When I first learned what God is, and that our real selfhood is made in His image and likeness.

The healing came slowly, for it was hard for me to realize that it was my own thinking that needed correcting. But one day when the practitioner was telling me, in the words of the apostle, "Now is the accepted time, behold, now is the day of salvation," I realized I was healed of blindness, and of the moving of the pupils of my eyes. Since then I have been able to read, and sew, all day long.

Later, I understood that I could not lack any needed substance. As Mrs. Eddy says (*Science and Health,* p. 301), "As God is substance and man is the divine image and likeness, man should wish for, and in reality has, only the substance of good, the substance of Spirit, not matter"; and with this truth I was healed of albinism.

Color came to my complexion, and my eyes, once pink, changed to blue. Also, the susceptibility to sunburn was healed at this time.

— *Journal,* May, 1942.

On December 4, 1913, a specialist pronounced my case to be tuberculosis in a very advanced condition, and said that immediate outdoor treatment must be commenced in a shelter on my lawn. This gentleman informed my partner that I could not recover, that I would pass on within six months. My local doctor supplemented this verdict by saying that I would never again be able to follow any employment or live in a normal way inside a house, even if this treatment was successful.

He further said that the best I could expect from it would be to prolong my existence a little while, because no treatment could replenish wasted organic tissue.

I commenced my life in the shelter about the middle of December. In the second week of January a lady visited me there, and told me I could be well if I would accept the teachings of Christian Science. My life in the shelter was lonely, tedious, and restless. My thoughts were chaotic. My hopes and ideals in life had all been shattered by this great shock, and I had no religious convictions to rely upon.

This lady's kindness and patience attracted me, but I felt sure that my views on religion could not suddenly be adapted by this new way of thinking. My doctors advised me to eat at all costs, even when I had no appetite. I struggled to obey; and sometimes my meals lasted an hour and a half in an effort to finish them.

After reading and rereading some Christian Science literature, I came to the conclusion it must be either a big lie or a big truth. I had lots of time for meditation; and my thoughts were gradually moving from my physical self—including mental pictures of diseased organs, germs, decay, and thoughts of death, with consequent fears—to a more spiritual realm.

I was having an awful mental upheaval. Sometimes I feared I could not survive it; but my appetite began to be normal, and step by step I gained a better evidence of health. I struggled hard to gain the substance of my new-found hope; but the way often seemed dark and too difficult for my understanding.

In March I was away on a farm where, in the quiet, I read Christian Science literature all my waking hours. I had help from a Christian Science practitioner in May and June; and, in the latter month, I commenced business with fear and trembling, but also with hope and thankfulness.

Adding together all the days from that time to the present, say a period of eight or nine years, I have not been away from business through sickness more than ten days. What a record! And how thankful I am for the normal life I now lead in a more congenial business! I am very strong, and the picture of health.

I have learned that being well is well being. I try to realize that a strong constitution is one constituted of right thoughts; that there is only one existence—namely, the spiritual—in which there can be no destruction or decomposition.

Jesus said, "I am come that they might have life, and that they might have it more abundantly." I have come out of a great tribulation with immense thankfulness for Christian Science.

—*Journal,* February, 1923.

One year we were spending our summer vacation on the Baltic Sea, and as there was continuous very hot weather we went bathing several times a day. After about three weeks our daughter was taken suddenly ill with vomiting and high fever. For days she refused all nourishment. Then she had difficulty in swallowing, her joints became swollen and stiff, and she was in great pain.

I tried with my own understanding of Christian Science to overcome this sickness, but she grew worse. I was told that the sickness was the result of her excessive ocean bathing.

In about a week my husband, who is not a Christian Scientist, insisted that a doctor be consulted. He came and identified the case as articular rheumatism. In the meantime I had written to a Christian Science practitioner and asked for help. But the sickness did not yield, the condition growing worse. The stiffness extended to the cervical vertebrae, and the child could not move her head, and was in great pain.

One day the sense of danger seemed especially great, the child being completely apathetic. When the doctor came he found his suspicion confirmed. He mentioned the danger of inflammation of the cerebral membrane, and a suspicion of cerebrospinal meningitis. . . .

Discouraged and perplexed, I remained alone with the child, as my husband meanwhile had had to go home. Despair threatened to seize me. I took the Christian Science textbook, and read. At the time I understood little of it, but I read on until I came to the passage which reads (p. 420), "Mind is the natural stimulus of the body."

I held on to this truth of which I was in need at that moment. I could not get beyond it, but read it over and over again. While I was pondering over these words, I had a vague, but yearning, desire, "If only the practitioner would work now!" Later I learned that the treatment I so desired was given at this time.

About half an hour later, suddenly, the child began to improve. She smiled at me, began to talk, sat up in bed, and in high glee showed me how she could move, and asked for some playthings and something to eat.

Others said it was "a miracle." But I knew it was no miracle, but the manifestation of Truth, and I am filled with gratitude for this proof of God's kindness. The doctor called a few times more, and could only confirm the quick recovery.

—*Sentinel,* January 25, 1936.

I am not a Christian Scientist. Last night's was the first visit I have ever paid to one of their churches.

I went early because I was told it was a Thanksgiving service—an annual event held on the last Thursday in every November. It is always crowded then, and it was no exaggeration—the vast church rapidly filled.

As the steady stream of people came in, I looked

around. It was all very strange; the high, dome-shaped roof, the semi-circular tiers of chairs, the four colossal arches that bounded the place, the high teak reading desk, with its teak canopy, and the colored pipes of the organ.

I read again and again the wall inscription: "With all thy getting, get understanding."

Then the rich tones of the organ filled the church, and after the voluntary, the congregation sang the "Mother's Evening Prayer," with its words by Mary Baker Eddy.

There was silent prayer; there were readings; and there was the Lord's Prayer. . . . Then the Reader said the gathering was open for testimonies.

I could not tell you how many people rose to testify; some spoke inaudibly, some clearly and ringingly, some almost vehemently. But . . . they were all earnest . . . and they were grateful, truly grateful.

A woman near me said, "It has helped me to be a better mother, a better wife, a better neighbor, and a better friend."

In front, a middle-aged man of the well-groomed business type said, "All the evidence of the past year has proved to me that physical sense must yield to Science. I have proved it time and time again, and I am deeply grateful. In my home it has brought good health, peace, and happiness. In times of stress, it has brought brightness."

There were many testimonies in which relief in unhappy cases was referred to, the blind man made to see, the tuberculosis victim eased, the drunkard saved.

For these, and other blessings, "joy, love, and protection," men and women paid tribute to "this glorious truth, the teachings of Mary Baker Eddy."

Out in the rain-sodden street people entered their big cars and drove away. I watched them leaving for a while. I imagined the quiet, happy city homes they were going to, for they all do seem to have gained happiness and contentment. Then I drove away, too.

On Sunday I shall return to my own church. In the meantime, I am glad I went to the Thanksgiving services.

If Christian Science has brought happiness to so many people there is a place for it in any community.

—Oliver Quain, in the *Daily News,*
Durban, Natal, South Africa.

CHAPTER FIFTEEN

Unless Youth Is Drawn

BELIEVING the Christian Science Movement to be in its beginnings, Mrs. Eddy permitted nothing to meddle with its beginnings. It was conviction that contained the capacity to look into countless tomorrows and see that unless youth is drawn to the same task that beckoned Isaiah and Jeremiah there is no devotion. It was assurance that left things for others to do—knowing that when the time comes for their doing, they will be done.

Illustrative of this is Mrs. Eddy's letter of January 21, 1906. This was the letter in which she advised Mrs. Mary Beecher Longyear to abandon the proposal to build a sanatorium because it was a matter that "properly belongs to The Christian Science Board of Directors to do"; and in which she indicated her own willingness to leave the decision of when to build in the care of the Directors—so sure was she that the time would come when "God's creation will appear."

As with the development of the sanatorium and The Christian Science Benevolent Association, so with the development of many things. When the challenge came, the way was open.

The growth of Christian Science among college students is one of these developments, and it illustrates the normal order of "first the blade, then the ear, after that the full corn in the ear."

Mrs. Eddy did not fear for the young. It was her wish to be with them in thought as they moved into deeper views. It was her counsel that the only way to progress is through preparation. It was her instruction that "to begin rightly enables one to end rightly, and thus it is that one achieves the Science of Life, demonstrates health, holiness and immortality." [1]

"On September 8 and 9," as reported in the *Sentinel*, December 3, 1955, "hundreds of university students gathered in the Original Mother Church in Boston, Massachusetts, for the first meeting to be held in the interest of Christian Science College Organizations. College students from England, Scotland, France, Switzerland, Australia, Canada and the United States, representing one hundred and forty-one different universities, attended the two-day session which was arranged by the Department of Branches and Practitioners with the approval of The Christian Science Board of Directors. . . .

"The steady increase in the number of new organizations, the splendid growth of their memberships, the improved quality of their work for the Cause of Christian Science, gave rise to the need for considering the 'what, how, whither' of the challenge at hand. The Mother Church accordingly provided for the gathering."

The subjects discussed were many. There was a workshop with its questions and answers; an evening seminar with specific matters pertaining to Christian Science; a speaker who knew Mrs. Eddy was heard; officials of The Mother Church and the Publishing Society talked of their work; the visitors were taken to the Board Room where they were introduced to The Christian Science Board of Directors; and, with the formal sessions ended, they visited Mrs. Eddy's

[1] *Miscellany,* p. 274.

home in Chestnut Hill, and other places of historial interest in Boston.

The representatives who gathered in The Mother Church in September, 1955, were not of the same mold as other students of Christian Science who, forty years before, were doubtful of the future of Mrs. Eddy's teachings.

No voices of capitulation were heard, such as were heard so soon after Mrs. Eddy's passing: "It is not possible for the church to survive under a set of rules which makes it impossible to keep in tune with the times." There was no complaining, such as before had reached many ears: "Mrs. Eddy could not have intended that we should be compelled to remain within fixed By-laws when she, herself, made changes to fit new conditions."

Doubts such as these had no place in the work of the representatives of one hundred and forty universities, located in seven countries. Meeting in Boston almost half a century after Mrs. Eddy made her final revisions, they had no trouble seeing that the walls of The Mother Church are held together by the *Church Manual*.

The existence of the *Manual* as a timeless instrument protecting The Mother Church is constantly disclosed; and a familiar road was traveled within a few weeks after the college organizations ended their meeting.

Early in the autumn of 1955, the Chairman of the Senate Subcommittee on Constitutional Rights announced that the subcommittee was preparing to conduct hearings on freedom of religion, as guaranteed by the First Amendment to the Constitution. The announcement, which was made in the newspapers, also informed the public that a questionnaire was available to all who wished to answer it.

From Boston came an immediate request for a copy of the questionnaire, and a voluntary offer to reply to all questions. Under date of October 8, 1955, the Senate Subcommittee sent its questionnaire and, on October 12, 1955, the Committee on Publication for The Mother Church replied. There were seven questions, all pertaining to the "religion clause" in the First Amendment to the Constitution with its guarantee that "Congress shall make no law respecting an establishment of religion, or prohibiting the free exercise thereof," and all seeking to determine, as asked in Question 5: "Have you observed any significant instances in recent years of a denial of the rights expressed in the religion clause? If your answer is Yes, kindly enumerate the instances."

The Committee on Publication replied at length, in part as follows:

"Christian Scientists find that the Constitutional guarantee of religious freedom is infringed where the following compulsions are enforced and there is no evidence that exemption on religious grounds would endanger the public welfare, provided isolation and quarantine regulations are observed:

"(a) Compulsory vaccination and inoculation.

"(b) Compulsory X-ray chest examination.

"(c) Compulsory physical examinations of school children.

"(d) Compulsory periodic medical examination for federal, state or local employees.

"(e) Compulsory study in public schools of medical disease theory, detailed descriptions of diseases and their symptoms; films, books, and other materials graphically portraying forms of disease or its effects; or of material which insists or infers that medical treatment is the only effective method of treating human ailments.

"(f) Requirement that the individual rely on medical

treatment for healing in order to qualify for disability benefits. This includes workmen's compensation, a proposal now
pending in Congress regarding Social Security benefits, and
other public supported systems.

"(g) Fluoridation of public water supply—a phase of compulsory medicine.

"(h) World Health Organization regulations.

"Compulsory medical care forces the Christian Scientist
to violate the sacred obligations of his religion; it invades
his communion with God, and interferes with his method
of prayer and worship.

"Christian Science teaches that the source of health is an
understanding of God and that all diseases can be healed by
means of systematic, scientific prayer.

"For the Christian Scientist, reliance on prayer to God for
healing is fundamental to his worship of God. It is insep-
arable from his worship. His worship of God is seriously
hampered—insofar as governmental law or administrative
regulations compel him to submit to medical diagnosis, the
use of drugs, or other medical treatment. . . .

"What is involved here is the right of the individual to
worship God according to his conscience—not the rights or
privileges of a religious denomination as such.

"All the Christian Scientists ask is exemption from local,
state, or federal programs of medical services or care, in-
doctrination or education, which, when compulsory, constitute an infringement of their religious freedom. The
Constitutional guarantee of individual freedom clearly prohibits the state from compelling the individual citizen to
adopt a particular method of treatment or healing especially
when this constitutes an invasion of his religious convictions
and practice.

"The right of Christian Scientists to depend upon their

religion for healing is quite widely recognized in actual practice. Where it is so recognized there is no significant evidence to indicate that this harms or endangers others or infringes their rights.

"Christian Scientists demand the right to be exempt from local, state and federal rules, regulations and laws as above indicated but in doing so they recognize the right of others to be protected from contagious and infectious diseases. Whenever there is reason to believe that a communicable disease has developed, they report it to the proper public authority. They observe strictly the regulations regarding isolation and quarantine. Where a Christian Scientist is employed as a food handler or in some similar work, and periodic physical examination is required for the protection of the public, we do not object. . . .

"As stated above, Christian Scientists quickly and willingly isolate themselves from others at the first indication of infectious or contagious disease. They feel that, where religious rights are involved, this method of controlling such disease is more in keeping with our American way of life than the attempt to establish universal compulsory medical examination and vaccination. They feel also that medical examinations in the schools tend to indoctrinate the children with medical teachings.

"It seems an unnecessary invasion of religious liberty for the schools to take on the responsibility of compulsory periodic medical examination—particularly when the children are in good health and when such examination is contrary to their religious convictions. . . ."

Unfortunately, the investigation of the Senate Subcommittee on Constitutional Rights was broken off almost before it was begun—but the sign of righting things was seen, nevertheless. It was seen because the question of religious freedom was raised. But, in spite of temporary abandonment, freedom to worship God is the destiny of mankind. It will come. Nor is it necessary to pass judgment on the materialism that delays its arrival. The only need is to see what is in the way.

Since 1866, when Mrs. Eddy was her own Committee on Publication, and since 1885, when she appointed others to help her, and since 1895, when she published the *Church Manual,* the obligation of Committees on Publication has been to see what is in the way, and to establish freedom for the practice of Christian Science—knowing that by establishing freedom for themselves, they will establish it for all mankind.

Mrs. Eddy saw the *Manual* as prophetic of the church she established. In the fifteen years that separated first publication and final revision, she waited, as she waited in all things, "for the watchword, and the revelation of what, how, whither" in full trust, as she added, that "God will do the rest." [2]

In *The Christian Science Journal,* April, 1922, Adam H. Dickey recalled this period:

Such changes as were made . . . by our Leader in the constitution of our church did not come without struggle. In this connection follows a statement from her own lips which the writer took just as she uttered it:

"I prayed God day and night to show me how to form my church and how to go on with it. I understand that He did show me, just as much as I understand that He showed me Christian Science, and no human being ever showed me Christian Science. Then I have no right or desire to change what God has directed me to do, and it remains for the church to obey it. What has prospered this church for thirty years will continue to prosper it."

[2] *Miscellaneous Writings,* p. 158.

Full-toned in its freedom from personal opinion, the *Manual* continues to prosper the church which began as a simple voluntary religious association, and so remains; which began by teaching that when thinking of God, mankind is sure to be thinking wrongly unless thinking in terms of perfection and Allness, and so remains; which began with no proselyting, and so remains—saying to all who contemplate joining to give to family, to pastor, and, if needs be, to friends, reasonable proof that the contemplated step is not hasty, but was reached through prayer.

Knowing that whatever is good is always under attack, Mrs. Eddy wrote the church By-laws in agreement with what she perceived to be the truth. Certain that truth provides freedom in rounded measure for all that is good, and perceiving that only the good is permanent, Mrs. Eddy was sure the same permanency would attend the *Church Manual*— and provide, in perpetuity, an open way to every fountain.

The fifty years of continued progress that have been added to the thirty years of Mrs. Eddy's testimony but underscore the evidence.

Mary Baker Eddy offered the world a simple religion—and sought for her teachings no acceptance without demonstration.

In her teachings, prayer seeks no gifts, asks no favors, pleads for no mercy, and makes no petitions for God to do this, or do that. In her teachings, prayer seeks only the presence of God.

To pray God to do more, when He has done all, is to misunderstand Him; and, in *Science and Health* (p. 3), she wrote:

Who would stand before a blackboard and pray
the principle of mathematics to solve the problem?

The rule is already established, and it is our task to work out the solution. Shall we ask the divine Principle of all goodness to do His own work? His work is done, and we have only to avail ourselves of God's rule in order to receive His blessing, which enables us to work out our own salvation.

It is emphasized in her teachings that when, in prayer, we close the door to all material senses, truth is revealed, we perceive it, and we know it. Emphasized, too, is the teaching that when we go to God in prayer we find that we are His reflection; not in part, but completely—and, in proportion to our acceptance, we come to Bethlehem.

To many, teachings such as these are abstractions because they are not of the human senses. To Mrs. Eddy, the Word of God is not an abstraction, and cannot be.

Knowing truth has no receptacle but itself, she believed that, in prayer, it is natural to hear the Word; and hearing, hear only what is true. Swedenborg also perceived this, and spoke of it: "It is no proof of man's understanding to be able to affirm what he pleases; but to be able to discern that what is true, and that what is false—this is the mark and character of intelligence."

Mrs. Eddy devoted an entire chapter, the first chapter, in *Science and Health* to the subject of prayer; and opened her book with this statement: "The prayer that reforms the sinner and heals the sick is an absolute faith that all things are possible to God,—a spiritual understanding of Him, an unselfed love." And, in *Rudimental Divine Science* (p. 10) she taught: ". . . God alone governs man; that His government is harmonious; that He is too pure to behold iniquity, and divides His power with nothing evil or material; that material laws are only human beliefs, which govern man wrongfully."

There is no doubt that in Mrs. Eddy's mind was the conviction that submission to material law will end and acknowledgment of spiritual law will prevail. Throughout her teachings runs the thought: suffering is the same as in the time of Jesus; truth is the same; God is the same—why, then, should not healing be the same? To grasp the truth of healing, she taught that pretense of every kind must be banished from the mind. When this is done, healing is inevitable, and immediate.

Mrs. Eddy understood the words, "Be ye therefore perfect, even as your Father which is in heaven is perfect," to be an individual responsibility. She was sure God's kingdom is of the spirit, and not of the flesh. She was equally sure that in His kingdom are no external forms—and no duality with purification of the flesh.

To offer a religion based on the perfection of God, and on the creation of man in the image of God, was to present an affirmation so elevated that even in Palestine, many years before, few embraced it. Perceiving this, she also saw that the wider the dissemination of the teachings of Jesus, the greater became their dilution for purposes of expediency.

That was why, in preparing the *Church Manual,* she so carefully defined the responsibilities of all who call themselves Christian Scientists. She knew that every dilution of the truth is an effort to establish what is not true, and give what is not true authority over mankind.

The real and the spurious travel together, and the more like the genuine the counterfeit can make itself, the less its risk of exposure. We all know that. We all know the counterfeit offers friendship, professes virtue, and travels widely—and, wherever it goes, introduces destruction. We all know that in money the counterfeit imitates the good; in government, the politician poses as the statesman; in commerce, the trickster acts the merchant.

In the vaster, more important realm of the spiritual, we are not so careful.

Here we find matter counterfeiting spirit, and promising love of God—but delivering sickness and poverty, hate, war, pestilence, and death; here we find matter arguing it is real—when its destiny is less than the dust; here in the vaster, more important realm of the spiritual, we find matter promising to lengthen the days of man upon the earth—in imitation of God's law of everlasting life.

That is the way of the counterfeit—it promises, but delivers on lower ground, on much lower ground.

In Mrs. Eddy's teachings, the greatest defense against the counterfeit is to know more about the real.

In *Miscellaneous Writings* (p. 61) she wrote:

> The education of the future will be instruction, in spiritual Science, against the material symbolic counterfeit sciences. All the knowledge and vain strivings of mortal mind, that lead to death—even when aping the wisdom and magnitude of immortal Mind,—will be swallowed up by the reality and omnipotence of Truth over error, and of Life over death.

It was in her acknowledgment of God as perfect and eternal that Mary Baker Eddy found her life and her work.

It was a conception that made of prayer more than an occasional thing; it was a conviction that to live in God is to understand not one truth, but all truth; and it was a certainty that it is only when we surrender ourselves to God that we win the final victory.

Mary Baker Eddy was not a halfway believer in God.

She refused to make any concessions in exchange for popularity, or compromises in exchange for numbers. Probably, more than any other factor, these refusals brought violent opposition to her, and to what she taught. But, no matter what was said, and no matter what was done, she healed the sick through prayer—and in the healings revealed the eternal life that is the testimony of His truth.

Appendices

1.

People v. Cole, Court of Appeals, State of New York
October, 1916. 219 N.Y. 98-113 NE790
The People of the State of New York, Respondent,
v. Willis V. Cole, Appellant.

Statement of Case

Public Health Law — Christian Science Practitioners — when statute does not prohibit offer of prayer for healing of disease in accordance with the tenets of the Christian Science church.

The Public Health Law, forbidding the practice of medicine by a person not licensed and registered as a physician, contains the qualification that the statute shall not be construed to affect the practice of the religious tenets of any church (p. 161-173). One of the tenets of the Christian Science church is the healing of physical disease by prayer; that prayer to God will result in complete cure of particular diseases in a prescribed, individual case. The defendant was not a licensed physician, but he was a member of the Christian Science church and one of its recognized practitioners, who, in the present case, assumed by silent prayer and for a money consideration to practice the healing of a patient of trouble with the eyes and a pain in the back. He testified that he was practicing Christian Science as laid down by the church and denied that he was practicing medicine. He made no diagnosis and prescribed no other remedy. On an indictment for violating the Public Health Law, *held*, that although defendant did "treat" the investigator by "any (some) means or method," as the word is used in the general prohibition contained in the statute (160, subd. 7), the statute is broad enough to permit offering prayer for the healing of disease in accordance with the recognized tenets of the Christian Science church.

The religious tenets of the church must, however, be practiced in good faith to come within the exception. When such practice is a fraud or pretense it is not excepted from the general prohibition, and when a person claims to be practicing the religious tenets of any church, particularly where compensation is taken therefor and the practice is apart from a church edifice or the sanctity of the home of the applicant, the question whether such person is within the exception should be left to a jury as a question of fact. Hence, the court erroneously charged the jury: "If you find from the evidence in this case that this defendant did engage in the practice of medicine as alleged in the indictment, within the definition which I have given you, it is no defense that he did what he did from any sense of duty, or that he did these acts in the practice of the religious tenets of the Christian Science church."

People v. Cole, 163, App. Div. 292, reversed.
(Argued June 5, 1916; decided October 3, 1916)

Appeal from an order of the Appellate Division of the Supreme Court in the first judicial department, entered July 10, 1914, which affirmed a judgment rendered at a Trial Term for the county of New York upon a verdict convicting the defendant of the crime of practicing medicine without lawful authorization and registration.

The facts, so far as material, are stated in the opinion.

Points of counsel

Samuel J. Elder, Herbert Noble, Henry D. Estabrook, Edmund A. Whitman and Clifford P. Smith for appellant. The definition of the "practice of medicine" in the act of 1907 was not intended to and did not enlarge the meaning of that phrase as then commonly understood, and was not intended to and did not include the practice of Christian Science in offering prayer for the sick.

(Bailey v. Mogg, 4 Den. 60; White v. Carroll, 42 N.Y. 161; People v. Somme, 120 App. Div. 20; 190 N.Y. 541; Martin v.

Baldy, 249 Penn. St. 253; People v. Phyfe, 136 N.Y. 554; People v. Rosenberg, 138 N.Y. 410; State v. Faratz, 83 Conn. 300; Verona Cheese Co. v. Murtaugh, 50 N.Y. 314; People v. Briggs, 193 N.Y. 457; Unwin v. Hanson, L.R. (2 Q.B. 1891) 115.) The conviction in this case cannot be sustained under the statutory definition of the practice of medicine because the acts of the defendant are expressly excluded therefrom by the words, "This article shall not be construed to affect ... the practice of the religious tenets of any church." (Public Health Law p. 173; United States v. Fisher, 2 Cranch 358; Comm. v. Poen, 195 Mass. 443; 196 Mass. 326; State v. Main, 69 Conn. 123; Hilton v. Roylance, 25 Utah 129; Weiss v. District Board, 76 Wis. 177; White v. Carroll, 42 N.Y. 161; Rogers v. Cady, 104 Cal. 288; People v. Mayes, 113 Cal. 618; Nix v. Holden, 149 U.S. 304; Brown v. Piper, 91 U.S. 37.)

Edward Swann, District Attorney (Robert C. Taylor of counsel, for respondent). The evidence showed practice of medicine by defendant. (People v. Smith, 51 Col. 270; State v. Peters, 87 Kans. 265; People v. Allcutt, 117 App. Div. 546; 189 N.Y. 517; People v. Mulford, 140 App. Div. 716; 202 N.Y. 624; Bragg v. State, 134 Ala. 165; O'Neill v. State, 115 Tenn. 427; State v. Buewell, 40 Neb. 158; State v. Marble, 72 Ohio St. 21; Singh v. State, 146 S.W. Rep. 891.) The exception in section 173 of the Public Health Law affords no defense. (Reynolds v. United States, 98 U.S. 145; Davis v. Beason, 133 U.S. 333; Mormon Church v. United States, 136 U.S. 1; People v. Smith, 51 Col. 270; State v. Peters, 87 Kans. 265; People v. Spinella, 150 App. Div. 923; 206 N.Y. 709.)

(Opinion, per Chase, J.)

Chase, J. On February 18, 1911, on an application therefor by the New York County Medical Society, a warrant was obtained against the defendant charging him with practicing medicine as defined by section 160 of the Public Health Law of the State of New York, without being duly licensed therefor. (People v. Cole, 25 N.Y. Crim. Rep. 350). On March 21, 1911, he was indicted by a grand jury of the county of New York. The indictment charges him with the crime of practicing medicine without lawful authorization and registration and alleges that such unlawful practicing of medicine occurred on the 19th day of January, 1911, and continually thereafter to and including the 28th day of January, 1911. The defendant was tried on such indictment in the New York Supreme Court Criminal Term, but the jury failed to agree and was discharged. Another trial was had in the same court and resulted in a verdict of guilty and a judgment was accordingly entered against the defendant on the 30th day of March, 1912. He appealed from such judgment to the Appellate Division where it was affirmed by a divided court. (People v. Cole, 163 App. Div. 292). An appeal was then taken from such judgment of affirmance to this court.

Practicing medicine when unaccompanied by acts that are in themselves evil, vicious and criminal, is not a crime at common law. Practicing medicine is not *malum in se*. It is important in the interest of public health and public welfare that a person holding himself out as a physician or healer of diseases, should have the education, training, skill and knowledge adequate for such purposes. Statutes designed to protect public health and general welfare by regulating the practice of medicine, in some part or all of the territory constituting this state, have been enacted from time to time since 1760.

When a person is charged with practicing medicine without a license it is necessary to examine the acts of the legislature to ascertain whether the practices complained of are in violation of the statute law.

The Public Health Law (Cons. Laws, ch. 45) of this state provides, and did provide at all the times mentioned in the indictment, that "No person shall practice medicine, unless registered and legally authorized prior to September first, eighteen hundred and ninety-one, or unless licensed by the regents and registered under article eight or chapter six hundred and sixty-one of the laws of eighteen hundred and ninety-three and acts amendatory thereto, or unless licensed by the regents and registered as required by this article ... (Public Health Law, p. 161.) "The practice of medicine is defined as follows: A person practices medicine within the meaning of this article, except as hereinafter stated, who holds himself out as being able to diagnose, treat, operate or prescribe for any human disease, pain, injury, deformity or physical condition, and who shall either offer, or undertake, by any means or method, to diagnose, treat, operate or prescribe for any human disease, pain, injury, deformity or physical condition." (Public Health Law, p. 160, subd. 7.)

The statute also provides: "This article shall not be construed to affect . . . the practice of the religious tenets of any church . . ." (Public Health Law, p. 173.)

Our Constitution provides: "The free exercise and enjoyment of religious profession and worship, without discrimination or preference, shall forever be allowed in this state to all mankind; . . . but the liberty of conscience hereby secured shall not be construed as to excuse acts of licentiousness, or justify practices inconsistent with the peace or safety of this state." (Constitution of the State of New York, Article 1, section 3.)

The defendant was never registered or licensed as a practitioner of medicine. He is a member of the Christian Science church and a recognized practitioner within the rules of that church. For about seven years he maintained an office in the City of New York. At the times mentioned in the indictment, his office was on the ninth floor of a building at Fifth Avenue and Madison Square. It consisted of two rooms; one, a reception room containing chairs, tables, a clock and literature; and an inner office containing a desk, two chairs, and a telephone. On the door of his office were the words: "Willis Vernon Cole, Christian Scientist."

The evidence taken on the trial consisted of the testimony of a woman who for seven years had been employed by and under the direction of the New York County Medical Society as an investigator, and the testimony of the defendant.

The investigator testified that at her first interview with the defendant on January 19, 1911, she waited in the reception room of his office with others until an opportunity arrived to see him and she then went into the inner office. She further testified as follows:

"I asked him if he was Dr. Cole. And he said he was Mr. Cole, a Christian Science healer. . . . I said . . . that I read about him in the newspapers; that I called to see if he could cure my eyes.

I had been troubled with eye trouble. And he said, 'How long have you been wearing glasses?' And I said, 'Ten years.' He said, 'You understand I do not give any medicine, I only give Christian Science treatment.' ... I said to him, 'What is Christian Science?' And he said, 'I cure by prayer.' He said that you must have faith in God; that God don't make us to have any disease; that we must be all love and all kindness and that God would cure the infidel as well as the confirmed believer in his Divine Power.' And I said what would be the fee? And he said $2 for the first treatment and all subsequent treatments, $1. ... The defendant then said, 'I will give you a treatment.' So Mr. Cole had his chair facing mine, and he closed his eyes and raised his hands up to his face and remained in perfect silence for fifteen or twenty minutes ... He said, 'That will do for today's treatment. You come back on Friday any time.' " On Friday, the next day, she returned to his office. Her testimony as to what occurred is as follows:

"I went in and he said to me, 'Why, you are looking very well.' And I said, 'I feel about the same.' And after that, why, he spoke about God is good and we must have love and faith in God. And then he says, why, he will give me a treatment. So that Mr. Cole placed his chair facing mine again, closed his eyes and put his hands up to his face and we remained in perfect silence for about fifteen minutes."

She further testified that before the treatment she said to him, " 'Mr. Cole, I have a pain in my back.' I then said that I had a porous plaster on my back at that time; and I said to him what did he think about the pain I had in my back. He said it was some kind of disease, but he could not tell me what kind it was; he said, 'I can cure it.' He said 'you must now take off that porous plaster because Christian Science cannot cure with plasters on.' He said that I must take off my glasses as well as remove the porous plaster from my back ... That I should have more faith and understanding; that I must have courage; that I should remove the glasses ... I said I must keep my glasses as I cannot go without them ... He said if I wanted to be cured by Christian Science I must remove the glasses ... I said, 'How can you cure locomotor ataxia?' He said, 'Just by prayer and by having faith in God.' He said 'When patients are given up by physicians they always turn to Christian Science for help.' " He told her to come back on Monday, January 23. She did so. She said to him, " 'I removed the plaster that was on my back as you told me to.' And he said, 'I want you also to remove the glasses.' I said, 'I have to keep the glasses on.' I said, 'When I eat bread and potato I would distress my stomach very much.' He said, 'Leave your stomach alone; you go home and eat anything you want to.' "

She returned again on January 27, and brought her little girl with her. The little girl wore glasses. She further testified, "I said to Mr. Cole that the child has been wearing glasses and she also has a cold. I said, 'Can you cure her by Christian Science?' And he said, 'Absolutely.' I said, 'Well, will you cure her?' And he replied, 'Absolutely.' So I said that the child had a pair of roller skates, and wearing glasses, why, if she should fall she would injure herself. And he said, 'You take the glasses off and let the child run and romp like other children;' that mothers should not put such fear in children." ... He gave them treatment similar to the one he had given her before.

The defendant during the interviews stated to the witness that she had as much power to heal disease as he had, and could do so as well if she would study the Bible and rely upon its promises and offer the prayer of understanding and faith. She understood him when he asserted that he could cure disease as saying that he could bring about the cure by means of prayer to Almighty God. He said to her that all diseases were alike to a Christian Scientist.

The defendant testified that at the first interview with the investigator "she told me that she had come to be treated for trouble with her eyes and stomach trouble. I informed her that Christian Science treatment was prayer to God, we did not believe in drugs, medical treatment, anything like that, and she asked me to give her treatment. Something was said in regard to the basis of Christian Science, and I told her substantially that Christian Science was the truth about God, and the truth about man and the truth about man's relationship to God and his birthright as a result of this relationship, which is the foundation of what we teach, and I told her that on this basis disease was no part of her birthright, or inharmony, and when she realized her oneness with God, and got in harmony with God that this was the treatment and was what we would do. I covered my face with my hands, or sat with my head partially bowed for fifteen minutes," in prayer.

He testified that at the second interview, "she spoke to me about taking off her glasses and I told her that there was no reason that she should not take off her glasses, and I casually spoke of my own healing, that I had worn glasses for many years . . . and taken them off . . . I told her I had had trouble with my eyes and had several other diseases, and that I had been to a number of physicians and I had been healed by Christian Science."

He further testified that on the second visit he told her "That Christian Science treatment was prayer to God. I told her that Christian Science realized that God was omnipotent, or all powerful; that He was omniscient, or all knowing; that He was omnipresent, or ever present; and that because God was omnipotent, and omniscient, and omnipresent, and God was good, that it must follow that evil, disease, inharmony, sin and discord were no parts of His Being and had no real existence, and I told her that man was the image and likeness of God, and was entitled to dominion, and that his birthright was dominion and that he had the right to affirm and secure immunity from discord of whatever name and nature, and that disease was like a shadow that flees before the light."

He says he told her that this result would follow from spiritual understanding. He says he spoke to her about keeping her life pure and Christlike and loving and good, and just and free from error. He says he then prayed again, and that prayer is a synonym for treatment.

He further testified that at the first interview, "I told her I could not cure her, that I had no more power to cure her than anyone else, that God was the only power, and the only healer . . . I told her that she could cure herself just as much as I could if she would study and purify her life, and her thoughts and cleanse from her consciousness fear and inharmony and false thoughts. I told her that by studying and gaining an understanding that she could apply the principle and law of Christian Science as well as anyone else, as well as I could ... I told her that I was nothing, and she was nothing, it was God."

His testimony as to what was said at the third interview was as follows: "We discussed Christian Science and I picked up *Science and Health with Key to the Scriptures* by Mrs. Eddy, which is recognized in Christian Science as the standard textbook; it is the original Christian Science textbook which we accept with the Holy Scriptures of which it is explanatory as the basis of our great religious truth. I asked her to procure a copy of this book."

He testified that he read to her from that book. " 'To be "present with the Lord" is to have, not mere emotional ecstasy or faith, but the actual demonstration and understanding of Life as revealed in Christian Science. To be "with the Lord" is to be in obedience to the law of God, to be absolutely governed by Divine Love,—by Spirit, not by matter.

" 'Become conscious for a single moment that Life and intelligence are purely spiritual—neither in nor of matter—and the body will then utter no conscious complaints. If suffering from a belief in sickness, you will find yourself suddenly well. Sorrow is turned into joy when the body is controlled by spiritual Life, Truth and Love.

" 'Entirely separate from the belief and dream of material living is the Life Divine, revealing spiritual understanding and the consciousness of man's dominion over the whole earth. This understanding casts out error and heals the sick, and with it you can speak "as one having authority." ' " [1]

He testified that he was practicing Christian Science as laid down by the church. He denied that he was practicing medicine.

It was conceded on the trial that Christian Science is a religion based upon the Scriptures and founded by Mary Baker Eddy in 1866, and that the church has about a million members. The alleged healing of moral, mental, and physical diseases by prayer was practiced by Christian Scientists in New York for more than twenty years before the times mentioned in the indictment. It

[1] *Science and Health*, p. 14.

was also conceded that in order to obtain entry upon the list of practitioners of the Christian Science church proof must be furnished satisfactory to the church of the character and qualifications of the applicant, but that the education and experience of the applicant is not an element in his qualifications. The church relies wholly upon the sincerity of the applicant and his reliance and faith in the power and efficacy of prayer to heal diseases.

It appears from the statute that we have quoted that a person practices medicine when he "holds himself out as being able to diagnose, treat, operate or prescribe for any human disease, pain, injury, deformity or physical condition, and who shall either offer or *undertake, by any means or method,* to diagnose, treat, operate, or prescribe for any human disease, pain, injury, deformity, or physical condition."

The language of the statute is very general. It bears evidence in itself that the words were chosen for the express purpose of prohibiting, except upon registration and authorization of the practitioner, as by the statute provided, every means and method that could thereafter be used or claimed to be used to relieve or cure diseases and infirmity by any person individually, or as a representative of a school, religious body or other organization.

It does not appear that the defendant attempted to diagnose the diseases which the investigator stated to him that she had; he not only in substance denied that she had any disease, but asserted that they rested in her imagination or were mere evidence of a lack of true relation to her God.

There was no inquiry on his part into the symptoms which the investigator claimed that she had as indicating the disease. There was no laying on of hands, manipulation, massage, or outward ceremonial. His direction to her to remove her glasses and to take off a porous plaster which she asserted she had upon her back were, as also asserted by him, simply to bring about complete reliance by her upon the power and willingness of God to heal her diseases.

Such directions were not, he asserts, intended as a prescription or as advice. It was a test of her faith. He, however, testified that prayer was a synonym for treatment. He habitually termed his interposition by prayer a treatment and such it would seem to have been in the ordinary meaning of the word. He had a place where interposition by prayer to God could be sought through him at a price, either as a compensation or as an honorarium. He asserts that he made interposition with God by prayer to take away diseases or what he alleges to be wrong relationships between persons having diseases and their God. His interposition with God as explained by him was to obtain such Divine action that the inharmony between the Divine Being and the person who sought to be relieved of diseases and infirmities might be adjusted. The duties of the defendant as a practitioner would seem to have been to handle the claim of those that came to him with their ills with a view to obtaining a Divine cure. Such interposition under such circumstances was, in the language of the defendant himself, a "treatment."

We are of the opinion that the defendant did "treat" the investigator by "any (some) means or method," as the word is used in the general prohibition contained in the statute.

The general and comprehensive definition of a person who practices medicine has an express exception. The descriptive words are preceded by the phrase "except as hereinafter stated." The exception concededly refers to the words in section 173 of the Public Health Law as follows: "This article shall not be construed to affect . . . the practice of the religious tenets of any church." The exception includes every person in the practice of the religious tenets of any church, and it is not in any way in conflict with the Federal or State Constitution.

The language quoted from said section 173 is not in any sense an affirmative license. It is, we repeat, an exception to the general prohibition. Whether the practice of the religious tenets of any church should have been excepted from the general prohibition against the practice of medicine unless the practitioner is registered and authorized so to do, or whether the exception should be continued therein, is a question for the legislature and not for the courts. The purpose of the general statute is to protect citizens and others of the state from being treated in their physical ailments and diseases by persons who have not adequate or proper training, education or qualifications to treat them.

The tenets of a church are the beliefs, doctrines and creeds of the church. The exception relates to the tenets of the church as an organized body as distinguished from an individual. It does not relate to or except persons practicing in accordance with individual belief.

It appears from the record that it is a tenet of the Christian Science church that prayer to God will result in complete cure of particular diseases in the prescribed, individual case. Healing would seem to be not only the prominent work of the church and its members, but the one distinctive belief around which the church organization is founded and sustained. It is claimed that the church extends its influence and spreads knowledge of its power by practical demonstration on the part of its sincere practitioners in securing the overthrow of moral, mental and physical disease.

It disclaims any reliance upon skill, education or science. In view of the tenets of the Christian Science church the exception to the prohibition in the statute is broader than the provision of the Constitution of this state which we have quoted, and which permits the free exercise and enjoyment of religious profession and worship without discrimination or preference.

The exception in the statute is not confined to worship or belief that includes the practice of religious tenets. If it was the intention of the legislature to relieve members of the Christian Science and other churches from the provisions of sections 160 and 161 of the Public Health Law to the extent of permitting them within the rules, regulations and tenets of a church to maintain an office and there offer prayer for the healing of the diseases of those that might come to such church members for treatment, and the defendant has in good faith acted in accordance therewith, he is not guilty of the crime alleged in the indictment.

The Christian Science church is in terms expressly excepted from the prohibition contained in the medical practice acts of many of the States. It is so expressly excepted in the statutes of Maine, New Hampshire, Massachusetts, Connecticut, North

Carolina, North and South Dakota, Kentucky, Tennessee and Wisconsin.

We think the exception in the statute in this state is broad enough to permit offering prayer for the healing of disease in accordance with the recognized tenets of the Christian Science church. It may be said that if the exception is so construed, it will lead to numberless persons assuming to cure diseases in the name of a church for the purpose of thereby maintaining a business and securing a livelihood.

The religious tenets of a church must be practiced in good faith to come within the exception. When such practice is a fraud or pretense it is not excepted from the general prohibition. When wrong is practiced in the name of religion it is not protected by Constitution or statute. (*Reynolds v. U.S.* 98 *U.S.* 145; *Davis v. Beason,* 133 *U.S.* 333; *Mormon Church v. U.S.* 136 *U.S.* 1.) Many of the decisions referred to by counsel may be explained by the fact that the persons therein severally considered were frauds and shams. (See *People v. Spinella,* 150 App. Div. 923; affd., 206 N.Y. 709.)

A person should not be allowed to assume to practice the tenets of the Christian Science or any church as a shield to cover a business undertaking. When a person claims to be practicing the religious tenets of any church, particularly where compensation is taken therefor and the practice is apart from a church edifice or the sanctity of the home of the applicant, the question whether such person is within the exception should be left to a jury as a question of fact.

In this case the court charged the jury: "If you find from the evidence in this case that this defendant did engage in the practice of medicine as alleged in the indictment, within the definition which I have given you, it is no defense that he did what he did from any sense of duty, or that he did those acts in the practice of the religious tenets of the Christian Science church."

We are of the opinion that the court was in error in so charging the jury. The exception was intended by the legislature to exclude from the prohibition the practice of the religious tenets of the Christian Science church and other churches. It was necessary as we have seen that the practice be of the tenets of a recognized church and the court, instead of charging the jury as stated, should have left to the jury the question whether the defendant was in good faith practicing the tenets of such a church within the meaning of the statutory exception.

The judgment should be reversed and a new trial ordered.

Cuddeback and Cardozo, JJ., concur; Willard Bartlett, Ch. J., concurs in the following memorandum: I concur in Judge Chase's construction of the Statute. But I would go farther. I deny the power of the legislature to make it a crime to treat disease by prayer; Collins, J., not voting; Hogan J., absent; Seabury, J., not sitting.

Judgment reversed, etc..

2.

People v. Vogelgesang, 221 N.Y. 290 — 116NE977 July, 1917
The People of the State of New York, Respondent,
v. Theodore J. Vogelgesang, Appellant.

Statement of Case

Physicians — practice of medicine without a license — a practitioner who prescribes and uses medicine for which he receives pay, not exempt from procuring a license as one engaged in practicing "the religious tenets" of his church.

A person who has no license to practice medicine, but, claiming to treat patients and cure diseases by means of the religious tenets of the Spiritualistic Church, uses liniments and prescribes medicines for internal use, which are compounded and patented by himself, for which he receives pay, is not exempt from the statute (Public Health Law, Cons. Laws, ch. 45, pp. 173) prohibiting the practice of medicine without a license, as one engaged in "the practice of the religious tenets of any church." While a healer inculcates the faith of his church as a method of healing he is immune, but when, as in this case, he goes beyond that, puts his spiritual agencies aside and takes up the agencies of the flesh by the use of remedies operating physically, his immunity ceases and a verdict convicting him of the illegal practice of medicine is sustained by the evidence.

People v. Vogelgesang, 173 App. Div. 919, Affirmed. (Argued June 13, 1917; decided July 11, 1917.)

Appeal, by permission, from a judgment of the Appellate Division of the Supreme Court in the fourth judicial department, entered April 11, 1916, which affirmed a judgment of the Erie County Court affirming a judgment of the City Court of Buffalo rendered upon a verdict convicting the defendant of the crime of practicing medicine without a license.

The facts, so far as material, are stated in the opinion.

Henry W. Killeen for appellant. The trial court committed error in excluding the defendant's substantial defense and in making the whole action hinge on the question of whether or not the defendant had received money for his ministrations to Haldeman. (People v. Cole, 219 N.Y. 98.)

Guy B. Moore, District Attorney (Clifford McLaughlin of counsel) for respondent. The court properly held through the trial and properly instructed the jury if they believed from the evidence that the defendant did for money attempt to treat or did treat and prescribe for any human disease, pain, injury, or physical condition, it was their duty to find the defendant guilty. (L 1909, ch. 49, p. 160.)

Opinion, per Cardozo, J.

J. Cardozo. The defendant has been convicted of the illegal practice of medicine. He says he is a spiritualist, and that he has practiced the religious tenets of his church. If that is all he has done, he has acted within his rights. We think he has done more.

In February, 1915, one Albert Haldeman, then suffering from fatal heart disease, visited the defendant's office. He paid four visits there, and received three visits at his own home. He died the next month. The defendant rubbed his body with a liniment, and gave him medicine for internal use. All this was done for pay. The patient's wife accompanied him to the office. She says the defendant never uttered a word about spiritualism. The defendant, who was a witness, does not assert that he did. A pamphlet, handed by him to his patient, is in evidence. The title on the cover gives the defendant's name, and adds the words "Specialist in all forms of chronic diseases; strictly confidential; consultation free." Within the covers is a sketch of the defendant's life. We are told that when eleven years old, "he would get herbs and give them to sick people, for he seemed to know what would be good for them."

In later years the Erie County Medical Society complained of him, and a fine was imposed. "After that," says the sketch, "he joined the New York State Association of Spiritualists." The sketch is followed by many testimonials from patients. All or nearly all acclaim the virtue of the medicines. Not one of them betrays a consciousness that the supposed cures have been wrought through the power of religion. This was the pamphlet by which the defendant accredited himself to Haldeman.

One cannot find here the picture of the religious devotee. One can find only the picture of the unlicensed practitioner. The picture is not changed when we read the defendant's testimony. On the stand he characterized himself as a therapeutic and spiritualist healer and dealer in patent medicines. He had patented them himself. He used a liniment, compounded of angle worms, turpentine, sweet oil and benzine. He says that, while massaging the patient with the liniment, he indulged in silent prayer.

He also prescribed for internal use a medicine compounded of wine, beef tea and citrate of iron. The same medicine was used for everyone. He argues that all this must be excused because he had become a member of the Spiritualist Church, and had been commissioned by that church as a spiritual healer. Some of the evidence which he offered on that subject was rejected. Enough was received, however, to prove that the church had recognized him as a healer, and that the practice of spiritual healing was a tenet of its faith. It would have been better if part of the rejected evidence had been admitted. But if all that was offered had been admitted, it could not justify the defendant's acts.

The state prohibits the practice of medicine without a license, but excepts from its prohibition "the practice of the religious tenets of any church." (Public Health Law, p. 173; Cons. Laws, ch. 45.) We held in *People v. Cole* (219 N.Y. 98) that the exception protected the practitioners of Christian Science, who taught as part of their religion the healing power of mind. Even then we said that there were times when the question of their good faith must be submitted to a jury.

But things were done by this defendant which no good faith could justify. He combined faith with patent medicine. If he invoked the power of spirit, he did not forget to prescribe his drugs. "It is beyond all question of dispute," said Voltaire, "that magic words and ceremonies are quite capable of most effectually destroying a whole flock of sheep, if the words be accompanied by a sufficient quantity of arsenic." (Morley's Critical Miscellanies, III p. 17.)

The law, in its protection of believers, has other cures in mind. The tenets to which it accords freedom, alike of practice and of profession, are not merely the tenets, but the *religious* tenets of a church. The profession and practice of the religion must be itself the cure. The sufferer's mind must be brought into submission to the infinite mind, and in this must be the healing.

The operation of the power of spirit must be, not indirect and remote, but direct and immediate. If that were not so, a body of men who claimed divine inspiration might prescribe drugs and perform surgical operations under cover of the law. While the healer inculcates the faith of the church as a method of healing, he is immune. When he goes beyond that, puts his spiritual agencies aside and takes up the agencies of the flesh, his immunity ceases. He is then competing with physicians on their own ground, using the same instrumentalities, and arrogating to himself the right to pursue the same methods without the same training.

The meaning of the act is made plain when we consider kindred legislation elsewhere. In varying phases immunity is granted to those who practice their religious tenets, but always in such a form as to confine the exemption to spiritual administration. The statutes are collated in the briefs in *People v. Cole,* supra. Thus, in Maine (Rev. Sts., 1903, ch. 17, p. 16, 1895 ch. 170) Massachusetts (R.L. ch. 76, p. 9) and Connecticut (Gen. Sts., 1902, p. 4514) the exemption is specifically declared to extend to those who practice Christian Science. In New Hampshire (L 1915, ch. 167, p. 17) it is declared to extend to "those who endeavor to prevent or cure disease or suffering by spiritual means or prayer." In Illinois (Hurd Rev. St., 1909, ch. 91, p. 11, p. 1474) the act does not apply to "any person who ministers to or treats the sick or suffering by mental or spiritual means without the use of any drug or material remedy."

Nearly the same language is used in the statutes of New Jersey (L 1915, ch. 271, p. 9), North Carolina (L 1903, ch. 697), Colorado (Rev. Sts., 1908, p. 6089), Virginia, (L 1912, ch. 237,

p. 11), and Michigan (L 1913, ch. 368, p. 8). There are like provisions in other states. Through all this legislation there runs a common purpose. The law exacts no license for the ministration by prayer or by the power of religion. But one who heals by other agencies must have the training of the expert.

If that is the true view of the meaning of this statute, the defendant on his own confession has violated the law. Errors which otherwise might be important are thereby rendered harmless. The court charged the jury that the defendant had not the right to practice his religion for pay. There was doubtless error in the ruling (*People v. Cole,* supra). It is impossible, however, that the error should have affected the result, and we disregard it as immaterial (Code Crim. Pr p. 542, *People v. Swersky,* 216, N.Y. 471, 481).

The defendant was justly convicted, and the judgment should be affirmed.

Cuddeback, J. (dissenting). I dissent. The City Court sentenced the defendant to imprisonment for six months. I think that when such extreme punishment is inflicted for a minor offense the rules of law in favor of the accused should be somewhat strictly followed.

The prevailing opinion says that the judge of the City Court excluded evidence to show the practice of healing followed by the Spiritualist Church which it would have been better to admit, and erroneously told the jury that a person has no right to practice his religious tenets for pay. Confessedly the defendant received pay for his services so the latter error left the jury no option but to convict the defendant. I am not inclined to overlook the errors, and I vote to reverse.

Hiscock, Ch J., Pound, Crane and Andrews JJ., concur with Cardozo, J., and Hogan, J., concurs in result; Cuddeback, J., reads dissenting memorandum.

Judgment affirmed.

3.

Deed of Trust

Be it known that I, Mary Baker G. Eddy of Concord, New Hampshire, in consideration of one dollar to me paid by Edward P. Bates, James A. Neal, and William P. McKenzie, all of Boston, Massachusetts, and in consideration of their agreement to faithfully observe and perform all the conditions hereinafter specified to be by them observed and performed, and for the purpose of more effectually promoting and extending the religion of Christian Science as taught by me, do hereby sell and convey to them, the said Bates, Neal and McKenzie, and their successors in the trust hereinafter established all the singular and personal property, goods, and chattels which were sold and conveyed to me by the Christian Science Publishing Society by its bill of sale dated January 21st, 1898, said property being located in the premises numbered 95 to 97 Falmouth Street in said Boston, including the publication called "The Christian Science Journal," (not including the copyrights thereof), the linotype, all pamphlets, tracts, and other literature conveyed to me by said bill of sale, the Hymnal, the subscription lists of "The Christian Science Journal" and of "The Christian Science Quarterly," all stationary fixtures, stock on hand manufactured or otherwise, machinery, tools, mailing lists, book accounts, notes, drafts, checks and bills, whether in process of collection or not, five United States bonds of one thousand dollars each, all cash and bank accounts and all personal property of whatsoever kind or nature which belonged to said Society and which were conveyed to me as aforesaid, excepting only such of said property as may have been used and disposed of since the date of said sale to me, *upon the following perpetual and irrevocable trust and confidence,* namely:

1. Said trustees shall hold and manage said property and property rights exclusively for the purpose of carrying on the business, which has been heretofore conducted by the said Christian Science Publishing Society, in promoting the interests of Christian Science; and the principal place of business shall be in said Boston.

2. The business shall be done by said trustees under the unincorporated name of "The Christian Science Publishing Society."

3. Said trustees shall energetically and judiciously manage the business of the Publishing Society on a strictly Christian basis, and upon their own responsibility, and without consulting me about details, subject only to my supervision, if I shall at any time elect to advise or direct them.

4. Said trustees shall keep accurate books of account of all the business done by them, and shall deposit in a responsible and reliable Bank or Trust Company all bonds, mortgages, deeds, and other documents or writings obligatory of every kind and nature for safe keeping; also all surplus funds over and above the sum necessary to defray the running expenses of the business, until the same shall be paid over to the Church Treasurer, as herein provided. No papers or monies shall be taken from said Bank or Trust Company excepting by and in the presence of a majority of said Trustees. Once in every six months the trustees shall account for and pay over to the treasurer of "The First Church of Christ, Scientist, in Boston, Mass.," the entire net profits of said business. The "net profits" shall be understood to mean

the balance remaining at the end of each six months after paying the usual and legitimate expenses incurred in conducting the business. No authority is intended to be confronted upon the trustees to expend the money of the trust for property not necessary for the immediate successful prosecution of the business, or to invest the same for purposes of speculation, or to incur liabilities beyond their ability to liquidate promptly from the current income of the business. Said treasurer shall hold the money so paid to him subject to the order of "The First Members," of said Church, who are authorized to order its disposition only in accordance with the rules and by-laws contained in the *Manual* of said Church.

5. The business manager shall present to the Trustees, at the end of each month, a full and correct statement of the receipts and expenditures of the month.

6. Said Trustees shall employ all the help necessary to the proper conduct of said business, and shall discharge the same in their discretion or according to the needs of the business, excepting that the business manager may call in at times if necessary such temporary help as will facilitate the business.

7. The Trustees shall employ such number of persons as they may deem necessary to prepare Bible Lessons or Lesson Sermons to be read in the Christian Science churches, the same to be published quarterly as has heretofore been done by and in the name of the *Christian Science Quarterly;* and they may, in their discretion, change the name or style of such quarterly publication as occasion may demand. They shall also fix the compensation of the persons so selected.

8. Said Trustees shall have direction and supervision of the publication of said *Quarterly,* and also of all pamphlets, tracts, and other literature pertaining to said business, using

their best judgment as to the means of preparing and issuing the same, so as to promote the best interests of the Cause, reserving the right to make such changes as I may think important.

9. Said trustees and their successors in trust shall not be eligible to said trusteeship or to continue in the same, unless they are loyal, faithful, and consistent believers and advocates of the principles of Christian Science as taught by me in my book, "Science and Health with Key to the Scriptures."

10. Whenever a vacancy shall occur in said trusteeship for any cause, I reserve the right to fill same by appointment, if I shall so desire, so long as I may live; but if I do not elect to exercise this right, the remaining trustees shall fill such vacancy. The First Members together with the directors of said Church shall have the power to declare vacancies in such trusteeship for such reasons as to them may seem expedient.

11. I also reserve the right to withdraw from said trust, if I shall so desire, the publication of *The Christian Science Journal,* but if I do not exercise this reserved option, then said *Journal* shall remain a part of the trust property forever.

12. Upon my decease, in consideration aforesaid, I sell and convey to said trustees my copyright of "The Christian Science Journal," to be held by them as the other property of said trust.

13. Said trustees shall each receive annually one thousand dollars for their services in that capacity, payable semi-annually in payments of five hundred dollars, or such salary as the said Church may determine from time to time.

14. The delivery of this instrument to, and its acceptance by, said trustees shall be regarded as the full establishment of the trust and as the agreement by the trustees to honestly

and faithfully do and perform all things to be done and performed by them within the terms, objects and purposes of this instrument.

WITNESS my hand and seal at Concord, New Hampshire, this twenty-fifth day of January, 1898.

(Signed) MARY BAKER G. EDDY. (Seal)

We accept the foregoing Trust.

(Signed) Edward P. Bates,
James A. Neal,
William P. McKenzie.

January 25, 1898.

4.

1395 Eustace v. Dickey
1402 Same v. Same
Exceptions of Emilie B. Hulin,
1415 Same v. Same
Appeal of Daisy L. Krauthoff et al.
1423 Same v. Same
Appeal of Daisy L. Krauthoff et al.

Rugg, C. J. — This is a suit in equity. The plaintiffs are three persons, who by succession are trustees under a deed of trust executed by Mary Baker G. Eddy, the founder of "Christian Science," so called, as donor, on January 25, 1898, to three persons therein named as trustees. The defendants are four persons alleged to be trustees under another deed of trust executed by Mrs. Eddy dated September 1, 1892, and also to be Directors of The First Church of Christ, Scientist, in Boston, Massachusetts, and two other persons, each alleged to be claiming to be a trustee and director in association with the other four. The basic question is whether the defendants have power to remove one of the plaintiffs from the position of trustee.

The answer to that question depends upon the true interpretation of these deeds of trust executed by Mrs. Eddy, and whatever other matters rightly may be considered in ascertaining their meaning.

The deed of Mrs. Eddy of January 25, 1898, whereby were created the trusts hitherto administered by the plaintiffs, hereinafter called the trust deed, related wholly to personal property. The declared object of that trust, related in the early part of the trust deed, is "for the purpose of more effectually promoting and extending the religion of Christian Science as taught by me." It transferred title to certain goods and chattels connected with the publishing business conducted for the promotion of the interests of Christian Science, which theretofore had been carried on by a corporation called the Christian Science Publishing Society. The grantees were three individuals, who accepted the transfers upon the trusts set forth in the deed. These are stated in paragraphs numbered from 1 to 14, both inclusive.

The first of these requires the trustees to use the property exclusively for carrying on the business, which had been conducted by the Christian Science Publishing Society, "in promoting the interests of Christian Science." Among these trusts were provisions to the effect that the trustees should energetically and judiciously manage the publishing business under the unincorporated name of "The Christian Science Publishing Society" on a strictly Christian basis and "upon their own responsibility and without consulting me (Mrs. Eddy) about details, subject only to my supervision, if I shall at any time elect to advise or direct them.," should account for and pay over the profits of the business every six months to the treasurer of The First Church of Christ, Scientist, in Boston, Massachusetts, subject to the order of "The First Members of said Church," who were empowered to make the final disposition "only in accordance with the rules and By-laws contained in the *Manual* of said Church," and should employ and fix compensation of necessary help, assistance and personnel to conduct the business and "to prepare Bible Lessons, or Lesson Sermons to be read in the Christian Science churches."

The annual compensation of the trustees was to be $1,000 each "or such salary as the said church may determine from time to time." The trustees were required at all times to be "loyal, faithful and consistent believers and advocates of the principles of Christian Science as taught by me in my book." Clause 8 of the trust deed is in these words: "Said trustees shall have the direction and supervision of the publication of said *Quarterly* and also of all pamphlets, tracts and other literature pertaining to said business, using their best judgment as to the means of preparing and issuing the same, so as to promote the best interests of the Cause, reserving the right to make such changes as I may think important." In clause 10 of the Trust Deed, it is provided that vacancies among the trustees should be filled by the donor, if she so elected, otherwise by the remaining trustees, and that "The First Members together with the directors of said Church shall have the power to declare vacancies in said trusteeship for such reasons as to them may seem expedient."

The facts are found by the master, in the light of which these words of this Trust Deed must be interpreted, Mrs. Eddy founded Christian Science. In 1879 she organized a church and became its pastor. In 1892, she reorganized the church. Under date of the first of September of that year she conveyed to four persons "as trustees as hereinafter provided and to their legitimate successors in office forever" land in Boston upon which within five years they were required to build a church edifice. It was provided that the "grantees shall be known as The Christian Science Board of Directors." Thus that board first was constituted, "The First Church of Christ, Scientist" was not organized until September 23, 1892. The deed declared that the grantees should "constitute a perpetual body or corporation under and in accordance with section one, Chapter 39 of the Public Statutes of Massachusetts. The master has found that the grantees never organized themselves as a corporation and never became such by virtue of their duties or similarity to deacons and wardens. The mere declaration of the grantor could not make them a corporation.

The directors were required, upon the completion of the church building, to "elect a pastor, reader or speaker to fill the pulpit who shall be a consistent Christian Scientist," to maintain public worship in accordance with the doctrines of Christian Science in said church and to that end they were "fully empowered to make any and all necessary rules and regulations." The directors were enjoined not to allow in the church building any preaching or other religious services not consonant and in strict harmony with the doctrines and practices of Christian Science as taught and explained by Mrs. Eddy. The directors also were required to maintain regular preaching, reading or speaking in the church on each Sabbath and to rebuild the church under conditions named. The number of directors named in the deed of September 1, 1892, was four. In addition to the duties imposed on them by that deed, they have exercised other powers and performed additional functions, assigned to them by the *Church Manual,* all of a highly important nature and covering a wide field. There was no rule fixing their number until February 1903, when a By-law was adopted, which has since continued in force, establishing their number at five. By the name "Christian Science Board of Directors" originally the four persons named as trustees by the deed of September 1, 1902, were described. As often, if not universally, used thereafter in the *Church Manual,* that name designates the board of five exercising powers and performing functions not derived from the deed but from the *Church Manual.*

The master also has found that the church has never become incorporated but has continued from the first an unincorporated religious association. It has worshipped regularly to the present in the edifice erected by the directors. "The First Church of Christ, Scientist, in Boston Mass." was organized on September 23, 1892, by eleven persons among whom were the four named as trustees and constituted directors in the deed of September 1, 1892. These eleven persons together with one other were voted to be "First Members of the First Church of Christ, Scientist." Others designated as "First Members" were added from time to time by vote of the "First Members." The voting power in the church always has been confined according to its policy to "First Members." Members of the church had no voting power. The First Church of Christ, Scientist, at the instance of the founder first adopted rules and By-laws in 1895. These were radically changed from time to time during the life of Mrs. Eddy and many different editions of them called the *"Church Manual"* have been published. In every edition the names of the Christian Science Board of Directors have been printed under the caption "Church Officers" together with the names of other officers of the church. This is true of those editions issued before January 25, 1898. At that time important functions of the church such as the election of all officers, the appointment of missionaries, the appointment and removal of readers of the church to conduct its services, amongst others, were vested in the board of directors by the *Church Manual.* Although it was not until 1908 that a By-law of the church expressly included a board of directors among the officers, it always has been provided by a By-law that all officers of the church should be elected by the board of directors.

The provisions respecting First Members in force at the time of the Trust Deed of January 25, 1898, were that their regular meetings were to be held semiannually, that they should vote on the admission of candidates and attend to the transaction of any church business that properly might come before them. Their number should not be permitted to fall below forty and seven constituted a quorum. It was provided in the *Church Manual* of 1898 that the number of First Members should not exceed fifty, and in several subsequent editions one hundred was fixed as the maximum number.

Subsequent events have introduced new factors with reference to which the trust deed must now be applied. In January 1901, the First Members adopted a By-law providing that "the business of The Mother Church (another name by which The First Church of Christ, Scientist was known) hitherto transacted by the First Members shall be done by its "Christian Science Board of Directors." This By-law was accepted and acted upon forthwith by the entire church membership without objection, and so has continued to be observed until the present. Almost immediately after the adoption of this By-law, at Mrs. Eddy's request or with her approval, a By-law, to the effect that vacancies among the trustees of the Christian Science Publishing Society (the trustees created by the Trust Deed of January 25, 1898) might be declared by the First Members and the directors, was changed so as to vest that power exclusively in the Christian Science Board of Directors. Every By-law or amendment since adopted was transmitted by Mrs. Eddy to the Board of Directors alone, by whom it was adopted. It is manifest that this procedure had the approval of Mrs. Eddy. After January 1901, the First Members never undertook to transact any business of the church and no new First Members were elected. In 1903, a By-law was adopted by the Board of Directors changing the name of "First Members" to "Executive Members" and in 1908 another By-law was adopted repealing all provisions concerning Executive Members and providing that "there being no further necessity for their organization, they shall be and hereby are disbanded."

This occurred about two years before the passing on of Mrs. Eddy, and was approved, if not originated, by her. There has been no objection or protest to this. No meetings of First or Executive Members have been held since that time. There has been continuous acquiescence in the binding force of this By-law by the entire membership of the church. All By-laws and provisions of the *Church Manual* were adopted during the life of Mrs. Eddy and substantially every one was suggested or proposed for adoption by her. So far as concerns the government of the church, treating it as an ecclesiastical organization, the First Members, who alone had voting power, have been abolished and have ceased to exist and the entire management has passed into the hands of the directors, a self perpetuating body, all this at the suggestion and with the approval of Mrs. Eddy.

The *Church Manual* in force in January, 1898, bore upon its title page "Church Manual of The First Church of Christ, Scientist, in Boston, Massachusetts by Mary Baker G. Eddy." With slight modifications, this has continued to be the title page of every edition of the *Church Manual*. The last several editions issued during the life of Mrs. Eddy contained provision that "This Manual shall not be revised without the written consent of the author." Since the *Church Manual* on its face purports to be the work of Mrs. Eddy as author and the master has found it to be proved that substantially all its provisions were suggested or proposed by her, it is apparent that there can now, since the decease of Mrs. Eddy, be no change in the provisions of the *Church Manual* in accordance with its terms.

The Trust Deed made provision for the removal of a trustee by the concurrent action of the First Members and the directors of the church. That is the effect of the clause conferring upon them "the power to declare vacancies in said trusteeship for such reasons as to them may seem expedient." In this context, the power to declare a vacancy is the equivalent of the power of removal.

The precise question to be decided is whether under these circumstances one of the trustees can be removed by the board of directors, since the First Members have been deprived of all ecclesiastical power and have been disbanded in accordance with the policy of the church.

Every instrument in writing, although it cannot be varied or controlled by extrinsic evidence, must be interpreted with a view to all the material circumstances of the parties at the time of its execution, in the light of the pertinent facts within the knowledge of those who signed it and in such manner as to give effect to the main end designed to be accomplished by the instrument. Best v. Berry, 189 Mass. 510. Polsey v. Newton, 199 Mass. 450. Simonds v. Simonds, 199 Mass. 552. Cotting v. Boston 201 Mass. 97. Bullard v. Leach, 213 Mass. 117. Tax Commissioner v. Putnam, 227 Mass. 522, 523, 524. Attorney General v. Methuen, 236 Mass. 564, 573. It is a cardinal rule in the interpretation of trust instruments that they are to be so construed as to give effect to the intent of the founder of the trust as manifested by the words used in the light of all the surrounding facts, unless inconsistent with some rule of law or repugnant to the terms of the instrument. McCurdy v. McCallum, 186 Mass. 464, 469. Ware v. Minot, 202 Mass. 512. Taft v. Stearns, 234 Mass. 273, 277. The decision of the question concerning any trust instrument depends upon the intention of the founder as manifested by the words used. An omission to express an intention cannot be supplied by conjecture. But if a reading of the whole trust instrument produces a conviction that a particular interest or power must have been intended to have been given not expressed by formal words, the court must supply the defect by implication, and so mould the language of the founder of the trust as to carry into effect the intention which it is of opinion has by the instrument as a whole been sufficiently declared. This principle has been chiefly invoked in the interpretation of wills but is equally applicable to a Trust Deed like that here involved. Metcalf v. Framingham Parish, 128 Mass. 370, 374. Boston Safe Deposit Co. v. Coffin, 152 Mass. 95, 100. Sanger v. Bourke, 209 Mass. 481, 486. Tibbetts v. Tomkinson, 217 Mass. 244, 252. Lamb v. Jordan, 233 Mass. 335, 340. The Trust Deed now under consideration must be construed and interpreted according to these principles. The avowed purpose of the Trust Deed of January 25, 1898, was for "more effectually

promoting and extending the religion of Christian Science."
The business of publishing was to be conducted "in promoting
the interests of Christian Science." The profits derived from that
business were to be paid to the treasurer of the church who was
authorized to dispose of it only in accordance with the *Manual*
of the church. Preparation of religious publications is the chief
business of the trustees.

It is manifest from the structure of the Trust Deed as well as
from its express words that the single and only design of the
founder was to promote and extend the religion of Christian
Science as taught by Mrs. Eddy. Every part of the Trust Deed
reenforces and makes even more plain the avowed purpose of
Mrs. Eddy that her sole and completely dominating aim in
establishing the trust was to promote and extend the religion
of Christian Science as taught by her. The administration of
the trust must continue to be directed exclusively to the accomplishment of that object alone. A trust of that nature cannot
be revoked or modified in the absence of reservation of an
express power to that end by the donor. Lund v. Thorp, 227
Mass. 474. The deed in question created a trust complete in
itself. By its own phrase it was declared to be upon the "perpetual and irrevocable Trust and confidence" therein set out. The
delivery by the donor of the Trust Deed and of the property
thereby transferred and the acceptance thereof by the grantees
and the performance by them of the trust thereby established
was an executed trust. It must be construed and applied according to its terms. Crawford v. Nies, 224 Mass. 474. Eliot v. Trinity
Church, 232 Mass. 517.

The clause at the end of paragraph eight which conferred
upon the trustees direction and supervision of the publication
of the *Quarterly* and all tracts and pamphlets, "reserving the
right to make such changes as I may think important," is not
a reservation of a general or special power of revocation of the
trust itself or of any of its terms or provisions. The context shows
that that clause refers only to the direction and supervision of
the trustees over publications. Its scope and force are confined
to the particular subject matter of that paragraph. It vested in
the donor the right of modifying and altering the publications

to be issued "to promote the best interests of the Cause." The power these retained concerned the publications and did not extend to the whole frame of the trust.

The words "First Members" occur twice in the Trust Deed, in paragraph four and in paragraph ten. The context in paragraph four is that the trustees shall keep accurate books of account and shall pay all expenses of the publishing business and "once in every six months shall account for and pay over to the treasurer of The First Church of Christ, Scientist, in Boston, Mass., the entire net profits of said business . . . Said treasurer shall hold the money so paid over to him subject to the order of 'The First Members' of said Church, who are authorized to order its disposition only in accordance with the rules and By-laws contained in the *Manual* of said Church."

The "First Members" of that church thus were constituted by the Trust Deed the sole body by which the net income of the publishing business as conducted by the trustees could be disbursed. Confessedly the net profits thus paid over have been very large in the aggregate. They must constitute a substantial element in the promotion and extension of Christian Science as taught by its Leader. The First Members were an integral part of the organization of "The First Church of Christ, Scientist." They were selected for that reason. They were not coordinate, subsidiary, ancillary trustees. They were too numerous to qualify as trustees. Their duty was to disburse the net income, not in conformity to their own judgment, but only in accordance with the rules and By-laws contained in the *Manual* of that church. In the earliest edition of the *Manual*, by which that church was governed, and in all subsequent editions, there is printed as a foreword an extract from the writings of Mrs. Eddy to the effect that the "Rules and By-laws in the Manual . . . were impelled by a power not one's own, were written at different dates and as the occasion required." The edition of the *Manual* in use on January 25, 1898, the date of the Trust Deed, was designated as the seventh. It was different in material particulars from those which had preceded it. It is manifest that the Trust Deed was intended to be made subject, so far as it concerned the officers of the church and their powers and duties touching the disbursement of the net income paid by the trustees to the treasurer of the church, to such changes as the occasion might require to be made in the *Manual*. If the words "First Members" in this connection in paragraph four are given a hard, fixed and unchangeable meaning, then the trust must come to an end when First Members are abolished as a part of the church. If "First Members" have been irrevocably established as an essential part of the machinery by which alone the trust can be carried out, and if for any reason that machinery breaks down or becomes incapable of operation, then the trust itself would fail. Bullard v. Shirley, 153 Mass. 559, 560. Teele v. Bishop of Derry, 168 Mass. 341, 342. Such a result ought not to be reached except for most compelling reasons, after the trust has been established and executed for so many years. No such compelling reasons are found in this record. The plain intent of the founder of the trust is that the net income must be used to promote the religion of Christian Science as taught by Mrs. Eddy even though First Members may pass out of existence. The conclusion is inescapable that in this connection the words "First Members" had no such hard and fast meaning, but were used in a broad sense to designate a body connected with and forming a part of that church, and to comprehend whatever body might from time to time exercise in accordance with the ecclesiastical laws of the Christian Science denomination the functions then exercised by the First Members. Since the First Members have been abolished and all their powers transferred to the Board of Directors, it must follow that the directors are authorized to exercise the functions vested in the First Members under paragraph four of the Trust Deed.

The meaning of the words "First Members" in this connection is a significant aid in determining the meaning of the same words upon their second occurrence in paragraph ten of the Trust Deed. It is a well recognized principle of interpretation that the same words used in different places in the same instrument commonly have the same meaning and effect unless another meaning is demanded by the context. Hall v. Hall, 209 Mass. 350, 353. Attorney General v. Armstrong, 231 Mass. 196, 211. Raymer v. Commissioner of Corporations, ante.

The second occurrence of the words "First Members" in the Trust Deed is in paragraph ten. The sentence there is "The First Members together with the directors of said church shall have the power to declare vacancies in said trusteeship for such reasons as to them may seem expedient." The precise point is whether the power of removal is gone if there are no longer any First Members. Although the trustees under the Trust Deed were given extensive powers concerning the publication of the so-called literature of the church, nevertheless they were not the final arbiters concerning these matters, because they might be removed from office by other church authorities "for such reasons" as to such other church authorities "may seem expedient." The soundness of the reasons for such removal is not made subject to review or revision by any other church tribunal, body or officer. The expediency of the reasons moving to that action are left by the deed wholly to the church authorities therein named. No discussion is needed to demonstrate that this power of removal was comprehensive, drastic and final. It is an important feature of the Trust Deed.

The power of removal of a trustee according to the Trust Deed was vested in the "First Members together with the directors of said church." These are ecclesiastical terms. They describe authorities of The First Church of Christ, Scientist, in Boston, as they were then constituted and established. Mrs. Eddy was the founder of that church. She was the pastor emeritus. It is manifest that so long as she lived the polity of that church might be modified or changed. Membership in the church, classification of members, voting rights, and officers, might be altered. Existing boards might be abolished and others created. The executive and disciplinary powers of the church, its officers and members, might be divided, consolidated and redistributed. They might be vested in one of several boards, officers, or bodies. Of course the terms of the Trust Deed cannot be varied, but its words are to be interpreted with reference to the subject matter to which they relate. It seems manifest to us that all parties to the Trust Deed used the words "First Members" and "directors" in paragraph ten of the Trust Deed with the significance which they had acquired in Christian Science usage, and with the knowledge that, according to the practice of that church, duties imposed on them might be shifted to others connected with the church. Those words comprehended at the time they were used all those possessed of authority to control the affairs of the church. They were used in a generic sense. They included such authorities even though their number and descriptive titles might change. The First Members did not include all members of the church. Those who united with the church by admission did not thereby become First Members. The First Members were those who were made such at the meeting for the organization of "The First Church of Christ, Scientist" and those who subsequently were by these First Members voted into their fellowship. First Members alone possessed voting power. The church was in its infancy as a religious sect. Its founder was active. The deed of January 25, 1898, is itself evidence of a hope and expectation of growth of the church and of the sect. It is a familiar principle of legislation, illustrated by numerous statutes, that one board, commission or other body may be abolished and its powers and duties transferred to other and succeeding officers. No doubt has been raised concerning the validity of such statutes. Ecclesiastical denominations have like power as to the establishment of their officials, the description of their duties, the limits of their authority and the modification and alteration of these matters according to their own system of government. The conditions attendant upon the execution of the deed of January 25, 1898, indicate that its words "First Members together with the directors of said church" were not used by the parties to the deed with the purpose of fixing inflexibly the persons or boards bearing those names in the church organization as alone capable of exercising power of removal of trustees. Thus to construe the words would be to stick to the form and ignore the substance. The fair interpretation of the words is that those possessing the ecclesiastical function at the time vested in First Members and directors should be the depositaries of the power of removal by whatever names they might be called, and however their numbers might fluctuate according to the policy of the church. In a more complete and accurate drafting of the deed of January 25, 1898, this might have been set forth in appropriate language. It is implied under all the circumstances from the words used. The intent of the parties to the Trust Deed as declared by the words used was not that the body known as First Members must be kept alive for all time in order that the power of removal of the trustees should continue. If at any time in the government of the church and in accordance with its practices it should be deemed wise to abolish First Members and transfer their duties to others. If such members should cease to exist under the church organization, the power of removal of a trustee would not thereby be extinguished. The parties to the instrument here in question were the founder of a sect of Christianity and three of her followers. The dominating purpose of the instrument was to promote and propagate the interests of that religious sect. As ancillary to that general object, power of removal of the trustees created by that instrument was established. It was invested in two constituent bodies of "The First Church of Christ, Scientist," then organized and existing. The power of removal of the Trustees was an essential part of the Trust Deed. The promotion of Christian Science as taught by Mrs. Eddy was the end and aim of the trust. To that regnant design all other provisions, not in themselves made fixed and unchangeable, must yield. Christian Science as thus taught was disclosed by the writings of the founder. The ecclesiastical organization established by her for the teaching and dissemination of Christian Science was "The First Church of Christ, Scientist." She did not reserve to herself the power of removal of the trustees but she reposed that authority in First Members and directors of that church. That church was the beneficiary of that trust. That church as shown by the *Manual* at the time of the execution of the Trust Deed of January 25, 1898, was the dominant church in Christian Science. It was the beneficiary of all net profits arising from the management of that trust. The Board of Directors was clothed with extensive powers concerning the management. Its *Manual* appears to be a vital part of Christian Science. The presumption is inevitable that all the parties to the Trust Deed of January 25, 1898, intended that the power of removal should be vested in the responsible representatives of The First Church of Christ, Scientist, however they might be described or denominated, provided they succeeded to the powers and exercised the functions of First Members and directors. The inference is irresistible that they had in mind the mutability of the names and functions of church officers and intended that the power of removal should vest in such representatives of The First Church of Christ, Scientist as might from time to time exercise according to the government of that church the functions and possess the powers of those named in the Trust Deed as having the power of removal. The vote of the First Members of January 10, 1901, embodied in a By-law to the effect that the business of the church hitherto transacted by them be done in the future by the directors, was not an attempt to delegate the trust powers to participate in the removal of a trustee vested in them by the deed of January 25, 1898. It did not stand alone. It was a part of a large transaction. It was one step in the process of change according to the polity of the church whereby First Members were abolished and their duties and authorities vested in the directors.

The number of First Members of the church on January 25, 1898, when the Trust Deed was executed, is not disclosed in the record. It is, however, fairly inferable that they were numerous, and liable to constant fluctuation by reason of death and election of new members. Therefore, Mrs. Eddy could not have placed special confidence in their discretion as individuals. The principle that, when the element of personal choice is found, the exercise of the power must be confined to the person or persons selected and is not transmissible has no application. Sells v. Delgado, 186 Mass. 25, 27. The naming of directors and First Members in paragraph ten of the Trust Deed as having power of removal was not an appointment of particular persons as repositories of authority but as designation of two classes of church functionaries in whom the power was to vest and survive, no matter who the individuals might be. The power conferred upon these two classes of church functionaries "to declare vacancies for such reasons as to them may seem expedient" imposes a continuing duty to maintain a certain intimacy of knowledge as to the work of the trustees in order to be able constantly to act intelligently. It was a power coupled with a trust. The obligation rested upon them to cause the provisions of the Trust Deed to be executed in accordance with its terms and the intent and purpose of the donor there expressed to be administered faithfully. This duty was given to the donees of the power by virtue of their respective positions in the church. In a sense this position was kindred to that of trustees clothed with a power coupled with an interest in the survivors of whom the authority continues for the purpose of effectuating the object of the power. Gould v. Mather, 104 Mass. 283, 286. Parker v. Sears, 117 Mass. 513. Chandler v. Rider, 105 Mass. 268. Coffin v. Attorney-General, 231 Mass. 579. Wilson v. Snow, 228 U.S. 217.

These circumstances distinguish the case at bar from Boston v. Doyle, 184 Mass. 373. In that case the holders of certain public offices had been designated in a trust instrument as members of a board of managers of a trust fund, and the offices thereafter were abolished and other offices created whose incumbents succeeded in most particulars to the same public duties. It was held that it became the duty of the court to appoint managers to take the places of those holding the original offices and designated by the donor as the board of managers.

The report of the master shows that the First Members have been disbanded according to the forms of church organization and government prevailing in "The First Church of Christ, Scientist." They are no longer in existence. They ceased to have any temporal power in 1901, and were disbanded in 1908. The means by which this was accomplished are not of consequence further than to know that they were those recognized, adopted and approved without dissent by the ecclesiastical body known as The First Church of Christ, Scientist. That result has been accepted by all Christian Scientists. It had the approval of Mrs. Eddy if it was not suggested by her. It would be difficult to conceive more convincing proof that the church as an organization had abolished First Members and conferred their powers, at least so far as related to removal of trustees, upon the directors. Votes and By-laws to that end were accepted with entire unanimity at the time and there has been unbroken acquiescence in their regularity for many years. The First Members have not become incapable of participation in the exercise of the power of removal of trustees merely as the result of their own act. The governing power of the church at the suggestion or with the approval of Mrs. Eddy has brought about their elimination in connection with the removals because substantially all their power has been transferred to the directors. That has been accomplished by ecclesiastical methods accepted without question by all the church. It is a matter as to which the action of the church according to its rules is final. So far as concerns the power of removal of a trustee under the Trust Deed of January 25, 1898, the organization of the church in accordance with its polity has consolidated those powers, previously shared by the First Members and the directors in concurrence, and placed them wholly in the directors. Interpreting the words of the Trust Deed according to their true meaning, we are of the opinion that the power of removal thereby survived and became vested in the board of directors. It exists in them by virtue of their office and the trust reposed in them by the deed of January 25, 1898, and the duties placed upon them by the church itself. Carter v. Papineau, 222 Mass. 464. Attorney-General v. Armstrong, 231 Mass. 196.

The board of directors, as those words are used in the Trust Deed of January 25, 1898, do not in our opinion refer to the board established by the deed of September 1, 1892, but to the officers constituting the ecclesiastical board of directors under the polity of the church. The reasons already stated respecting First Members lead to this conclusion. No reference to the deed of September 1, 1892, is found in the Trust Deed of January 25, 1898. The latter deed throughout relates to those connected with The First Church of Christ, Scientist either as First Members or directors. These terms are ecclesiastical when therefore the board of directors under the practice of the church was increased in membership, it became vested with powers formerly exercised by the four directors, so far as concerns the power of removal in the Trust Deed of January 25, 1898. It is unnecessary to determine in this connection whether the board of directors constituted a corporation or not. For the purpose of this decision the finding of the master that they never became a corporation is accepted.

The result is that the board of five directors have the power, if they act in accordance with law and with the terms of the Trust Deed of January, 1898, to effect removal of a trustee under that deed.

The conclusion that the power of removal of a trustee is now vested in the board of five directors is contrary to that of the master, but it is in substance and effect the application of different legal principles to the facts found by the master. The facts found by him are accepted in their entirety. The result which has been stated follows in law from those facts.

One being absent and one refusing to vote, the three remaining directors adopted a resolution removing the plaintiff Rowlands from his position as one of the trustees under the deed of January 25, 1898. This resolution is somewhat long and recites numerous reasons. One of these is that Rowlands "evidently has other interests which prevent him from giving sufficient time and attention to the business of the Christian Science Publishing Society." Respecting this the master was "unable to regard the charge made as one actually believed to be true, by the directors who made it, after due inquiry into the facts, or as one which they would have considered sufficient for his removal if they had not desired to remove him for other reasons." The other reasons assigned in the resolution of removal grew out of a controversy arising some years after the death of Mrs. Eddy, between the trustees and directors regarding the extent to which the former were subject to the control and supervision of the latter. Seemingly the controversy started because the directors requested that a pamphlet called "Purification" be not sent out until authorized by them. Nevertheless the business manager sent out the pamphlets on the ground that it was "his highest understanding of Principle to follow the original order of the Trustees" to that effect notwithstanding the request of the directors. Then the controversy widened into a general discussion of the respective powers and duties of the two boards under the deed of trust of January 25, 1898, and under the *Church Manual*. The controversy appears to have centered about the meaning of certain sections of the *Church Manual* and the extent to which its provisions authorized the directors to supervise the matter to be printed and sent out by the trustees, and to what extent the trustees were required to heed the provisions of the *Church Manual*. Into the details of that controversy, it is not necessary to enter. Out of it has grown the present litigation. The finding of the master is that "I am unable to hold either that the final authority claimed by the directors is so clearly established by the deed itself and the provisions of the *Manual* that no reasonable denial of it was possible—or that the Directors' determination that they had such final authority was conclusive upon the trustees. Whatever the right conclusion may be upon the question whether such final authority belonged to the Directors or not, it was by no means a question regarding which no honest difference of opinion was possible." This is another way of saying that an honest difference of opinion was possible. Therefore, if the directors were honest in their view, they cannot be said to be without authority to decide that it was expedient with reference to the welfare of the trust to remove one of the trustees.

The words of the Trust Deed are that vacancies in the trusteeship may be declared "for such reasons as to them may seem expedient." That is a broad phrase. Expediency is a word of large import. It comprehends whatever is suitable and appropriate in reason for the accomplishment of the specified object. In this connection it includes whatever may rationally be thought to conduce to the welfare of the trust. It means that the genuine judgment of the named church authorities honestly exercised is to prevail. The discretion of those possessing the power of removal, when applied in good faith, is not subject to re-examination in respect to its wisdom. The judgment of the court cannot be substituted for the discretion of the constituted authorities, when fairly exercised. Whether the decision be right is not for the courts to decide. The power of removal cannot be put forth maliciously, or capriciously. The function of the court is to ascertain whether the terms of the deed of trust have been observed, whether the proceedings have been regular, whether the cause assigned is sufficient to warrant removal, whether fair opportunity has been accorded the trustee to present his side of the matter so as to satisfy the requirements of natural justice, whether the decision is within the scope of the power conferred and whether the final action appears to have been in exercise of good faith and an honest judgment or to have been arbitrary and lacking in the ordinary elements of fairness. Proctor v. Heyer, 122 Mass. 525, 529. Grosvenor v. United Society or Believers, 118 Mass. 78, 91. Leverett v. Barnwell, 214 Mass. 105, 108. Richards v. Morison, 229 Mass., 458, 461. This does not necessarily imply that a formal hearing must be had before removal. O'Dowd v. Boston, 149 Mass. 443. Attorney General v. Donahue, 169 Mass. 18, 22. Sims v. Police Commissioner, 193 Mass. 547, 549. Circumstances may be conceived to exist, which would render a hearing futile. Nevertheless a hearing ordinarily is important to the decision of such a question. Burgess v. Mayor and Aldermen of Brockton, 235 Mass. 95, and cases collected at page 100. Smyth v. Phillips Academy, 154 Mass. 551, 557. Gray v. Christian Society, 137 Mass. 329, 331.

It hardly can be held to be a capricious or arbitrary exercise of power for the directors to determine that, because a radical difference of opinion as to the interpretation of the *Church Manual* existed between them and the trustees, the welfare of the trust required the removal of one of the trustees. It is not for us to pass upon the wisdom of such action. The only question is whether it was arbitrary and capricious and not in good faith. One of the grounds stated in the resolution of removal was that Mr. Rowlands did not recognize the importance of "promoting the interests of Christian Science by following the directions given by Mrs. Eddy in our Church By-laws" and had shown a disposition to pervert their meaning and annul their effect.

Respecting the good faith of the directors in this matter, the master finds that "So far as the assigned reasons accuse Rowlands of failure to devote time enough to the Publishing Society's business, or were made to appear as reasons requiring his removal only, and not equally the removal of his co-trustees, it may be said that they were not reasons assigned in good faith. But that the Directors who adopted the resolution honestly believed themselves to be exercising a power belonging to them, and for sufficient reasons, whether those assigned or not, I find no reason to doubt." The directors cannot be said to have acted arbitrarily or capriciously in removing only one of the trustees, because the same grounds appear to have existed for removing all the trustees. Sound judgment may have dictated the removal of one, and not all. The last sentence of this finding to the effect that the directors honestly believed they were acting within their power and honestly believed their reasons to be sufficient is inconsistent with bad faith or fraud in its common acceptation. This is a finding of good faith on the part of the directors as to all the reasons stated except the one for failure to devote time enough to the business. It is not a finding that the other reasons given were tainted or affected by the one as to failure of Mr. Rowlands to devote time enough to the business. Those other reasons honestly assigned were such as, within the power vested in the directors, warranted them in making a removal. It is their honest judgment upon the question of expediency in this regard which must prevail and not that of any other body or magistrate.

The circumstance that no formal hearing was held is not decisive against the validity of the removal. While ordinarily one, whose conduct is called in question, ought to be given an opportunity to be heard in his own defense, it is apparent that the long controversy between the trustees and the directors had brought out clearly the points of difference between them. The grounds of removal, on which the actions of the directors can stand, had been in substance fully debated orally and in writing and Mr. Rowlands had stated his point of view forcibly and at length.

A majority of the directors were present at the meeting and voted for the removal. That was sufficient in form to effect a removal. A unanimous vote was not required. The result is that upon the application of the principles of law to the facts found by the master the removal of Mr. Rowlands as one of the trustees was effected.

While the case was pending before the single justice the Attorney General filed a petition for leave to intervene and to file an answer. That was denied. No exceptions were saved. No appeal was taken. Before the full court the Attorney General has filed a suggestion that the court is without jurisdiction to

determine the issues raised in this record or to enter a final
decree on the ground that the suit relates to a public charitable
trust or trusts and that the Attorney General as the representative of the public beneficiaries is a party essential to jurisdiction over the subject. The point thus presented is not whether
the Attorney General may be a proper party or whether in the
exercise of the judicial discretion he ought to be permitted to
become a party. Those questions were raised by his petition
to intervene and, having been decided adversely to his contention without reservation of any right of review, cannot now be
considered.

The court has taken jurisdiction of numerous cases, indis-
tinguishable in this particular from the case at bar, to which
the Attorney General was not a party. Carey v. Bliss, 151 Mass.
364. Morville v. Fowle, 144 Mass. 109. Teele v. Bishop of Derry,
168 Mass. 341. Worcester Missionary Society v. Memorial
Church, 186 Mass. 531. Codman v. Brigham, 187 Mass. 309.
Hubbard v. Worcester Art Museum, 194 Mass. 280. Ware v.
Fitchburg, 200 Mass. 61. Crawford v. Nies, 220 Mass. 61. S. C.
224 Mass. 474. First African Association v. Worthy, 232 Mass.
331. It is the duty of the court of its own motion to examine
its jurisdiction before proceeding to any decision. Eaton v.
Eaton, 233 Mass. 351, 364 and authorities there collected. It is
hardly to be thought that so many cases arising over so long a
period of time could have been decided inadvertently. These
adjudications without joining the Attorney General as a party
are almost conclusive of the jurisdiction of the court even
though the point has not been discussed.

The issue here to be settled (as has been already stated) is
whether one of the trustees under the deed of January 25, 1898,
can be and has been removed by the directors. The public interests must be directly and essentially, rather than remotely and
accidentally involved as to some distant issue in order to prevent
the cause from proceeding to a decision without the presence
of the Attorney General as a party. Jackson v. Phillips, 14 Allen,
539, 579. McKenzie v. Presbytery of Jersey City, 67 N. J. Eq.
625, 683 to 686. Esquimalt and Nanaimo Railway v. Wilson,
1920 A. C. 358.

Whether the power of removal of one of the trustees has been exercised according to law is a matter of direct interest to the parties to the present proceeding. The absence of the Attorney General does not affect the jurisdiction of the court to proceed to a final determination on the merits of the issues raised between the immediate parties. Such decision will not directly pass upon interests of which the Attorney General in his official capacity is the representative.

No question is involved in this suggestion of the Attorney General either under the Constitution of the Commonwealth or under the Fourteenth Amendment to the federal Constitution. Cases like Riverside Mills v. Menefee, 237 U.S. 189 and McDonald v. Mabee, 243 U.S. 90 plainly depend upon a principle different from that here raised.

On April 6, 1920, after the filing of the master's report, Daisy L. Krauthoff and Edwin A. Krauthoff petitioned, in behalf of themselves and such other members of "The First Church of Christ, Scientist" as might elect to come in, for leave to file exceptions to the master's report, a motion to recommit to the master and a motion to postpone. They sought to except to the report on objections filed but omitted from exceptions by the defendants. A decree was entered denying this petition and the petitioner claimed an appeal. The petitioners were not parties to the proceeding and therefore had no standing to present such a motion. The master's report was filed March 6, 1920. The time allowed by equity rules 31 and 32 for filing exceptions thereto had expired. Smedley v. Johnson, 196 Mass. 316. They had no right to appeal from the denial of their motion. Martin v. Tapley, 119 Mass. 116. Ex parte Leaf Tobacco Board of Trade, 222 U.S. 578.

On October 20, 1920, which was about two months after the reservation of the case for decision by the full court, Mr. and Mrs. Krauthoff filed a motion in behalf of themselves and such other members of the church as might desire to join, to be admitted as parties to the suit and to refile the motions before filed and denied. There was no error in the denial of this motion. The case was pending before the full court. The single justice could not then deal with such questions. Burbank v.

Farnham, 220 Mass. 514, 515, 516. Old Dominion Copper Mining & Smelting Co. v. Bigelow, 203 Mass. 159, 221. The motion also was addressed under the circumstances disclosed on the record to the discretion of the court, which cannot be held to have been abused. New York Bank Note Co. v. Kidder Press Manufacturing Co., 192 Mass. 391, 408. Credits Commutation Co. v. United States, 177 U.S. 311, 314 to 317. Opinion by Lurton Circuit Judge in Toler v. Tennessee, Virginia & Georgia Railway, 67 Fed. 168, 172. City of New York v. Consolidated Gas Co., 253 U.S. 219. There appears to have been an adversary relation between the petitioners and the directors. It was the duty of the latter to protect the interests of the members of "The First Church of Christ, Scientist." John Hancock Mutual Life Ins. Co. v. Lester, 234 Mass. 559-562.

The result is that the exceptions of the defendants to the master's report so far as they relate to his rulings that the directors had no power under the deed of January 25, 1898, to remove a trustee and that the removal of Mr. Rowlands was ineffectual must be sustained. On the facts found by the master, in the light of the principles of law here found to be controlling the plaintiffs cannot maintain their bill.

In order to decide the fundamental issues raised on this record, it is unnecessary to consider the question whether Mr. Dittemore or Mrs. Knott is a director. That issue is directly involved in another suit.

The exceptions of Emilie B. Hulin have been waived and will not be considered.

Suggestion of the Attorney General denied.

Both appeals of Mr. and Mrs. Krauthoff dismissed.

Exceptions of Emilie B. Hulin waived.

Bill dismissed, November 23, 1921.

5.

The Parkside
18 Gramercy Park
New York City
March 23, 1937.

Directors of The Mother Church,
    Boston, Massachusetts.

Gentlemen:

As the result of experience over a period of years and a great
deal of serious study devoted to the science of government, I
have come to the humble conclusion that I made a great mistake
in allowing personal differences of opinion and the feelings that
developed therefrom, to influence me to the extent which they
evidently did after Mrs. Eddy passed on.

We were all greatly affected by her demise and held divergent
views regarding the policies to be pursued when she was no
longer here to direct us. And while I acted on convictions which
I regarded as right at the time, I have since been led to see, and
am anxious to go on record as admitting it, that I was wrong in
letting personal opinion and matters of policy induce me to
depart from Principle.

God's law does not divide and separate men; it unites them,
enabling them to work together and perpetuates this unity.
Personal differences that appear irreconcilable disappear as we
grow in the understanding of His law and the ability to demonstrate it. Man is properly self-governed only as he enthrones this
mighty law in his heart and mind. It annihilates everything
unlike itself and I find it has destroyed all sense of personal
animosity, all desire to justify self, and brought instead the
sincere desire to acknowledge my mistake in organizing what
was naturally regarded as an opposition movement, opposed to
the Cause of Christian Science, to Mrs. Eddy and her teachings.

I recognize and revere her as having restored to humanity primitive Christian healing and acknowledge The First Church of Christ, Scientist, in Boston, Mass., as the first church in history to stand for the spiritual and the scientific significance of the life of Christ.

I am happy to forward you this letter to use as you may see fit and to sincerely announce as my fervent desire that the Cause which you represent may continue to grow and prosper under your direction.

Yours in Truth,
John V. Dittemore.

6.

Statement from The Christian Science Board
of Directors, read by Ezra W. Palmer, at the
annual meeting (1938) of The Mother Church.

In one of our Leader's inspired statements she tells us that
"Mind measures time according to the good that is unfolded"
(*Science and Health*, p. 584). When thus considered, the day set
aside for the annual meeting of The Mother Church becomes
something more than an event to measure the passing of another
year or an occasion to recount achievements and listen to reports
on the general welfare of the Church.

It becomes, in fact, a day of thanksgiving and spiritual reckon-
ing, a day when Christian Scientists, wherever located, may
properly withdraw into the privacy of their own thought and
offer up a prayer of gratitude to God, the Giver of all good, for
what Mrs. Eddy has aptly described as "the marvelous speed of
the chariot-wheels of Truth," and "the steadfast, calm coherence
in the ranks of Christian Science." (*Miscellany*, p. 127). It is
gratifying for us to be able to say that the statement just quoted
accurately describes conditions within the movement today.

The "chariot-wheels of Truth" continue to turn with the
same "marvelous speed," and the ranks of Christian Scientists
remain calm and coherent, and unswerving in their loyalty to
Mrs. Eddy as the one divinely commissioned to give to the world
the final and complete revelation of the Christ. (*Science and
Health*, p. 107.)

Our Church has grown substantially in numbers during the
past year. It is united, harmonious, and without debt. Its affairs
and the affairs of its allied trusteeships, including property interests, the Benevolent Homes, and the important operations of
The Christian Science Publishing Society are conducted with
an efficiency and economy consistent with the best interests of
the movement as a whole.

More important than all, however, is the marked success with which the healing ministry of Christian Science is being practiced throughout the world. This not only is important in itself, but is highly significant as a sign of the times. This success of the healing ministry indicates among other things that the spiritual, indestructible nature of man's real life is being more universally recognized, and the basic fact accepted that life conceived of humanly is not a physical thing, to be destroyed by sin, disease, and death, but is a condition of thought to be corrected and transformed.

It also indicates that the day is approaching when responsible heads of governments will see that undue reliance upon material means and methods to accomplish their ends inevitably results in failure and defeat. They will then realize that no nation is stronger than the moral fiber of its people, and that a nation can become truly great and permanently endure only to the extent that spiritual qualities are cultivated in the thoughts of its citizens and permitted freely to operate in the government of their lives.

The history of the past teaches that nations whose governments have been conceived largely in selfish ambitions and brought forth by human force are literally "of few days, and full of trouble." As expressions of economic and political systems they were essentially as fleeting and unsound as the mentalities which gave them their birth. Nothing remains of them but the briefest possible records of material achievements, and their apparent greatness is little more than a passing shadow on the dial of time.

In spite of the material tendencies of the past, there were always a few who courageously stood for the development in national life of individual initiative, integrity, and high moral standards. In much the same way there are thoughtful men and women today who are concerned when the state undertakes to subordinate religious interests to social and economic expedience.

Such men and women are the hope of the race, the bulwark and inspiration of every nature. Without them civilization would perish and freedom of thought and action would disappear from human experience. These courageous individuals, strengthened by the truth that frees, stifle aggression, preserve peace and freedom, and promote the brotherhood of man. They represent the type of thought which in some degree has been touched by spiritual truth, and among them will be found Christian Scientists.

As students of Christian Science we have a definite responsibility in respect to the unfolding of such fundamental issues of life as the cultivation of good will and the preservation of a system of government which protects the civil rights of its people, and insures to them freedom of speech, of the press, and of religious worship.

This special responsibility is imposed upon us primarily because we know that the divine qualities of thought which constitute realities in life, righteousness in government, and unity among men, are not something to be denied or bestowed by the will of man, but belong alike to all. They emanate from infinite Principle, and are as universal in their operation, and as permanent in their character as Principle itself.

We also know, and are daily demonstrating that the obstructive forces which would deprive man of a free and full enjoyment of these blessings are unreal in their nature and powerless in their effect. They are, as Isaiah tells us, nothing, and "a thing of nought." In reality they belong to nobody and operate nowhere. Understanding this, it manifestly becomes our duty to apply what we know to the betterment of world conditions, prayerfully and with love for God and man, and do it with the same diligence and consistency which we commonly employ in working out a solution of personal problems.

Individuals, like nations, however, are prone to become so engrossed in purely personal or local affairs that they take little or no account of conditions which they believe do not concern their immediate welfare. While we should not magnify error or become unduly alarmed by the present-day suggestions of war and disaster aggressively presented through many channels, we must be keenly alert not to allow a false sense of security to lull us to sleep and make us indifferent to situations of national and international character which, unless corrected, are destined to affect our interests as directly as if the scene of their action were within the bounds of our own community.

The rousing words of our Leader on page 177 of "Miscellaneous Writings" are particularly fitting at this time. She says: "Never was there a more solemn and imperious call than God makes to us all, right here, for fervent devotion and absolute consecration to the greatest and holiest of all causes." And she adds: "Will you give yourselves wholly and irrevocably to the great work of establishing the truth, the gospel, and the Science which are necessary to the salvation of the world from error, sin, disease, and death? Answer at once and practically, and answer aright!"

7

Youth Forums

Among the numerous contributions of *The Christian Science Monitor* to better understanding among people, and especially among younger people, are the Youth Forums. Since 1946, when the groups were brought together, and a headquarters established in Boston, they have multiplied until there are more than six hundred Forums in twenty-one countries. As announced in the *Sentinel,* August 17, 1946, the purpose of the Youth Forums is:

"To provide young Christian Scientists with an opportunity for understanding *The Christian Science Monitor;* to promote the ideals for which it stands, namely, 'to injure no man, but to bless all mankind' (The First Church of Christ, Scientist, and *Miscellany,* by Mary Baker Eddy, p. 353), and to provide cooperative, cultural, and social activity."

Membership is restricted to young people between the ages of sixteen and thirty years. Each group elects its own officers, raises its own funds, maintains its own meeting places, and advances its own social and cultural opportunities under the sponsorship of the *Monitor.*

Unique among the activities is a Travelship Fund. The Fund is used to bring Forum members closer together in a world-wide educational program. Contributions to the Fund are made by individuals, and awards are made on individual records, and abilities. Award winners select the city and country they wish to visit. They pay their own ocean transportation costs, but are given adequate money from the

Fund to meet travel expenses in the countries and cities visited.

To date, about ten Travelship awards have been made each year.

8.

Christian Science Board of Lectureship

Allan, Gavin W.	— 1925-28, '30-33, '35-38, '40-43.
Appleton, Helen	— 1948, '49, '53-57.
Aultman, Lela May	— 1952-55.
Ayres, Frank C.	— 1950-52.
Bailey, Arch	— 1953, '55-57.
Bathurst, Algernon Hervey	— 1922-27, '31-34.
Beck, Herbert W.	— 1942, '43, '45.
Bell, Frank	— 1915, '22-26, '28-31, '33-36, '38-41.
Biggins, Peter B.	— 1935-38, '40-44, '47-51, '54.
Booth, W. Stuart	— 1925-28, '30, '31.
Braithwaite, John Sidney	— 1916-20, '22.
Brookins, Mary	— 1903-10.
Brown, Hon. Wm. E.	— 1924-29, '31-33, '35-37.
Browne, Harry C.	— 1942-45, '54.
Buskirk, Hon. Clarence A.	— 1904-15.
Campbell, Hugh Stuart	— 1944.
Carey, Archibald	— 1946-50, '53-55.
Carney, Leonard T.	— 1944-46.
Carr, Eric W.	— 1942, '43.
Carr, Dr. John R.	— 1939, '40.
Castle, Ralph	— 1947-49, '51, '54-57.
Cern, Jules	— 1953, '55-57.
Chadwick, Clarence W.	— 1913-20, '22.
Channing, George	— 1938-40, '45-48, '53, '55-57.
Clarkson, Judge Joseph R.	— 1899, 1900.
Comer, Gordon V.	— 1944, '45.
Cook, George Shaw	— 1914-20, '22-24.

Cook, Louise Knight Wheatley	—	1935-38, '40-42.
Cooper, W. Norman	—	1956-57.
Corby, Blanche K.	—	1918-20, '22, '23.
Coulson, Lucia C.	—	1923-25, '27-30, '38, '39-42.
Craig, Clayton Bion	—	1945-48.
Davis, Richard J.	—	1924, '25, '29-32, '34-37, '40-43, '48, '49.
Davis, Will B.	—	1943-46, '49-52.
DeCamp, Arthur P.	—	1929, '30-33, '35.
de Lange, Dr. Hendrik J.	—	1929-33, '35-38, '40-43, '46-50.
Denton, Cecil F.	—	1947-51.
Doorly, John W.	—	1915-20, '22-24, '26-28.
Dunn, John Randall	—	1916-19, '23-26, '28-34, '36-39, '42.
Eaton, Clarence C.	—	1905-17.
Eddison, Colin Rucker	—	1936-39, '41-43.
Ewing, Mary G.	—	1918-20, '22, '23, '25.
Ewing, Judge Wm. G.	—	1899-1910.
Exo, Harold H.	—	1953-55.
Farlow, Alfred	—	1898.
Fell, Col. Wm. E.	—	1913-15.
Flinn, John J.	—	1922-26, '28, '29.
Fluno, F. J.	—	1899-1918.
Gale, Mary Wellington	—	1955-57.
Garrett, Emma Louise	—	1951.
Gilmore, Dr. Albert F.	—	1930-32.
Glenn, Margaret Murney	—	1923-26, '28-31, '33-37 (*See* Matters, Margaret)
Graham, Rev. Andrew J.	—	1918-20, '22-24, '26-29.
Greene, Judge Samuel W.	—	1918-20, '22-24, '29-32. '34-37, '39, '41-43.
Gross, Willis F.	—	1910-20.
Hammond, Edward H.	—	1898, 1903, '04.
Hanna, Judge Septimus J.	—	1902-13.
Harsch, Paul A.	—	1926-29, '31-35, '37-40, '43-45.

Hart, Salem A.	—	1925-29, '31, '32.
Hay, Ella H.	—	1953-57.
Hering, Prof. Hermann S.	—	1905-20, '22, '23, '25-29, '31-36, '38, '39.
Herzog, Anna E.	—	1942-45.
Heywood, Evelyn F.	—	1944-47, '51, '52.
Hickman, Adair	—	1939-42, '49-51.
Hill, Judge Frederick C.	—	1922-27, '29-34, '36-39, '42, '43.
Hoag, Ella W.	—	1918.
Holdship, Aimee	—	1942, '43.
Holloway, Mary C.	—	1952-55.
Hooper, E. Howard	—	1952-55.
Hord, Frank	—	1951-54.
Hubbard, Dr. H. Walton	—	1916-20, '22-25, '37-39, '48, '49.
Hurley, Thomas E.	—	1938-41, '44-46, '50-52.
Jandron, Francis Lister	—	1935-37.
Jarvis, Charles E.	—	1927-30.
Kantack, Walter W.	—	1951, '52.
Karpen, Louise S.	—	1956-57.
Kennett, Lowell F.	—	1956-57.
Ker-Seymer, Violet	—	1926-28, '39-41, '45.
Key, Lt. Col. Robert Ellis	—	1945-47.
Kilpatrick, Wm. D.	—	1917-20, '22-27, '29-34, '36-39, '42-44.
Kimball, Edward A.	—	1899-1909.
Knapp, Bliss	—	1904-20, '27-29.
Knott, Annie M.	—	1898-1902.
Kolliner, A. Sim	—	1945-48.
Lathrop, John C.	—	1918-20, '22, '23, '29.
Lee, Richard Knox	—	1945, '51-54.
Leonard, Frank H.	—	1904-12, '19, '20, '22, '23.
Lewis, B. Palmer	—	1944-46.
Lewis, J. Hamilton	—	1956-57.
Linscott, John Freeman	—	1900, '01, '04.
Martin, George W.	—	1942-45, '50.

Matters, Margaret	—	1942-45 (*See* Glenn, Margaret Murney)
MacRae, Harry B.	—	1947-51, '54-57.
McCloud, Earl	—	1941-44, '47-49.
McCrackan, Wm. D.	—	1904, '09-16.
McKenzie, Rev. Wm. P.	—	1898-1914.
McReynolds, James Harry	—	1945-49, '54-57.
Middaugh, Florence	—	1938-41, '44-47, '50-54.
Miller, Wm. N.	—	1899-1909.
Mims, Sue Harper	—	1898-1910.
Molter, Harold	—	1946-49, '52, '53.
Morrison, Margaret	—	1935-37, '41-43, '47-51.
Nay, George	—	1952-55.
Nichols, Henry Allen	—	1951-54, '56-57.
Noee, Grace Jane	—	1950-53.
Norton, Carol	—	1898-1903.
Norwood, Elisabeth	—	1946-49.
Nunn, Herschel P.	—	1943-46, '49-52, '55.
Nysewander, Clifford R.	—	1956-57.
Ohrenstein, Charles I.	—	1915-20, '22-24, '26-28.
Palmer, Ezra W.	—	1916-20, '22-24.
Peeke, Oscar Graham	—	1941-44, '46, '48-51.
Perrow, Arthur	—	1948-51.
Pickett, John D.	—	1952-55.
Poling, Sylvia N.	—	1956-57.
Porter, Wm. W.	—	1916-20, '22-27, '29-33, '36-38.
Preller, Friedrich	—	1955-57.
Ramsey, Robert	—	1943.
Rathvon, Wm. R.	—	1911-17.
Rauthe, Claire	—	1948-52, '55-'57.
Ritchie, Nelvia E.	—	1925-28, '30-33.
Rogers, Cyrus S.	—	1927-30.
Ross, Peter V.	—	1922-26, '28-31, '33-36, '38-43.
Ross, Robert Stanley	—	1924-28, '30-35, '37, '39, '40, '43-46, '49-52.
Rowell, James G.	—	1927-30, '32-36, '38-43.

Sammons, John S. — 1945-49, '52-55.
Sampsell, Maj. Chauncey Whitney — 1947.
Sawyer, Silas J. — 1900-05.
Scholfield, Ralph B. — 1930-34, '40-42.
Scott, Elisabeth Carroll — 1946-50, '53, '55-57.
Sedman, John Ellis — 1927-30, '32-36.
Seeley, Paul Stark — 1916-20, '22-27, '29-33,
'35-38, '40-42, '48-52,
'55-57.
Selover, John J. — 1952-55.
Shield, Jacob S. — 1914, '15.
Simms, Earl E. — 1946-50, '53, '55.
Smith, Judge Clifford P. — 1911-13.
Snyder, Jean M. — 1950-53.
Strickler, Virgil O. — 1911-20.
Sulcer, A. A. — 1899-1901.
Symonds, Walter S. — 1950-53, '56-57.
Tennant, Charles W. J. — 1942.
Tennant, Georgina — 1953, '55-57.
Thomson, Elizabeth McArthur — 1938-41.
Tomkins, George — 1898.
Tomlinson, Rev. Irving C. — 1898-1904, '06-08, '32-34.
Tutt, Dr. John M. — 1918-20, '22-27, '29-31,
'33-36, '38-41, '44-46.
VanAtta, Robert S. — 1946-49, '52-55.
Verrall, Richard P. — 1944-47, '50-52.
Vosburgh, Rev. Arthur R. — 1899-1910.
Wagers, Ralph E. — 1946-50, '50, '53, '55-57.
Wallach, Theodore — 1951, '52, '55-57.
Watt, James — 1955-57.
Weer, John Henry — 1936-39.
Whitcomb, M. Ethel — 1930, '31.
Whitney, Arthur C. — 1944-47, '50-53.
Winn, Charles V. — 1929-35, '37-40, '47, '48.
Wood, J. Lingen — 1956-57.
Wuth, Arthur P. — 1955-57
Young, Bicknell — 1903-16, '20, '22, '23, '25,
'26, '32-37.

Index

A

Abbott, Willis J., 189
Abortion, 58
Adams, George Wendell, 26
Adams, William, 115
Addison, W. Marlborough, 250
Africa, 229
  (*See also* East Africa; South Africa)
Alabama, 227
Alcoholism, 52
Allergies, 290
American Medical Association, 39-40, 43
Arkansas, 228
Armstrong, Joseph, 185n., 270, 281
Army camps (*see* United States Army)
Army Chaplains' School, 250
Asia, 253
  (*See also* names of countries, as China)
Australia, 39, 229, 318
Austria, 236, 237, 241, 254
Austria-Hungary, 98

B

Babson, Roger, 27
Baker, Abigail (mother of Mary), 116-117, 119
Baker, Alfred (brother of Mary), 118-119
Baker, Alfred A., 131n.
Baker, Gen. Henry M. (cousin of Mary), 142-143, 210n.
Baker, Mark (father of Mary), 112, 116-119
Baker, Rufus (cousin of Mary), 112
Baker homestead, 112-114
Bartlett, William M., 102
Bates, Edward P., 146n.
Bates, Gen. Erastus N., 128
Bates, John L., 174
Beck, Herbert W., 102
Belgium, 229, 244, 254
Bell, Frank, 285n.
Bench and Bar, 72
Benzecry, Mrs. Frances, 53, 56-62, 65
Berlin, 237, 243
Bible, the, 6, 60, 122, 259, 299
  distribution of, 255
  in World War II, 252
  (*See also* Scriptures)
Bible Lesson Committee, 189
Bible Lessons in Braille, 206
Bigotry, 8
Bill, Mrs. Annie C., 191n.
Black, the Rev. James, 206-207
Blindness, 309-310
Bone fractures, 301-303
Bonner, George R., 102

Boston, 30, 124n., 135, 136, 140, 212, 248, 267
Boston Herald, 158, 160, 210-212
Boston Transcript, 3
Bouton, the Rev. Nathaniel, 121
Bow, New Hampshire, 112, 116
Bowlegs, 303-304
Braille, 232
  Bible Lessons in, 206
  Science and Health in, 201-202
Braithwaite, John Sidney, 247n.
Braley, Justice, 162
Brazil, 229
British Isles, 86, 98-99, 106, 110, 207, 224-225, 232, 255, 263, 318
British War Relief Society, 248
Brookline, Massachusetts, 208, 214n.
Brooklyn Eagle, 72
Brussels, 253-254
Buffalo, New York, 75
Buffalo News, 69-70
Bulgaria, 276
Burgess, Samuel W., 106
Burma, 251
Burnham, the Rev. Abraham, 121
Burr, Hudson C., 270n.

C

Cabot, Richard C., 207
Cairo, 229
California, 224, 226, 263
Camp Edwards, Massachusetts, 248
Canada, 38, 86, 110, 207, 227, 229, 263, 318

Cancer, 294-295
Cardozo, Benjamin N., 77
CARE food packages, 254
Carver, Horace J., 270n.
CCC camps, 233
Cedar Rapids (Iowa) Evening Times, 3
Censorship, 258
Chamberlain, Neville, 225
Charitable Institutions Fund, 222
Charity, 208, 210, 216
Chase, Stephen A., 38
Chestnut Hill Sanatorium, 215-219, 224
China, 251, 254, 276
Christ and Christmas, Eddy, 205, 269
Christian Healing, Eddy, 201n., 206
Christian Intelligencer (New York), 72
Christian Science Benevolent Association, 93, 207-217, 219, 222-223, 226, 317
Christian Science Board of Directors, The, 5-6, 12, 19-21, 26, 38, 224-226
  appointment of, 173, 183
  appointment of committees by, 263-264
  authority of, 22, 53n., 171-174, 178-180, 183, 195
  duties of, 93-94
  election of, 173
  election of committees by, 263
  first woman member of, 158n.
  lecturers appointed by, 284-285

and publications, 93-94, 144-154, 160-173, 187-188
responsibility of, 13, 17-18, 23-24, 133, 142, 176
suits brought against, 160-180
support of, by members, 168
Christian Science Board of Education, 129-131
Christian Science Board of Lectureship, 283-285
list of lecturers, 384-388
Christian Science Board of Missionaries, 284
Christian Science chaplains, 100-102, 104-107, 248-250, 256
Christian Science Church, branches of, 24-25, 59, 80, 82, 93-94, 97, 104, 199-201, 229, 254-255, 263
charter for, 134-135
dissolution of, 129, 139, 192, 194
effect of lawsuits on, 180-181, 190
foreign, 38-39, 80-81, 86, 98*n*., 181, 199-200, 238-239, 241-246, 253-255
founding of, 127, 134-136, 138, 267-268
naming of, 134*n*.
organization of, 8-10, 13, 15, 31, 33, 38-39
rebellions in, 168, 191, 196
written word in, 258-259
(*See also* First Church of Christ, Scientist, The, Boston)
Christian Science dispensaries, 208

Christian Science Heralds, Braille, 233
Dutch, 233
French (*Hérault*), 93, 160, 168, 189, 200, 233, 237, 252
German (*Herold*), 93, 160, 168, 189, 200, 233, 237, 252, 270, 272, 307
Scandinavian, 233
Christian Science Hymnal, 232, 308
foreign editions of, 206, 243
revision of, 279
Christian Science Journal, 30, 85*n*., 89*n*., 93, 160, 166-167, 189, 220, 259, 267
circulation of, in 1922, 180, 186
in 1933, 232-233
in World War II, 252
enlargement of, 206
founding of, 127, 138, 269, 271-272
listing of nurses in, 217
listing of practitioners in, 62, 66-67, 200, 201, 254
quoted, 12, 23, 163-164, 288-289, 309-310, 323
Christian Science lecturers, 201, 202, 283-285
list of, 384-388
Christian Science literature, 185, 198*n*., 270
authority over (*see* Trust Deed)
in Braille, 201-202, 206, 232
distribution of, 201
in World War I, 104, 109-110
in World War II, 244

reliability of, 168-169
sale of, 167
(*See also* names of, as *Science and Health*)
Christian Science Ministers, Wartime, 248-250
Christian Science Monitor, 85n., 104, 110, 163-164, 166n., 167, 180, 182, 186-187, 189, 201, 206, 220, 247, 264, 271-276
circulation of, 273, 275
in 1933, 232-233
European Bureau of, 277
founding of, 212, 270
naming of, 272
Youth Forums of, 382-383
Christian Science Movement, in colleges, 230-232, 317-319
criticisms of, 3, 8, 18-20, 89-91, 210, 258
effect of lawsuits on, 191
foundation of, 27-28
founding of, 6
future of, 4
provision for (*see* Church Manual)
speculation about, 3-4
growth of, 3, 38-39, 80, 181, 199-200, 229, 238-239, 260
imitators of, 127-128
legislation and, 39, 46-79, 86-87, 207, 265
and medical profession (*see* Medical profession)
Mrs. Eddy's passing and, 3-4
and the Mother Church, 13
as a spiritual movement, 7
(*See also* Christian Science Church)

Christian Science nurses, 200, 201, 216-217, 238, 308
Christian Science Parent Church of the New Generation, 191n.
Christian Science periodicals, circulation of, in 1925, 206
editors of, 158-161, 166-167, 189-190, 270
subscriptions to, 167-169, 180, 186-187
Christian Science practitioners, 80, 200, 201, 294-296, 300-302, 305-306, 314
in Army camps, 103-104
as chaplains, 99-101, 104-108
early, 39, 47-68, 86-87
foreign, 86-87, 98n., 238, 241, 243-245, 254
Christian Science Publishing Society, 26, 93, 94, 185-189, 238, 268, 270n., 277
Board of Trustees of, 182-189
removal of, 144-151, 156-165, 169-180, 365-375
European Bureau of, 277
founding of, 270
new building for, 277-279
Christian Science *Quarterly*, 168, 221, 310
foreign editions of, 206, 243-244, 251
founding of, 269
Christian Science readers, 21, 172n., 263
Christian Science Reading Rooms, foreign, 237, 241
founding of, 127, 138

Christian Science Sentinel, 89n., 91, 93, 97, 148, 160, 166, 182, 189, 199n., 247, 277
  change in size of, 279
  circulation of, in 1922, 180, 186
    in 1933, 232
    in World War II, 252
  founding of, 221, 270, 272
  naming of, 270n., 271-272
  quoted, 96, 99-100, 148, 163-164, 183-184, 196-198, 213-215, 221-223, 229-230, 233, 236-239, 258, 291-303, 307-309, 313-314, 318
Christian Science societies, 80, 97, 104, 181, 199
  foreign, 241, 244-246, 254
Christian Science teachers, 128-131
  foreign, 245
Christian Science versus Pantheism, Eddy, 206
Christian Science War Relief Shipping Depots, 247
Christian Science Wartime Committees of The Mother Church in the United Kingdom, Canada, and France, 247
Christian Science Weekly, 270n.
Christian Science Welfare Committee, World War I, 103-104
Christian Scientist Association, 9, 30-32, 137, 257
  Committee on Publications, 127, 138
  constitution of, 137
  dissolving of, 129, 139-140

  membership in, 137-138
  organization of, 127, 136-137
  in relation to church, 138
Christian Scientists, 4, 8, 39, 51, 68, 74
  duties of, 90
  foreign, 81
  persecution of, 238, 242-245
  responsibilities of, 326
  testimonials of (*see* Testimonials)
  in World War I, 96-111
  in World War II, 235-255, 273-275
Christmas for the Children, Eddy, 230
Church Manual, 9, 19, 22-25, 130-132, 141, 192-193, 195, 222, 243, 255, 269, 283, 319, 323, 326
  in Braille, 201n.
  By-laws of, 5, 7, 11-13, 19, 22, 82-83, 131, 141, 148-149, 167, 174-175, 177, 184, 191, 194-195, 212-213, 221, 231, 257, 261, 263, 324
  deletion of title "Pastor Emeritus" from, 19
  importance of, 10, 17, 260
  legality of, 142-158, 162-167, 176-180, 182
  obedience to, 12-13, 24-26, 141-142, 169
  provisions for government of church in, 4-7, 18, 82
  rebellion against, 191, 193-196
  sales of, 205
Churchill, Chester L., 277n.

Cole, Willis Vernon, 46, 53-54, 78, 80, 180
    arrest and conviction of, 47-51, 54-74
    text of case against, 329-342
Colleges, Christian Science organizations in, 230-232, 317-319
Communion, Eddy, 89-91
Communism, 235-236
Conant, Albert F., 92
Concord, New Hampshire, 30, 85*n.,* 116, 128*n.,* 212, 221
Concord (New Hampshire) *Monitor,* 89*n.*
Concordance to Other Writings, Conant, 92
Congregational Church, 116, 118*n.,* 124
Congressional Record, 41-42
Cook, George Shaw, 131*n.*
Cooper, Dora, 247*n.*
Copeland, Royal S., 228
Copenhagen, 181
Corning, Charles W., 85*n.*
Corser, the Rev. Enoch, 120
Cosmopolitan Magazine, 230
"Country Seat, The," Eddy, 119-120
Crosby, John C., 183
Cross, Walter S., 102
Curtice, the Rev. Corban, 121
Czechoslovakia, 229, 254, 276

D

Daily Prayer, 94
Daily Times Journal (Ontario, Canada), 102

Daniels, Josephine, 105
Davis, Richard J., 104, 106, 131*n.*
Death, 287, 294-295
Deformity, 303
Denmark, 232, 244, 254
    (*See also* Copenhagen)
DeWitt, Lt. Gen. John L., 274*n.*
Dickey, Adam H., 12, 38, 85*n.,* 161, 164, 193-194, 323
    text of case against, 353-375
Dickey, Edward W., 101, 161, 164
Disability benefits, 320-321
Disease, Christian Science in treatment of, 217-218
    contagious and communicable, 62-63, 302, 322
    fear of, 13
    study of in schools, 320
    (*See also* Healing)
District of Columbia, 227, 264
Dittemore, John V., 38, 85*n.,* 151-154, 158*n.,* 165-167, 170, 179, 180, 190-191*n.,* 375-377
Divine love, 10
Dixon, Frederick, 166*n.*
Doctors (*see* Medical profession)
Dodge, Frederic, 162, 166, 170
Dresden, Germany, 233
Dudley and Hodge bindery, 276-277
Dunn, John Randall, 285*n.*
Durban (Natal) *Daily News,* 316
Dutch East Indies, 245

E

East Africa, 229
Ecclesiasticism, 7-8, 33

Eddy, Asa G. (husband of Mary), 128*n.*

Eddy, the Rev. Daniel C., 136

Eddy, Ebenezer J. Foster (adopted son of Mary), 128, 270

Eddy, Mary Baker, beliefs of, 13-16

charity of, 208, 210, 216, 226

childhood and youth of, 114-120

and the clergy, 114-115, 117-121, 124-126, 135, 206-207

copyrighting of books by, 4

criticism of, 8, 89-91

discovery of Christian Science by, 123

as editor, 196

education of, 120

enemies of, 196

eulogy of, 35-36

founding of church by, 127, 134-135

and future of church, 4-7, 12-13

gavel presented by, 20

healing of, 6, 16, 28, 117, 123, 135

health of, 117, 121-122

home of, 289

intelligence of, 120

as lecturer, 136, 284

letters of, 196-198

made Pastor Emeritus, 19, 202-203

memorial to, 19*n.*, 112-114

passing of, 19, 34-35

effect of, on church, 3-4

as pastor, 196, 203

as a person, 26-31

poems of, 119-120

as practitioner, 123-124

prose writings of, 4, 11, 27, 74, 84-91, 94, 178, 185-186, 188, 196-199, 204-206, 252, 268-269

(*See also* names of, as *Science and Health*)

repudiation of, 32

ridicule of, 8, 33

as teacher, 37, 128-129, 196

will of, 9, 85*n.*, 94, 186-188

wisdom of, 82-83, 131-133, 182

and young people, 317-319

Edwards, Jonathan, 116

Egypt, 229

England (*see* British Isles)

Estabrook, Henry D., 51-52, 54, 59, 68-69

Esthonia, 236-237, 244*n.*

Europe, 38, 96, 229, 233-238, 254-255

(*See also* names of countries)

Eustace, Herbert W., 94, 150-151, 157, 183

Eustice v. Dickey, text of case, 353-375

Ewing, Mary C., 131*n.*

Excommunication, 89

Executive Members, 22, 172*n.*, 173, 358

Eyes, injury to, 308-309

F

Farlow, Alfred, 257

Fear, 296-300

Fernald, Josiah E., 85*n.*, 142*n.*, 210*n.*

Filler, Harry K., 102

Finland, 236-237, 244*n.*

First Church of Christ, Scientist, The, Boston, 9, 11, 13, 19, 82, 114
  annual meetings of, 200, 234, 255, 378
  auditorium for, 21-22
  authority of, 174-175
  building of, 135, 220, 268
  Church Manual of (*see* Church Manual)
  Committee on Christian Science Nursing Homes, 225
  Committee on Publications, 138*n.*, 158, 194, 228, 233, 257, 259-260, 263-266, 320, 323
  establishment of, 25, 129, 140, 173, 192, 194
  excommunication by, 89
  Executive Members of, 22, 172*n.*, 173, 358
  First Members of, 21-22, 172-174, 178, 356-358, 361-368
  government of, 21-23, 169, 183, 195
  insured against impropriation, 140-143
  membership of, 20-21, 24, 131, 199
  President of, 20
  property of, deed of, 173*n.*
  regular meetings of, 23
  as relief agency, 247
  voting power in, 21

First Church of Christ, Scientist, Eddy, 84-86, 91, 206

First Church of Christ, Scientist, New York City, 168

Fletcher, Richard, 118

Fluoridation of water supply, 321

France, 98-99, 110, 206, 232-233, 244, 254, 318

Frederic, Harold, 86-87, 89

Freedom of religion, 49-51, 228, 234-236, 238, 241-245, 265, 319-323

Freedom of speech, 236

Frye, Calvin A., 143

G

Gale, Frank W., 131*n.*

Gamaliel, 44-45

Garrison, William Lloyd, 40

General Association of Teachers, 141

German prisoners-of-war in the United States, 251

Germany, 80-81, 98-99, 108, 206, 233, 236-239, 241-244, 253
  gift of books to, 254

Gestapo, 253

Gilman, Don C., 102

Gilmore, Albert F., 189

God, Christian Science concept of, 6-7, 13-16, 27-29, 33, 37, 57, 60-63, 66, 78-79, 83-84, 123-126, 267, 287-292, 300-301, 305-306, 310, 321, 325-328
  love of, 10, 15, 29, 38
  obedience to laws of, 12, 16
  understanding of, 17
  (*See also* Jesus)

Goodwin, Mrs. Isabelle, 46

Greece, 229, 244*n.*, 254

Greene, Eugene H., 131*n.*
Gustav V of Sweden, 81

H

Hague, The, 245
Halifax, Nova Scotia, 102-103
Hanna, Septimus J., 131*n.*, 143, 257
Hannover, Germany, 80
Harsch, Paul A., 109*n.*
Harvard University, 230
Harvey, Paul, 183
Havana, Cuba, 181
Healing, 43-46, 50, 67*n.*, 72, 88, 136
    increased recognition of, 227-228, 232
    institutional, 216
    by practitioners, 47, 54-58, 60, 62, 68-71, 78-79, 86-87
    principle of, 6-7, 14-16, 61-62, 69-70, 72-75, 117, 123-124, 265, 328
    spiritualistic, 75-77
    testimonials of (*see* Testimonials)
Health department, national, 39-42
Heresy, 117
Hering, Hermann S., 80*n.*, 285*n.*
Hiroshima, 256
Historical Sketches, Smith, 116, 120
Hitler, Adolf, 233, 236, 238, 241-242, 245
Hoag, Mrs. Ella W., 131*n.*, 158, 166, 189-190
Hodges, William L., 248

Holland, 98-99, 206, 232-233, 244-245, 254
Holland, Maj. Gen. Spencer E., 247*n.*
Homeopathic School of Medicine, 43
Hongkong, 245
Hoover, Herbert, 232
Hughes, Charles Evans, 147*n.*, 170-172, 178*n.*
Hulin, Mrs. Emilie B., 131*n.*, 169, 179, 353, 375
Hungary, 237
Hunt, Harry I., 185-186, 270*n.*, 276
Hunter, Charles, 207

I

Illinois, 170
Impartiality, 10, 26, 38
Independent Statesman (New Hampshire), 89*n.*
India, 251, 276-277
India paper, 276
Indiana, 227
Inoculation, compulsory, 320
Insanity, healing of, 124
Insomnia, 307
Intellectualism, 7-8
Ireland, 263
Italy, 98, 244, 254

J

Jackson, Martin F., 101-102
James, William, 8
Japan, 245, 254, 256
Jarvis, Charles E., 151, 158, 190

Jerome, William Travers, 47n.
Jesus, 7-8, 10, 14, 38, 45, 124-125, 128, 292
Jews, persecution of, 242
Johnson, Julia M., 131n.
Journal of the American Medical Association, The, 8, 41, 86-87
Jugoslavia, 237

K

Kenya, 229
Key, Lt. Col. Robert Ellis, 131n., 247n.
Kilpatrick, William D., 285n.
Kimball, Edward A., 131n., 284
Knapp, Bliss, 285n.
Knapp, Ira O., 38
Knott, Mrs. Annie M., 158, 161, 164, 167, 170, 179, 375
Korea, 256
Krauthoff, Daisy L., 169, 179
  text of appeal of, 353-375
Krauthoff, Edwin A., 169, 179, 374, 375

L

Lamson, Fred M., 183, 186, 188
Lathrop, Laura, 131n.
Latvia, 236-237, 244n.
Lesson-Sermon news items, 228
  preparation of, 264
Life of Mary Baker Eddy, Wilbur, 120n.
  foreign edition of, 206
Lódź, Poland, 241

London, 86, 97, 207, 263-264
  Committee on Christian Science Houses in, 224
Longyear, Mrs. Mary Beecher, 208-209, 213, 214n., 317
Lord, James F., 112
Lord's Prayer and interpretation of in foreign languages, 232
Los Angeles, 246, 254
Luther, Martin, 8
Lynn, Massachusetts, 122, 124, 135, 137, 208, 210, 285

M

McClintock, John N., 121n.
McCrackan, William D., 97-98, 156-161
McKenzie, William P., 156, 159, 166, 183, 186, 188-189, 284
McLellan, Archibald, 38, 74-75, 85n., 91, 99, 142n., 143, 178n., 210-211, 270-271
Manchester, England, 229-230
Manitowoc (Wisconsin) *Daily Herald,* 3
Mary Baker Eddy and Her Books, Orcutt, 280n., 282
"Mary G. Baker Eddy's Charitable Fund," 211
Maryland, 227
Massachusetts, 134-135, 140, 226, 264
  religion in, 115-116, 227
  (*See also* names of cities in)
Massachusetts Metaphysical College, 30, 128, 258
  closing of, 128-129
  founding of, 127

Massachusetts Supreme Judicial Court, 165, 183, 190, 197
suits brought in, 144-155, 162-167, 169-180
Materialism, 7-8, 10, 16, 27
Medical examinations, compulsory, 320, 322
Medical groups and national health department, 40-41
Medical profession, 294-295, 301-302, 304, 311, 313
Christian Science and, 39-44, 47-79, 86-89, 207, 227-228
Medicine, compulsory, 320-321
practice of, and Christian Science, 55-56, 60, 68
and Spiritualism, 75-77
Mein Kampf, Hitler, 236
Mental Digestion, Eddy, 192
Mental environment, treatment and, 217-218
Merrill, the Rev. Nathaniel, 115
Message to The Mother Church, Eddy, in 1900, 206
in 1901, 121, 206
in 1902, 206
Minnesota, 227
Miscellaneous Writings, Eddy, 84-85, 91, 205
quoted, 5, 11, 29-31, 44, 82, 122-123, 132, 164, 166, 216, 220, 226, 235, 323, 327, 381
Miscellany, Eddy, 84-86, 206
quoted, 11-12, 20, 27-29, 83, 88-91, 127, 129-130, 192-193, 195, 230, 318, 378
Missouri, 227
Morals, 17

Mother Church, The (*see* First Church of Christ, Scientist, The, Boston)
"Mother's Evening Prayer," Eddy, 315
Munich, 244
Mussolini, Benito, 236

N

Nairobi, 229
National League for Medical Freedom, 41-42, 44
Navy Chaplains' School, 250
Nazis, the, 236, 241
Neal, James A., 85, 161, 164
Nervousness, 307
New Guinea, 251
New York City, 51
first Christian Science practitioner in, 46-47
New York County Medical Society, 47, 52-54, 59, 68, 72, 78
New York Post, 3
New York State, 55, 64, 68
Constitution of, 49-51
Court of Appeals of, 67-72, 75-77
Court of General Sessions of, 52, 54, 66
Court of Special Sessions of, 52, 54
Public Health Law in, 50, 64
New York State Association of Spiritualists, 75
New York Sun, 67, 87, 89n.
New York Times, 69, 72
New York World, 105
New Zealand, 39, 200, 229

Nixon, William G., 269
No and Yes, Eddy, 206, 269
Normal Classes, 128-131
Norton, Carol, 284
Norway, 206, 232-233, 244, 254
Nursing homes, foreign, 224-225
  (*See also* Sanatoriums)

O

Ogden, David B., 94, 150-151, 165, 183n.
Ohio, 227
Old age, care in, 219-220
Orcutt, William Dana, 269, 279-282
Owen, Robert L., 39, 42

P

Paine, Gustavus S., 102, 166n.
Palmer, Ezra W., quoted, 378-381
Paralysis, 304-306
Pastor Emeritus, title of, bestowed, 19, 202-203
Patton, James E., 183, 186, 188-189
Paul, Charles C., 250
People's Idea of God, The, Eddy, 206
Per capita tax, in England, 255
  in Germany, 238
Permanency of the Mother Church and Its Manual, Smith, 8-9
Personality, Eddy, 27
Philippines, 245-246, 254
Physical examinations, compulsory, 320

Pierce, Franklin, 118
Pierce, Henry B., 134
Pilsbury, Ellen C., 123
Pittman, Alfred, 270n.
Pleasant View farm, 220-221
Pleasant View Home, 220-223, 255
Poems, Eddy, quoted, 119-120
Poland, 229, 236, 241, 254, 276
Portland, Oregon, 246
Prayer, 8, 16, 26, 47, 50, 66, 68, 77, 109, 121, 267-268, 325-328
  healing by (*see* Healing)
Primary Classes, 130
Prisoners-of-war, 251-253
Prose Works, Eddy, 205
  resetting of, 279
Pulpit and Press, Eddy, 205-206, 269
Pure food laws, 41, 44

Q

Quain, Oliver, 316
Quimby, Phineas P., 121

R

Radio broadcasting, 260-261
Rathvon, William R., 142-143, 161, 164
Reader's *Quarterly,* 206
Religion, 287
  Christian Science as, 6-7, 48, 81, 88-89, 100-101
  freedom of, 49-51, 227, 234-236, 238, 241-245, 265, 319-323
  superstition and, 3

Religious persecution, 234, 242-245

Resort, proposed, 208-214

Retrospection and Introspection, Eddy, 205, 269, 284

in Braille, 201*n*.

foreign editions of, 232

quoted, 116-117, 120, 122, 127, 136-137, 192, 259

Rheumatism, 313

Rhode Island, 227

Ross, Robert Stanley, 285*n*.

Roumania, 237, 244*n*., 276

Rowlands, Lamont, 94, 145-146, 148-151, 162-163, 170-171, 176, 179, 180, 183, 369, 371-372, 375

Rudimental Divine Science, Eddy, 201*n*., 206, 269

quoted, 325-326

Rugg, Chief Justice, 172-173

Ruskin, John, 79

Russia, 236-237, 276

S

St. Paul, 31-33, 36-37

Salem, Massachusetts, 134*n*.

San Francisco, 224

Sanatoriums, 255, 317

at Brookline, 217-219

chartering of, 215

requirements for admission to, 215-216

at San Francisco, 224-226

Sanbornton Bridge, New Hampshire, 118

Sanitation, 41, 44

Sargent, Laura E., 131*n*.

Science and Health with Key to the Scriptures, Eddy, 18, 24-25, 60, 85, 122, 128, 135, 142, 168, 195, 220-221, 243, 259, 268-269, 276, 288-292, 299, 303, 305-307, 325

binding for, 276

Braille edition of, 201-202

concordances to, 92-93

deletions from, 132*n*.

distribution of, in World War II, 252

foreign editions of, 80-81, 94, 251, 276*n*.

quoted, 13-15, 37, 61-62, 79, 123, 125-126, 131-132, 140*n*., 148, 203, 215, 217-218, 230, 292, 309-310, 324-325, 378

resetting of, 279-282

sale of, early, 204-205

increase in, 205

sold by mail-order houses, 232

Subscription Edition of, 282

title changes in, 205*n*.

Science of Man, by Which the Sick are Healed, Eddy, 268

Science et Santé, Eddy, 94

Scotland, 206, 318

Scriptures, 83, 154-155

spiritual understanding of, 15-17

study of, 33, 61

(*See also* Bible)

Second Church of Christ, Scientist, Manchester, England, 229

Seeley, Elisha B., 217

Seeley, Paul Stark, 285*n*.

Senate Subcommittee on Constitutional Rights, 319-322
Seven Poems, Eddy, 201*n.*
Shanghai, 233, 245
Shannon, Clara, 142
Shields, Drummond, 207
Shipman, Emma C., 131*n.*
Sinclair, Duncan, 131*n.*, 190
Singapore, 181, 245
Smith, Clifford B., 67-68, 116, 120, 131*n.*, 137*n.*, 158, 160-162, 239, 259
Smith, Clifton P., 8-10
Social Security benefits, 321
South Africa, 200, 227
South America, 38
Spiritualism, 75
Stalin, 241
Steinmetz, Charles P., 27
Stetson, Mrs. Augusta E., 168, 191
Stewart, Allison V., 85, 185, 270*n.*
Stockholm, 81
Story of Christian Science Activities, 1939-46, 249*n.*
Strawn, Silas H., 147*n.*
Sunday services, notice of, 228-229
Superstition, religion and, 3
Sweden, 81, 206, 232-233, 244
Swedenborg, 325
Switzerland, 81, 98-99, 244, 318
Syracuse (New York) *Journal,* 71

T

Tasmania, 200
Television, 262

Testimonials, 288-316
broadcast over radio, 261-262
Texas, 227
Tientsin, 245
Titanic, sinking of, 296-300
To the Christian World, Eddy, 86-89
Tomkins, the Rev. George, 284
Tomlinson, the Rev. Irving C., 131*n.*, 257, 271, 284-286
Travelship Fund, 382
Trust Deed, 144, 147-149, 163, 169, 171-173, 175, 177-179, 183, 188, 210*n.*, 261, 354-355, 357-370
text of, 348-352
Tuberculosis, 311-313
Tutt, John M., 131*n.*, 285*n.*
Twain, Mark, 8
Twelve Years with Mary Baker Eddy, Tomlinson, 271, 286

U

Ukraine, the, 237
United States, college organizations in, 318
growth of Christian Science in (*see* Christian Science Movement, growth of)
laws of, against Christian Science, 86, 207
on health, 320-322
United States Army, Christian Science work in, 100-104, 106-110
United States Congress, 39
United States Constitution, 49-50, 227

United States Navy, Christian Science work in, 104-106
Unity of Good, Eddy, 201n., 205, 269
quoted, 294
University Press, Boston, 204-205, 269, 280
Untermeyer, Samuel, 51-52, 54-55, 58-59, 63, 65-68

V

Vaccination, compulsory, 320, 322
Vernon, the Rev. Edward T., 207
Veterans, free Christian Science treatment for, 253
Vogelgesang, Theodore J., 75, 180
text of case of, 343-347

W

Walker, Mrs. Emily Hart, 250
Wallace, Arthur J., 109n.
War Relief Fund, World War I, 96-100, 102-103, 109
World War II, 236-237, 247
Warsaw, Poland, 241
West Virginia, 227
Whipple, Sherman L., 147n.
Whitney, Arthur C., 102, 106-107
Wilbur, Sibyl, 120n., 206

Wilson, John, 204-205, 269, 280
Wilson, Woodrow, 101
Winslow, Ole Elizabeth, 115n.
Winslow, Wentworth Byron, 52
Woman's National Daily, St. Louis, 35
Woodbury, Mrs. Josephine, 89-91
Workers for the Blind, world conference, 1931, 232
Workmen's compensation laws, 321
Works, John D., 42
World Health Organization, 321
World War I, 96-111, 276
World War II, 235-254
chaplains in, 248-250
ministers in, 248, 250
relief and rehabilitation work after, 254-255
Relocation Centers in, 273-275
volunteer workers in, 251

X

X-ray chest examinations, compulsory, 320

Y

Young, Bicknell, 131n., 285n.
Youth Forums, 382-383
Youth and Young Manhood, Eddy, 230